Modern Critical Views

Edward Albee
African American Poets Volume I
American and Canadian Women Poets, 1930–present
American Women Poets, 1650–1950
Maya Angelou
Asian-American Writers
Margaret Atwood
Jane Austen
James Baldwin
Samuel Beckett
Saul Bellow
The Bible
William Blake
Jorge Luis Borges
Ray Bradbury
The Brontës
Gwendolyn Brooks
Elizabeth Barrett Browning
Robert Browning
Italo Calvino
Albert Camus
Lewis Carroll
Willa Cather
Cervantes
Geoffrey Chaucer
Anton Chekhov
Kate Chopin
Agatha Christie
Samuel Taylor Coleridge
Joseph Conrad
Contemporary Poets
Stephen Crane
Dante
Daniel Defoe
Charles Dickens
Emily Dickinson
John Donne and the 17th-Century Poets
Fyodor Dostoevsky
W.E.B. Du Bois
George Eliot
T. S. Eliot
Ralph Ellison
Ralph Waldo Emerson
William Faulkner
F. Scott Fitzgerald
Sigmund Freud
Robert Frost
George Gordon, Lord Byron
Graham Greene
Thomas Hardy
Nathaniel Hawthorne
Ernest Hemingway
Hispanic-American Writers
Homer
Langston Hughes
Zora Neale Hurston
Henrik Ibsen
John Irving
Henry James
James Joyce
Franz Kafka
John Keats
Jamaica Kincaid
Stephen King
Rudyard Kipling
D. H. Lawrence
Ursula K. Le Guin
Sinclair Lewis
Bernard Malamud
Christopher Marlowe
Gabriel García Márquez
Cormac McCarthy
Carson McCullers
Herman Melville
Molière
Arthur Miller
John Milton
Molière
Toni Morrison
Native-American Writers
Joyce Carol Oates
Flannery O'Connor
Eugene O'Neill
George Orwell
Octavio Paz
Sylvia Plath
Edgar Allan Poe
Katherine Anne Porter
J. D. Salinger
Jean-Paul Sartre
William Shakespeare: Histories and Poems
William Shakespeare: Romances
William Shakespeare: The Comedies
William Shakespeare: The Tragedies
George Bernard Shaw
Mary Wollstonecraft Shelley
Percy Bysshe Shelley
Alexander Solzhenitsyn
Sophocles
John Steinbeck
Tom Stoppard
Jonathan Swift
Amy Tan
Alfred, Lord Tennyson
Henry David Thoreau
J. R. R. Tolkien
Leo Tolstoy
Mark Twain
John Updike

Modern Critical Views

Kurt Vonnegut
Alice Walker
Robert Penn Warren
Eudora Welty
Edith Wharton
Walt Whitman
Oscar Wilde
Tennessee Williams
Thomas Wolfe
Tom Wolfe
Virginia Woolf
William Wordsworth
Richard Wright
William Butler Yeats

Modern Critical Views

E. L. DOCTOROW

Edited and with an introduction by

Harold Bloom

Sterling Professor of the Humanities

Yale University

CHELSEA HOUSE PUBLISHERS

Philadelphia

Printed and bound in the United States of America

10 9 8 7 6 5 4 3 2 1

Library of Congress Cataloging-in-Publication Data

E.L. Doctorow / edited and with an introduction by Harold Bloom
p. cm. — (Modern critical views)
Includes bibliographical references and index.

ISBN 0-7910-6451-4 (alk. paper)
1. Doctorow, E.L., 1931---Criticism and interpretation. 2. Historical fiction,
American--History and criticism. I.Bloom, Harold. II. Series.

PS3554.O3 Z618 2001
813'.54--dc21 2001042341

Chelsea House Publishers
1974 Sproul Road, Suite 400
Broomall, PA 19008-0914

http://www.chelseahouse.com

Contributing Editor: Pam Loos

Contents

Editor's Note

This book brings together a representative selection of the best criticism published to date upon the fiction of E. L. Doctorow. The essays are reprinted here in the chronological order of their composition.

My Introduction is devoted to Doctorow's most recent novel, *City of God*, his most ambitious work so far and, in my judgement, his best. I have centered upon Doctorow's complex argument with God, in a Jewish tradition that goes from Job to the Hasidic masters.

Sam B. Girgus begins the chronological sequence of criticism with an examination of *The Book of Daniel*, which he sees as a moral history of the American Jewish identification with the Old Left, after which Geoffrey Galt Harpham emphasizes Doctorow's concern with technological history which is also a development in the technology of narrative.

In Paul Levine's overview, Doctorow is seen as a historical moralist working in the literary mode of the romance, while Cushing Strout usefully brings together Mark Twain's *A Connecticut Yankee in King Arthur's Court* and *Ragtime*, finding in Hank Morgan a less tragic precursor of Coalhouse Walker.

Doctorow's personal memories are judged by John G. Parks to be the essence of *Lives of the Poets* and *World's Fair*, after which Christopher D. Morris considers the complexities of illusions compounded with illusions in *Ragtime*.

Billy Bathgate, one of my favorite romances by Doctorow, is judged by Douglas Fowler to show Doctorow's nostalgia for the criminal existence he never experienced, while Marshall Bruce Gentry reflects upon the struggle both in Doctorow and in Philip Roth to represent women at a time when feminist pressures are inexorable.

The stories of *Lives of the Poets* are read by Stephen Matterson as further instances of Doctorow's ongoing quest for authenticity, after which John Williams considers aspects of the critical reception of *Welcome to Hard Times* and *The Book of Daniel.*

Billy Bathgate returns in Matthew A. Henry's essay, which broods on issues of "truth" and the fictive, while Michelle M. Tokarczyk concludes this volume with an analysis of the splendid *The Waterworks* as an American political novel.

Introduction

Having read all of, and admired most of, E.L. Doctorow's previous fiction, I was surprised by my first reading of *City of God*, a surprise that has not worn away with rereading. I would not have expected the author of *The Book of David*, *Ragtime*, *Billy Bathgate* and *The Waterworks* to compose a book as spiritually ambitious as *City of God*, a wholly appropriate title for this religious romance. I use the term "romance" deliberately because that, rather than novel, is the accurate term for Doctorow's mode of fiction. We have debased "romance" so that almost no contemporary writer of eminence would now use it as a genre description, and the title page of *City of God* explicitly says it is: "a novel." But Sir Walter Scott, Nathaniel Hawthorne, the three Brontë sisters, and William Morris wrote romances, and so does their distinguished successor, Doctorow. Northrop Frye, in his *Anatomy of Criticism*, is very helpful on the distinction between the novel and prose romance:

> In novels that we think of as typical, like those of Jane Austen, plot and dialogue are closely linked to the conventions of the comedy of manners. The conventions of *Wuthering Heights* are linked rather with the tale and the ballad. They seem to have more affinity with tragedy, and the tragic emotions of passion and fury, which would shatter the balance of tone in Jane Austen, can be safely accommodated here. So can the supernatural, or the suggestion of it, which is difficult to get into a novel. The shape of the plot is different: instead of manoeuvering around a central situation, as Jane Austen does, Emily Bronte tells her story with linear accents, and she seems to need the help of a narrator, who would be absurdly out of place in Jane Austen. Conventions so different justify us in regarding *Wuthering Heights* as a different form of prose fiction from the novel, a form

> which we shall here call the romance. Here again we have to use the same word in several different contexts, but romance seems on the whole better than tale, which appears to fit a somewhat shorter form.
>
> The essential difference between novel and romance lies in the conception of characterization. The romancer does not attempt to create "real people" so much as stylized figures which expand into psychological archetypes. It is in the romance that we find Jung's libido, anima, and shadow reflected in our hero, heroine, and villain respectively. That is why the romance so often radiates a glow of subjective intensity that the novel lacks, and why a suggestion of allegory is constantly creeping in around its fringes. Certain elements of character are released in the romance which make it naturally a more revolutionary form than the novel. The novelist deals with personality, with characters wearing their *personae* or social masks. He needs the framework of a stable society, and many of our best novelists have been conventional to the verge of fussiness. The romancer deals with individuality, with characters *in vacuo* idealized by revery, and, however conservative he may be, something nihilistic and untamable is likely to keep breaking out of his pages.

By these criteria, *City of God*—like so much previous by Doctorow—is essentially a romance, through much that is novelistic is mixed in. Individuality counts for more than personality in Doctorow, as it does also in Hawthorne, or in John Bunyan's *The Pilgrim's Progress*. The protagonists of *City of God*—a New York City novelist who might as well be Doctorow himself, an innovative Episcopalian rector, and a young woman rabbi of "Evolutionary Judaism"—do not wear societal masks. They are individualistic questers, seeking to redefine God in the post-Holocuast world, and in the city which, more than Jerusalem (as Doctorow sees, and teaches) must now be taken as the City of God.

It fascinates me to compares Doctorow's romance with Robert Stone's *Damascus Gate*, which is a religious novel set in contemporary Jerusalem, and which also seems to me Stone's most interesting work to date. Part of the large difference between *City of God* and *Damascus Gate* is the difference between romance and novel, but part is the very diverse auras of Manhattan and of Jerusalem. Stone, as is appropriate for Jerusalem, introduces Kabbalah or Jewish mysticism into his story, and creates a remarkable blend of international thriller and theosophy. Doctorow weaves together theology,

Holocaust survivors, Albert Einstein, the philosopher Wittgenstein, and the three questers—novelist, minister, rabbi—into another astonishing fusion.

The central event of *City of God* is the vanishing of a large brass cross that hung behind the altar of a Episcopal church in lower Manhattan, and the subsequent finding of the cross on the roof of an Upper West Side synagogue. Thomas Pemberton, rector of the church of the missing cross, is informed by Rabbi Joshua Gruen that the cross has found its way to his roof. Gruen's wife, Rabbi Sarah Blumenthal, is the romance's third protagonist, who ultimately will be married to Pemberton, well after her first rabbinical husband is murdered in Vilna, when in pursuit of the ghetto archives that are a final memorial of the Vilna Jews, butchered by the Germans and their Lithuanian helpers.

In one sense, Doctorow has written what he knows to be an unwritable book, which despite its distinction is never going to be a popular success. Perhaps he over-reaches in *City of God*, but what could be more heartening? Only his surrogate, the narrator Everett the novelist, persuades us at times of his personality, but I repeat that authentic literary romance scarcely trades in such persuasion. Visionary place can count for most in romance, and Doctorow's New York City is immensely persuasive. It can be rather too persuasive, when Doctorow runs it as an apocalyptic movie:

> —The movie from this: And now more and more people are born into it. The wretched of the earth stream into it. All at once it passes its point of self-containment. Its economy is insufficient. It becomes less able to employ, to house and feed the crowds that hunker about in its streets. As the smog thickens and the rising global temperatures bring on intolerable heat waves, droughts, hurricanes, and monumental snowfalls, the sustaining rituals of the society break down and ideas of normal daily life erode. The city begins to lose its shape, its outlines blur as its precincts expand, and the class distinctions of its neighborhoods are no longer discernible. Crimes against property increase. The food supply is erratic, power blackouts come with greater and greater frequency, the water arrives contaminated, the police forces are armed like soldiers, and inflation makes money useless. Prophets arise in their clerical robes to speak of evil, to speak of irreverence and blasphemy. They announce that the wrath of God has come down on the city of unnatural pride, the earthly city. They call upon the pious to destroy the city. And the

unremarked God, the sometime-thing God, is alive once again, resurrected in all His fury.

Politicians arise who decide the city is adaptable to any political abstraction impressed upon it. Strange diseases appear for which the doctors have no cure. Schools are closed. They become neighborhood armories. Plagues break out, hospital corridors become morgues, the elected leaders declare martial law, troops are everywhere, and the befouled shantytowns that have sprung up on the metropolitan outskirts are routinely swept by machine-gun fire. When the God-soaked impoverished mobs rush upon the city, they are massacred. The military mount a coup, the elected leaders who called them in are jailed, a governing junta closes down all television and radio stations, home computers are declared illegal, and around the beleaguered enclaves of the wealthy, high walls are built with periodically spaced guard towers.

It becomes a political commonplace resisted not even by theorists of the democratic left that totalitarian management, enforced sterilization procedures, parentage grants issued to the genetically approved, and an ethos of rational triage are the only hope for the future of civilization.

This is more monitory than prophetic, and possibly attaches more to *City of God*'s problematical spirituality than to Doctorow's own socio-economic convictions (whatever they may be). There are two centers of true concern in the book: the Holocaust and the status of New York City as the new City of God. *Ragtime* enchants its readers (and audiences) because it is an all-but-perfect historical romance, wonderfully consistent with itself in tone, idea, and ethos. *City of God* does not enchant anyone, but it is a troubling book, highly deliberate in its imperfections. A crucial moment in it is Pemberton's meditation upon the transfer of the cross from church to synagogue, a transfer that he himself will follow, when he becomes a Jew, a rabbi, and the husband of the widowed Sarah:

> Pem had chosen the hospice across the East River as an appropriate dead end for his professional life. He was already working around in his thinking to a meaningful transition, to what he did not yet know, but he felt himself changing, and if he had any faith left, it was his conviction that when the brass cross of St. Tim's appeared on the roof of the Synagogue of Evolutionary Judaism, something momentous was announced.

> This was not a proposition he was prepared to argue with anyone—he had regretted mentioning it to me because, on the one hand, it belonged to a mode of thought characteristic of the ancient prophetic communications which he could no longer countenance and, on the other, because he felt, with the stunning power of superstition, that to discuss it, to speak of it, was for it to lose its light. He did not think of the sign as necessarily unearthly but as so cryptic as to render the motives of the human beings who had arranged it entirely beside the point.

Doctorow has, despite all his inventiveness, a normative consciousness: by temperament he is closer to the central Jewish traditions than are Philip Roth or Cynthia Ozick. One wants to urge the Kabbalah of Nathan of Gaza on him, even if it is the doctrine of the false Messiah, Sabbetai Zevi. A degraded Godhead may be the only path out of post-Holocaust dilemmas, which seems the suggestion of Tony Kushner in *A Dybbak*. But Doctorow, in *City of God*, has written a normative Jewish romance, consonant with his earlier work. That seems the basis for Pemberton's anxious demands for theodicy in his climactic speech to Sarah's congregation:

> ...I think we must remake You. If we are to remake ourselves, we must remake You, Lord. We need a place to stand.

Good luck to Pemberton, but the Yahweh of the Jews is recalcitrant and will hardly consent to being remade. Pemberton and Sarah are not looking for Yahweh, and would be unable to accept him if found. They need the stranger or alien God of the Gnostics, who is exiled from our solar system, and wanders out in the interstellar spaces. Unable to accept that we were thrown into this world by demiurges and archons, they will seek to remake what they were given. Doctorow's bold, spiritual romance deserves the answer of William Blake:

> Though thou art worshiped by the Names Divine
> Of Jesus and Jehovah: thou art still
> The Son of Morn in weary Night's decline
> The Lost Traveller's Dream under the Hill.

SAM B. GIRGUS

A True Radical History: E. L. Doctorow

Although E. L. Doctorow is not the same kind of public personality as Mailer, the quality of his commitment to the role of the New Jeremiah in the tradition of the New Covenant is as strong and as significant as Mailer's. Like Mailer, Doctorow writes from the perspective of a moral consciousness to reexamine the meaning of the American experience and to revivify our moral imagination. His concern for the relevance of America as a myth and ideology has led him to write a form of "metahistory" that builds upon the poetic and linguistic origins of historical understanding. Moreover, it can be argued that as metahistory, in Hayden White's sense of the term, Doctorow's work can be compared with Nietzsche's philosophy of history. According to White, Nietzsche attempted "to translate history into art." Doctorow shares Nietzsche's interest in, as White says, returning "consciousness to the enjoyment of its Metaphorical powers." Much of Nietzsche's discussion in *The Use and Abuse of History* of the objectives and responsibilities of the historian could serve as a model for Doctorow. Nietzsche insists that the "real value" of history "lies in inventing ingenious variations on a probably commonplace theme, in raising the popular melody to a universal symbol and showing what a world of depth, power and beauty exists in it." To achieve such a level of creativity, the historian, Nietzsche argues, must function and think like an artist. The historian, he says, must develop "above

From *The New Covenant: Jewish Writers and the American Idea.* ©1984 by The University of North Carolina Press.

all a great artistic faculty, a creative vision from a height, the loving study of the data of experience, the free elaborating of a given type." Based on this artistic theory of rendering history, Nietzsche goes on in *The Genealogy of Morals* to establish something like guidelines for an approach to history that emphasizes openness and invention.

The elements of myth and symbol, as well as art and invention, are the important factors in Nietzsche's thinking about history that elucidate Doctorow's work. For Nietzsche, myth and symbol constitute the heart of a culture and its history and must, therefore, be contrasted with the fictions derived from ordinary history. History and culture without myth turn man into an abstraction. Man's loss of myth, Nietzsche writes in *The Birth of Tragedy*, leads to "abstract man stripped of myth, abstract education, abstract mores, abstract law, abstract government; the random vagaries of the artistic imagination unchanneled by any native myth; a culture without any fixed and consecrated place of origin, condemned to exhaust all possibilities and feed miserably and parasitically on every culture under the sun." In contrast to such abstraction, Nietzsche hopes to return culture to its "mythic home, the mythic womb." He associates the power of myth to define the essence of culture with the power of music to stimulate men to operate and think beyond their usual capacities. Both myth and music come together for him in a truly exciting culture. Through the revivification of the metaphoric consciousness, he seeks to establish in cultural history "the mythopoeic power of true music." Nietzsche's understanding of history in terms of myth, metaphor, and music is, as White says, the "notion of historical representation as pure story, fabulation, myth conceived as the verbal equivalent of the spirit of music." *Ragtime* represents the most obvious example of Doctorow's attempt to develop the narrative structure of the historical novel in what can be described as a Nietzschean mode that uses music as the metaphor to best dramatize an era and a people. Thus, Doctorow indicates his interest in the idea of history as, in White's words, "pure story, fabulation, myth" when he says of *Ragtime* that "there's no more fiction or nonfiction now, there's only narrative. All the nonfiction means of communication employ narrative today."

However, there are also major differences between Nietzsche and Doctorow. Most importantly, Doctorow rejects the nihilistic implications of Nietzsche's philosophy. As White indicates, in Nietzsche's "conception of history, the prospects of any *community* whatsoever are sternly rejected." "In Nietzsche," White says, "no historical grounds exist for the construction of any specific *political* posture except that of antipolitics itself. Thought is liberated from responsibility to anything outside the ego and will of the individual, whether past, future, or present." Although certainly aware of such implications in contemporary thought, Doctorow remains committed to community and politics, to a moral vision that includes individual responsibility, and to history itself, meaning a belief in the necessity of trying to understand the past as a means for attempting to deal intelligently with the present and future. Such humanistic concerns also put Doctorow in opposition to a modern school of apocalyptic writers. Harry Henderson's list of these writers includes Nathanael West, John Barth, Joseph Heller, and Thomas Pynchon. Henderson believes that these writers have an "apocalyptic historical imagination" that entertains the "idea of an apocalyptic Day of Doom, an end to history that is foreshadowed by the exhaustion of the historical imagination that their parody signifies." Although the ending to Doctorow's first novel, *Welcome to Hard Times*, resembles this kind of apocalyptic catastrophe, the spirit of the hero and narrator suggests a hope for human communication, truth, and love that characterizes Doctorow's literature and philosophy in general.

Welcome to Hard Times also indicates Doctorow's important interest in working with universal figures and classic motifs in a mythic pattern. In the novel Doctorow places classic western types in a traditional setting and narrative. The absence of surnames for the characters reenforces their universality. They clearly are intended to stand for general personality types that fit into the mythic scheme of "the Western." For example, the stock figure of the bad man who destroys the town of Hard Times and massacres its residents is cast simply as the Man from Bodie. The hero is known as Blue, depicting the low key, almost maudlin, mood of the piece. He is also called mayor since he assumes a kind of clerical and administrative responsibility for the town. From being a record keeper of sorts, he eventually achieves a judicial and prophetic role. His consciousness and vision make the town a community. Condemning himself for his initial cowardice in failing to stand up to the bad man, he restores the town and establishes something of a family. However, he finds himself forced to confront the return of the Bad Man from Bodie, who once again destroys everything. The mayor blames himself. He says, "I can forgive everyone but I cannot forgive myself. I told Molly we'd be ready for the Bad Man but we can never be ready. Nothing is ever buried, the earth rolls in its tracks, it never goes anywhere, it never changes, only the hope changes like morning and night, only the expectations rise and set. Why does there have to be a promise before destruction?"

However, even in the face of the evil and the destructiveness of the Bad Man, Blue cannot surrender his humanistic priorities, which include at the top of the list the need to conclude his history. In spite of his awareness of what we can call the epistemological difficulties and uncertainties entailed in attempting to know and transmit the truth, Blue feels compelled to complete his project. The only meaning the events can have will be provided by Blue as the historian whose work will make them part of human consciousness. Rather than confirming the nihilism of the apocalyptic vision, the destruction of Hard Times seems to demand of Blue just the opposite of a concession to death. In spite of his fears and self-doubts, Hard Times for Blue requires a reassertion of his individual moral responsibility. He says, "And now I've put down what happened, everything that happened from one end to the other. And it scares me more than death scares me that it may show the truth." Blue admits that he cannot be sure of the final meaning of his account given the difficulty of figuring out "which minutes were important and which not." He asks, "Does the truth come out in such scrawls, so bound by my limits?" His actions, however, along with his fulfillment of the obligation to record history, stand as the final moral judgment upon Blue. Thus, as he takes his last look upon the destruction of the town, he notes that wood for reconstruction remains available. He says, "And I have to allow, with great shame, I keep thinking someone will come by sometime who will want to use the wood." So, even in death, he continues to be the builder, the pioneer, the American.

Blue's questions concerning his dilemma about being caught up as a man, a citizen, and a historian in the making and writing of his own history achieve brilliant elaboration and discussion in Doctorow's most successful and important novel to date, *The Book of Daniel*. Issues about history, myth, human values, and individual moral responsibility that are suggested in *Welcome to Hard Times*, and to a lesser degree in *Big as Life*, reach maturity in *The Book of Daniel*, a largely neglected work that may yet receive deserving recognition as a major work of contemporary literature. There are reasons for this neglect. First of all, with the important exception of Stanley Kauffmann in the *New Republic*, most reviewers have failed to see much beyond the novel's most obvious intention of dramatizing the story of Julius and Ethel Rosenberg, who were convicted and executed by electrocution as spies for stealing atomic secrets for the Russians in the early 1950s. In the novel the names of the Rosenbergs are changed to Paul and Rochelle Isaacson, and the story is told through the consciousness of their son, Daniel Isaacson. In addition, other novels in the Doctorow canon, especially *Ragtime*, have received far more critical attention from major reviewers and scholars. Doctorow's dazzling insertion of real characters in the fictional setting of *Ragtime* and his experimentation in that novel with a kind of verbal and imagistic syncopation have intrigued both popular and critical audiences, but it has also distracted them from much of the inventiveness and originality of *The Book of Daniel*, which also experiments with the form of the historical novel. In terms of sparkle and glitter, *The Book of Daniel* cannot compete with *Ragtime*'s use of such figures as Evelyn Nesbit, J. P. Morgan, Freud, Houdini, and Emma Goldman. As Barbara Foley indicates, *Ragtime* departs radically from the historical novel's practice of dealing only plausibly with historical figures. Foley writes, "Events so audaciously 'invented' as Freud's and Jung's trip through the Tunnel of Love at Coney Island or Emma Goldman's massage of Evelyn Nesbit clearly violate this canon of historical decorum. Doctorow is doing something quite different here: he is utilizing the reader's encyclopedic knowledge that a historical Freud, Jung, Goldman, and Nesbit did in fact exist in order to pose an open challenge to the reader's preconceived notions about what historical 'truth' actually is. Asked on one occasion whether Goldman and Nesbit ever really met, Doctorow has boldly replied, "They have now!'" Other critics such as Leonard Kriegel and John Seelye also have expressed their great admiration for the cleverness of Doctorow's technique in *Ragtime*. Kriegel considers the novel "intriguing" and says, "In Dos Passos' great trilogy, the biographical is used as a counterweight to the fictional. In Doctorow, the stuff of J. P. Morgan is, indeed, the stuff of fictional life." Also relating *Ragtime* to Dos Passos, Seelye notes that "perhaps Doctorow's most significant borrowing is from continental, not American literature, namely, his use of Heinrich von Kleist's historical novel *Michael Kohlhaus*." Seelye further states that *Ragtime* "manages to syncopate materials borrowed from other radically oriented novels of the '30s, including Roth's *Call It Sleep* and George Milburn's forgotten *tour de force*, *Catalogue*."

The experimentation in *The Book of Daniel* is of a more traditional sort than in either *Ragtime* or the more recent *Loon Lake*. In *The Book of Daniel*, Doctorow, like Philip Roth, develops the idea of the self-consciousness of modern literature and art so that the process of creativity and production becomes a subject in itself. However, while Roth writes fiction about writing fiction, Doctorow writes fiction about writing history. At the beginning of the novel, we learn that Daniel Isaacson is writing his history dissertation at Columbia University and that we will be watching him watching himself as he progresses on it. In fact, Daniel's history will take the form of the very book in our hands. We also see that Doctorow, through the persona of Daniel, really writes a special kind of history that imbues Daniel's prophetic narration with the rhetoric of the jeremiad in a linguistic achievement that projects a vision of justice and truth upon American culture. In effect, then, Doctorow demands of himself a literary work of initiation that includes the stories of Daniel and his family and, for want of a better term, Daniel's inner spirit or sense of being; an intellectual and social history that establishes the ideals, values, trends, and mores of America from the period of the depression until the era of the Great Greening of America in the late 1960s; a political study of modern radical movements and thought; a moral history that lives up to the rhetorical tradition of the jeremiad. Putting all of this together—Daniel's own story plus the story of his people and their times in America—Doctorow, by adhering consistently to the complex consciousness and multidimensional point of view of his young Columbia graduate student, writes one of the great Jewish novels of our times.

Two figures are especially important examples to Daniel in his effort to write such a history—Edgar Allan Poe and the Prophet Daniel. Our Daniel—Daniel Isaacson—sees Poe as an important literary and cultural model of the power of the alienated artistic consciousness to instigate a revolution in the values and thought of his times. In Poe, art and alienation go hand in hand. Thus, Daniel calls Poe "the archetype traitor, the master subversive Poe, who wore a hole into the parchment and let the darkness pour through" by virtue of his drinking, his relationship to his thirteen-year-old cousin, and his poetry. He says, "A small powerful odor arose from the Constitution; there was a wisp of smoke which exploded and quickly turned mustard yellow in color. When Poe blew this away through the resulting aperture in the parchment the darkness of the depths rose, and rises still from that small hole all these years incessantly pouring its dark hellish gases like soot, like smog, like the poisonous effulgence of combustion engines over Thrift and Virtue and Reason and Natural Law and the Rights of Man. It's Poe, not those other guys. He and he alone. It's Poe who ruined us, that scream from the smiling face of America." Daniel believes that Poe would understand him as a complex and divided consciousness who has been trained by his parents to be "a small criminal of perception" and "a psychic alien," meaning someone whose point of view and ideas of reality always will be difficult and multidimensional. Daniel also believes that Poe provides an original lesson in American culture of the cost of such a complex consciousness. Poe demonstrates how an alien vision becomes a double-edged sword. Though a complex consciousness allows Daniel to function with great perspicacity and imagination on many different levels and through many creative forms, it also can be a self-destructive and nonproductive force in the manner of much of modern nihilism. The tendency in art to carry such alienation to its nihilistic extreme interests Daniel and becomes an ideology in itself. Daniel finds a symbol for the nihilistic potential of his own perspective in the mutilation of a woman's eye in "a classic surrealist silent film by Buñuel and Dali." In the movie a man brings his straight razor toward a woman's face and her eyeball. Daniel says, "And just as you, the audience, have settled for this symbolic mutilation of the woman's eye, the camera cuts back to the scene, and in closeup, shows the razor slicing into the eyeball."

The counterpart to Daniel's psychological and aesthetic alienation as represented by Poe is the moral alienation of the prophetic and righteous visionary in a corrupt land as embodied in the biblical story of Daniel. The biblical Daniel stands as a symbol, or a "type" in the Puritan sense of the word, for the Daniel in the novel. His moral vision and his story establish a standard and a pattern for our Daniel. Through Daniel the Prophet, the novel attempts to transcend historical limitations and extends itself to a higher realm of moral authority. However, the psychological credibility for the moral consciousness of Daniel and his sister derives from the abrasive onslaught of continuous preaching from their parents. The obsessive moralism of their parents' left-wing politics, values, and views has taught Daniel and Susan to see even ordinary matters as ultimate moral issues. Moreover, Daniel recognizes important parallels between his own situation and that of the biblical Daniel, of whom he says, "It is a bad time for Daniel and his co-religionists, for they are second-class citizens, in a distinctly hostile environment. But in that peculiar kind of symbiosis of pagan kings and wise subject-Jews, Daniel is apparently able to soften the worst excesses of the rulers against his people by making himself available for interpretation of dreams, visions or apparitions in the night." Similarly, as Jews and Communists, Daniel's parents consider themselves to be second-class citizens, and Daniel also feels like an alien in his own country. In addition, he sees an existential connection between himself and the biblical Daniel. As someone who inherits an awesome guilt and loss through his parents, Daniel can sympathize and identify with the biblical Daniel's feeling of having been chosen. God, according to Daniel, "enlists the help of naturally righteous humans who become messengers, or carriers of his miracles, or who deliver their people. Each age has by trial to achieve its recognition of Him—or to put it another way, every generation has to learn anew the lesson of His Existence. The drama of the Bible is always in the conflict of those who have learned with those who have not learned." The biblical Book of Daniel, therefore, operates as a moral metaphor for our Daniel's history.

Daniel's moral vision achieves additional depth and specificity through the character of Susan, who functions as an alter—or more precisely a super-super—ego for Daniel, forever torturing him with ever increasing moral demands. Their intimate relationship as almost a single mind or psyche becomes solidified when circumstances unite them against the world. This special relationship emerges after the arrest and the death of their parents. Thus, she becomes capable of sending a "signal" to him "from the spasm of soul." He says, "Susan and I, we were the only ones left." At times he tries to treat her moral intensity facetiously, but in fact her moral authoritarianism operates as a kind of tourniquet upon his personality. He says that she has become "a dupe of the international moralist propagandist apparatus" and has been made into a "moral speed freak." Significantly, her moral position is heavy with political content because she identifies ferociously with her parents and vehemently maintains a radical ideology. She attacks Daniel for defaming the memory of their parents and argues that his decision to attend graduate school is an act of cowardice and of treason against them and the left. " 'What did they die for?' " she exclaims as a curse against Daniel. He, of course, assumes the guilt and responsibility for her eventual breakdown and death. "There is" he says, "some evidence that she was driven finally to eradicate him from her consciousness by the radical means of eradicating her consciousness."

Whereas Susan radiates radical moral righteousness, Daniel usually responds to situations with the defensive detachment of a student of radicalism. In contrast to Susan, whose radicalism recoils against herself, Daniel vents his frustration in his writing. The scattered inclusion of Daniel's interpretations of history, politics, and thought within *The Book of Daniel* is one of the novel's major accomplishments. Doctorow presents a relatively traditional Marxist historical methodology and perspective within the broader concept of history represented by the book in its entirety. By expanding upon the studies and ideas of established radical and revisionist historians such as William Appleman Williams, Daniel develops an interesting framework through which to interpret history in terms of class oppression, organized violence, bourgeois control of society's institutions, and capitalist domination of the means of economic production and distribution. Daniel expounds upon this point of view in a series of statements dealing with diverse periods and events in diplomatic, political, and social history, all of which ultimately contribute to and explain the background and meaning of his parents' execution. Some of Daniel's leftist disquisitions include an explanation and justification of Stalin's leadership based on E. H. Carr's interpretation of the dictator's role in revivifying Russian nationalism; an argument that all men are inherently both victims and enemies of all governments because "the final existential condition is citizenship. Every man is the enemy of his own country"; a revisionist argument entitled "A True History of the Cold War: A Raga" that maintains that the cold war was initiated by America in the hope of using atomic weapons as a means for controlling Russia and that the Truman Doctrine and the Marshall Plan were thinly veiled disguises to protect and advance American capitalistic interests; and a belief "that the basis of all class distinctions in society is corporal punishment. Classes are created by corporal punishment, and maintained by corporal punishment." Daniel develops the latter argument along classic Marxist lines. He writes, "As societies endure in history they symbolize complex systems of corporal punishment in economic terms. That is why Marx used the word 'slavery' to define the role of the working class under capitalism." Daniel's obsession with the authoritarian power and brutality of the state motivates his dramatic history of civic and governmental torture and punishment that includes drawing and quartering, smoking, knouting, and burning at the stake, which he offers to strengthen the argument for the martyrdom of his electrocuted parents.

On the other hand, Daniel's personal experiences with people on the left and his proclivity to temper his radicalism and Marxism with self-criticism and pragmatic intellectualism tend to challenge Susan's ideological rigidity. Although he identifies with the left, he frequently views it ironically and critically. From his perspective the left seems more pathetic than ominous. In fact, it appears to be a danger only to those people like his parents who let their belief in it become a new kind of orthodoxy that inflates their sense of importance, disguises their vulnerability, and encourages a kind of moral myopia, which confuses immediate self-interest, personal status, and convenience with universal truth and justice. The novel offers innumerable examples of the failure of thought and character by members of the left, many of them most powerfully dramatized by his parents and their friends. His parents are filled with an enormous sense of their own importance and knowledge. They believe their access to historical truth makes them part of a psychological, moral, and intellectual elite. Ironically, such self-elevation puts them in opposition to the very masses they are supposed to serve. The fact of their political irrelevance and impotence in the face of such reputed power contributes to a sense of frustration that further increases their feeling of internal weakness and ineptitude. Thus, Daniel remembers how mixed motivations inspired the idealism of his parents. Daniel writes, "They rushed after self-esteem. If you could recognize a Humphrey Bogart movie for the cheap trash it was, you had culture. If you discovered the working class you found the roots of democracy. In social justice you discovered your own virtue. To desire social justice was a way of living without envy, which is the emotion of a loser. It was a way of transforming envy into constructive outgoing hate."

Unfortunately, such hatred became a characteristic way of being in the world for his parents. He writes, "The thing about the Isaacson family, the thing about everyone in our family, is that we're not nice people." The wife of the lawyer who lost his health in his tireless efforts on their behalf understandably resents the impact of the Isaacsons upon her own life. "'I have no love for the memory of your parents,'" she tells Daniel. "'They were Communists and they destroyed everything they touched.'" Accusing his parents of being unkind to everyone, she also feels that "'they were not innocent of permitting themselves to be used. And of using other people in their fanaticism.'" Furthermore, during the trial his own mother comes to recognize many harsh facts about the left and the people in it. She ironically fails, however, to see similarities between herself and her friends. She thinks, "My God how I hate them all, how I despise their pompous little egos and their discussions and resolutions and breast-beating; with their arrogance as they delivered to us each week the truth, the gospel according to 11th Street. Always they treated Paul like a child and with his mind! a mind so fine, so superior to theirs except in the grubby self-serving politics of the Party. He was always being censured, he was never quite in step. All he did was slave for them, believe for them. Communists have no respect for people, only for positions. . . . You blind them with your ideals and while they are looking up you stab them in the belly for the sake of your ideals." Thus, for Daniel, the major lesson of the left in America as rendered by his parents was self-destruction, partly through self-delusion. "But you see," he says, "I was learning. I was learning how to be an Isaacson. An Isaacson does things boldly calculated to bring self-destructive results."

One of Daniel's most bitter accounts of the contrast between his parents' sense of self-importance as radicals and the reality of their pathos concerns the search of his home and the arrest of his father by the Federal Bureau of Investigation. As the FBI empties the house of its miserable belongings, Daniel sarcastically warns the reader to be alert to the scene "so that you may record in clarity one of the Great Moments of the American Left. The American Left is in this great moment artfully reduced to the shabby conspiracies of a couple named Paul and Rochelle Isaacson." The extent of their real power and contribution to the left probably is best summarized by a *New York Times* reporter, who tells Daniel that they "'had to have been into some goddam thing. They acted guilty. They were little neighborhood commies probably with some kind of third-rate operation that wasn't of use to anyone except maybe it made them feel important. Maybe what they were doing was worth five years. Maybe.'"

Daniel's understanding of the complexity of his parents' relationship to the old left influences his perception of the people and program on the new left. When his sister proposes to use a trust fund that had been established on their behalf to advance a "New Left" cultural revolution, Daniel seems uncertain. Later in the book he thinks, "THEY'RE STILL FUCKING US. . . . The Isaacsons are nothing to the New Left." Moreover, as a product of the more conventional moralism of the old left, Daniel feels basically uncomfortable with certain new left character types who live a kind of self-centered existence. The superiority such people express over the previous generation of Isaacson radicals further alienates Daniel from them. They render an easy view of the failures of the past that are part of Daniel's own personal history. Thus, after receiving a beating on the historic 1967 Washington march on the Pentagon, he assures his wife that the wounds are not major. He says, "'It looks worse than it is. There was nothing to it. It is a lot easier to be a revolutionary nowadays than it used to be.'"

In their attitude toward his parents, many of those Daniel encounters on the new left simply share the so-called dominant culture's disdain for his parents. In a sense, the Isaacsons were born guilty. They are guilty of being losers, guilty of being poor Jews, guilty of not being quite smart enough or powerful enough to escape or transcend the limitations of their environment, guilty of being used and of using others. At the same time, their attitude in death gives them a moral strength that elevates them above their enemies both on the right and the left. For Daniel, they achieve a quality of martyrdom and sacrifice that rises above their political and personal causes and failures. Daniel says, "But they stuck to it, didn't they, Daniel? When the call came they answered. They offered up those genitals, didn't they, Dandan? Yes, they did. There were moments when I thought he would crack, I had my doubts about him. But I knew she would take it finally, to the last volt, in absolute selfishness, in unbelievably rigid fury." In order for Daniel to find a meaning and significance for their death, he must go beyond its political context. He puts their death, as we shall see, in a Jewish framework. As a Jew, he finds a structure through ritual to express and contain his grief, his mourning, his sense of inadequacy, and his guilt as an heir to the pain and burdens of the past.

Throughout the novel, Daniel thinks of his parents as representatives of a lower-middle-class Jewish subculture of radicalism. Their backgrounds, values, life-style, behavior, thought, language, tastes, and opinions epitomize the particular world view of the Jewish left in New York that developed early in the century, reached its peak during the depression and the war years, and quickly declined during the late 1940s and early 1950s. As Stanley Kauffmann says, "The novel faces up squarely and intelligently to the Jewishness of its subject." Jewish identity provides an important frame of reference to help Daniel comprehend his history and the tragedy of his family. The symbol for Daniel of his Jewish past as both a burden and dynamic heritage can be found in his grandmother, Rochelle's mother. She stands for him as an exuberant and eccentric life force. She appears early in the novel as the neighborhood's crazy woman whose story is told in part through the Bintel Brief, or "Bundles of Letters" section of the Jewish Daily Forward, which served as both an outlet for expression and a rare source of comfort and advice to thousands of immigrants. The strengths, dedication, deprivation, and psychological trauma in the immigrant generation are evoked in her character. Daniel conjures up a vision of her during which she reminds him that "'this placing of the burden on the children is a family tradition. But only your crazy grandma had the grace to make a ritual of it.'" During this ghostly visit, she reminds Daniel that he inherited from her the "'shimmering fullness of stored life which always marks the victim. What we have, too much life in each of us, is what the world hates most. We offend. We stink with life. Our hearts make love to the world not gently. We are brutal with life and our brutality is called suffering. We scream into our pillows when we come.'"

However, the Jewish experience in America as presented in this novel includes more than insights into Jewish radicalism and portrayals of the immigrant generation. The novel deals with the meaning of America to the Jews, and one of the novel's deepest ironies concerns the significance to Daniel's family and people of the idea of America. Nothing represents the hold of the American Way more dramatically than Paul Isaacson's belief, almost until his last breath, in the principles, ideals, and purposes of the American system. He demonstrates the power of the American idea to displace dissent by directing it into a framework of the ideology's own terms. Isaacson typifies Sacvan Bercovitch's thesis that the rhetorical structure of the myth and ideology of America integrates opposition into a consensus of belief in the very ideals and values that comprise the American Way. Thus, Isaacson internalizes the ideology of America even while fighting it. The depth of his bitterness about America makes him a target of its legal system. As a Communist, he oppugns the validity of the American idea. Nevertheless, he believes in America. "It's screwy," Daniel says as he describes how his father's generation of Communists could both challenge and believe so desperately in America. He says, "Lots of them were like that. They were Stalinists and every instance of Capitalist America fucking up drove them wild. My country! Why aren't you what you claim to be? If they were put on trial, they didn't say *Of course, what else could we expect*, they said *You are making a mockery of American justice!* And it was more than strategy, it was more than Lenin's advice to use the reactionary apparatus to defend yourself, it was passion." In other words, in terms of the New Covenant, even Paul cannot dissociate himself from the rhetoric of the jeremiad in his radical politics. His Americanism helps to drive him toward a foreign ideology in order to achieve those things he believes to be most American. Daniel remembers his father "eating [his] heart out" while listening to Radio Town Meeting of the Air because the program so perfectly exemplified the failure of American democracy to live up to itself. "He used to turn that on at home," Daniel says. "It would make him furious." Daniel insists that "the implication of all the things he used to flagellate himself was that American democracy wasn't democratic enough. He continued to be astonished, insulted, outraged, that it wasn't purer, freer, finer, more ideal." In a sense, Paul's belief in America follows the pattern of the family's drive toward self-destruction. It could be argued that his undiminished belief in those American ideals that his more "patriotic" and "American" persecutors defame and corrupt leads to his electrocution as a traitor and spy. In the Death House at Sing Sing he says to his children, who a moment before had hysterically insisted upon being searched by a guard before the visit, "'You cannot put innocent people to death in this country. It can't be done.'"

Daniel's life as an Isaacson represents only one phase of his life and one aspect of the Jewish experience in America. It gives him roots in the radical and immigrant-based subculture of the Jewish left. That phase culminates for Daniel when his mother says that her execution should serve as a bar mitzvah, or day of initiation into manhood, for him. At the time of her execution, she says, "'Let my son be bar mitzvahed today. Let our death be his bar mitzvah.'" Considering the significance of the bar mitzvah in Jewish life, as well as Daniel's general helplessness at the time, the words amount to a curse on his head. They are an act against the living that helps propel her son into a life of anguish. The mother's words also conclude what had been a period of devastation for the children, including the arrest of the father, the steady isolation of the family, the horrible failure of the mother to return home one day after saying good-bye to them because she also has been arrested, the sense of abandonment that leaves the children with almost no emotional support and love, the loneliness of living with an inept and grotesque aunt, and the nightmare of a public shelter in which Susan screams at night and recedes into old habits like wetting the bed. At one point during this period, Daniel from his own place in the shelter believes that he can hear his sister scream from another part of the building. He soon masterminds their escape, and they return to their old house as though believing that everything can be made normal and safe in the old surroundings. Instead, of course, they find nothing and in turn are found alone in the house by the Isaacson's lawyer, a stream of the girl's urine on the floor.

Following the execution, a new phase begins for the Isaacson children with their adoption by a liberal law professor and his wife. However, since the novel defies traditional chronological plot development, we know from the beginning that this new phase marks just a temporary reprieve for the children. Their new parents are ideal in conventional middle-class terms. They can give the children a new life, but they cannot rewrite the history the children already have had. Nevertheless, in terms of the Jewishness of the novel and its success in rendering the meaning of the story of the Jews in

America, the new parents, Robert and Lise Lewin, are vitally important. While Paul Isaacson believes devoutly in the aspect of the American idea that relates to social justice and equality, Robert Lewin adheres with comparable vigor to another view of the American idea. Together, for Daniel, they move his book closer toward presenting a total view of the relationship between the Jews and America. Daniel directly addresses the question of Lewin's significance as a bond between Judaism and Americanism in a comment about a letter he receives from him. Daniel writes, "It is interesting to note, aside from everything else, the operating pressure of fatherhood in Robert Lewin's letter. He wants to stabilize me with responsibility. That is a true blue american puritan idea. In that idea is the fusion of the Jew and America, both of them heirs of the ancient seafarers: you ride the sea best with lead in your keel. My lawyer father is no accident, and it is no accident that he loves American Law, an institution that constantly fails and that he constantly loves, like a bad child who someday in his love will not fail, stabilized with responsibility."

The marriage between the Jews and America that Lewin represents is further developed through the character of Jacob Ascher, the defense counsel for the Isaacsons and the law partner of Lewin's father. Ascher served as the children's only real friend and companion throughout the period of the trial. Daniel writes, "Ascher was a pillar of the Bronx bar. He was not brilliant, but his law was sound, and his honor as a man, as a religious man, was unquestionable. He was an honest lawyer, and was dogged for his clients. I picture him on Yom Kippur standing in the pew with his homburg on his head, and a tallis around his shoulders. Ascher could wear a homburg and a tallis at the same time." The symbols of the tallis, or Jewish prayer shawl, and the homburg combine to form one symbol of the union between the American Way and the Jewish Way in thought and life-style. Daniel writes, "Ascher was not a political man, you could imagine him voting for anyone he found morally recognizable, no matter what the party. If anything, he was conservative. He perceived in the law a codification of the religious sense of life. He was said to have worked for years on a still unfinished book demonstrating the contributions of the Old Testament to American law."

The prominence of Ascher and Lewin in the novel emphasizes the point that *The Book of Daniel*, like its biblical model, is the story of the Jews in a foreign land. However, through them Doctorow is also able to dramatize the marriage between American and Jewish life and thought. In a sense, the novel suggests that the Jews have become the modern archetypal Americans. They are almost super Americans. Accordingly, the Isaacsons' saga in the history of America becomes literally a Jewish story of America. Isaacson himself talks of the Jewishness of the event during his trial. However, from his point of view they all have become slaves bowing before the enemy. He writes to Rochelle, "My darling have you noticed how many of the characters in this capitalist drama are Jewish? The defendants, the defense lawyer, the prosecution, the major prosecution witness, the judge. We are putting on this little passion play for our Christian masters. In the concentration camps the Nazis made guards of certain Jews and gave them whips. In Jim Crow Harlem the worst cops are Negro." His hatred is particularly directed toward the Jewish judge named Hirsch and the Chief U.S. Attorney General, Howard "Red" Feuerman. "Feuerman," he writes, "in his freckles and flaming red hair, this graduate of St. John's, the arch assimilationist who represses the fact that he could never get a job with the telephone company—Feuerman is so full of self-hatred HE IS DETERMINED to purge us. Imperialism has many guises, and each is a measure of its desperation." As told in this part of the novel through Paul's perspective, his judgment upon these two lawyers seems just. He thinks, "Hirsch has heard more cases brought by the government in the field of subversive activities than anyone else. He is Jewish. He wears a striped, ivy league tie, the knot of which can be seen under his judicial robe." It is commonly believed, he reports, that the judge hopes his role in the trial will earn him a place on the Supreme Court. The insensitivity and vulgarity of Hirsch and Feuerman do not diminish the moral authority of either Ascher or Lewin. Nor do they weaken the Isaacsons' passion for justice. However, they do round out the Jewishness of the story in a way that avoids sentimentality. *The Book of Daniel* does not turn all Jews into American heroes, but it does dramatize the significance of their role in American culture.

To adequately tell this story of the marriage between two cultures required Doctorow to unite in one form history, literature, and moral prophecy while he wove into a single web stories of initiation, crime and punishment, self-destruction, courage, and moral triumph. In a sense, the whole story turns the Jews into a prophetic tribe of Daniels casting multiple perspectives on the totality of the American experience. The result is an ingenious reconstitution of the myth of regeneration in America. Daniel is ultimately rescued and saved. Moreover, he gives himself three choices of how to dramatize his regeneration. The first two endings deal with Daniel's ability to confront and transcend his past and express a form of reconciliation. In the first suggested ending, he returns to the old house in the Bronx that was the scene of his youth. As he observes a family of strangers in the house, Daniel seems able to leave, finally, that part of his life. The second ending proposes two funerals. In the first funeral, both he and Susan bury their parents. In the second, Daniel and his new parents bury his sister. In this scene, which recalls the command of his grandmother to remember the dead, Daniel initiates one of the most important rituals in the Jewish religion, a Mourner's Kaddish, or prayer for the dead. The moment reveals Daniel's sense of himself as a Jew as well as his ability to use Judaism as a way to confront his experience. It thereby becomes an act of integration of his Jewish and American selves as part of a reconciliation between his sense of the past and his hope for the future. At his sister's grave, he dismisses "the company rabbi" but calls together the other Jews at the cemetery—the kind of souls who make their living as Jews by praying for a fee for other Jews—and they say Kaddish. Daniel suddenly becomes part of this community of mourners, and, as they pray, he finds himself forcing them to continue. Throughout the entire novel Daniel has had to be a rock. However, in this graveside scene he turns into a human. He writes, "The funeral director waits impatiently beside his shiny hearse. But I encourage the prayermakers, and when one is through I tell him again, this time for my mother and father. Isaacson. Pinchas. Rachele. Susele. For all of them. I hold my wife's hand. And I think I am going to be able to cry."

Both endings suggest freedom for Daniel, but the third ending discusses the subject of freedom itself. In this ending, Daniel is in the library at work on *The Book of Daniel* and trying to conceive of an ending for it. Suddenly a man interrupts Daniel's work to order him to leave because the students are closing the library as part of their protest against the university. The intruder shouts, "'Close the book, man, what's the matter with you, don't you know you're liberated?' " Daniel feels compelled to smile at this announcement of his new freedom by a stranger. "It has not been unexpected," he writes.

Daniel is free. Not because of the student rebellion but because of his ability to complete his book, he achieves a form of liberation. He has freed himself from the task of the book. He has written a book of freedom—a lesson in freedom—because through it he gives everything of himself to fulfill his obligations to his parents and his sister, to his present, and to his hopes for the future. He liberates his life by humanizing it through the exertion of his moral and historic consciousness. Not just an animal or a victim, he overcomes his mother's cry and achieves his own form of bar mitzvah by initiating himself into the realm of those willing to accept moral responsibility for themselves. It is as though Daniel has been striving to achieve a degree in humanity and finally receives it. He writes, "DANIEL'S BOOK: A Life Submitted in Partial Fulfillment of the Requirements for the Doctoral Degree . . . " The final words in the book are in italics and come from the biblical Book of Daniel (12: 1–4, 9). They say that Daniel has done all that he can for his own deliverance and for the deliverance of his people: "*and there shall be a time of trouble such as never was since there was a nation . . .*

and at that time the people shall be delivered, everyone that shall be found written in the book. . . . But thou, O Daniel, shut up the words, and seal the book, even to the time of the end. . . . Go thy way Daniel: for the words are closed up and sealed till the time of the end."

In *The Book of Daniel* and in his subsequent novel *Ragtime*, Doctorow achieves a level of literature that fits Warner Berthoff's category of the mythic. Berthoff writes, "That work of fiction, in brief, has most authority which most abundantly opens itself to the modality of the mythic. But to be a mythmaker, to move toward myth, is not simply to invent new fictions, including exploratory or ironic reconstructions of famous individual myths. It is rather to compose by way of continuously refreshing the substance of what people characteristically say in each other's presence up and down the whole range, or some great part of it, of purposeful human utterance." Both novels are attempts to relate fiction to myth in Berthoff's sense of transforming the language and thought of an era into an art form that reflects and touches all aspects of culture. Doctorow again endeavors in *Loon Lake* to develop and modernize "famous individual myths" for the purpose of capturing the essence of American culture.

In *Loon Lake*, Doctorow elaborates upon the mythic, historical, and cultural significance of a fictional geographic landmark in a way that attempts to re-create and modernize the relationship between the landscape and the American imagination. He invents a geographic region to demonstrate how such a space becomes a region of the mind. The physical space functions as a means of cultural self-identification only to be corrupted by the culture itself, which fails to live up to the meaning it implanted into its own geography. As a fictional reenactment of this process, the novel attempts to get to the heart of the American spirit. In a Nietzschean manner we get history as a symbol. Moreover, Doctorow inhabits this region of the mind with characters and images that are themselves products of the American mythic and literary imagination. Parallels and interesting connections between *Loon Lake* and such works as *Walden*, *The Great Gatsby*, and *U.S.A.* abound.

Thus, in *Walden* the loons become symbolic of both Thoreau's and the pond's independence. He writes, "I am no more lonely than the loon in the pond that laughs so loud, or than Walden Pond itself. What company has that lonely lake, I pray?" In another part of his narrative, Thoreau describes in detail his attempts to chase down a loon who keeps hitting the surface from flight and disappearing under the water, only to emerge again at an unexpected place in the lake. The loon seems to mock Thoreau's attempts to understand him. He sends forth loud "demoniac laughter" that taunts Thoreau with its suggestion that the loon possesses some unique knowledge.

Thoreau writes, "While he was thinking one thing in his brain, I was endeavoring to divine his thought in mine. It was a pretty game, played on the smooth surface of the pond, a man against a loon." The loon's ability to thrive on all three realms of the lake—above the water, on the surface, and below—demonstrates the bird's possession of special gifts. Thoreau writes, "How surprised must the fishes be to see this ungainly visitor from another sphere speeding his way amid their schools!" Thoreau also notes "that loons have been caught in the New York lakes eighty feet beneath the surface, with hooks set for trout." It is at such a lake situated in the Adirondacks in New York that Doctorow picks up the mystery of the loon.

As in *Walden*, the history of the meaning to mankind of *Loon Lake* goes back to the time of the Indians, and the story of the lake symbolizes the continuing profanation of the purity of the natural environment by society. In the novel, a poet named Warren Penfield functions as the consciousness who describes the meaning of the lake. Naturally, his book is called *Loon Lake* so that the physical landmark merges with the poetic and intellectual construct. Penfield writes, "All due respect to the Indians of *Loon Lake* / the Adirondack nations, with all due respect. / What a clear cold life it must have been." Penfield the poet sees the loons as symbolic of an eternal process of death and rebirth. The image of the loons connects the past of the Indians with the present. "The loons they heard were the loons we hear today," Penfield writes. The representation of the lake in the poem as the embodiment of the natural and spiritual purity of America contrasts with the current uses of the lake. Following the invasion of the Adirondacks by artists and painters who helped invent "the wilderness as luxury" business, the lake became the property of a wealthy industrialist named F. W. Bennett. Under Bennett, the wilderness of *Loon Lake* changes into a beautiful mountain camp where leading celebrities as well as the corrupt and the criminal are entertained. As though to dramatize the change, a loon appears from nowhere while gangsters speedboat along the lake's surface. The loon catches in midair a cigarette that the wind had "whipped out" of the mouth of one of the gangsters. "The crazy bird" seems almost trained to do it, as though they are now part of the entertainment for the corrupt company at the camp.

The novel's best example, however, of the change to the new America of industrial exploitation and waste can be found in a character named Joe who functions as the most significant consciousness in the novel. Born Joseph Korzeniowski, he is called Joe Paterson after his native city. Primarily through Joe's consciousness, we get compact, intense, and personal visions of experience that remind one of the "Camera Eye" sections of Dos Passos's *U.S.A.* A wanderer and loner, Joe also seems modeled after several Dos Passos types, especially Joe Williams, who represents in U.S.A. the consciousness of the common-man victim. Thus, in style and substance, Doctorow recognizes and consciously elaborates upon the mythic constructs in much of modern American literature. Joe Paterson's story, however, seems most related to that of F. Scott Fitzgerald's Gatsby. The pattern of Joe's development and metamorphosis follows the one established by Gatsby, and the cultural implications that Gatsby's story embodies are duplicated by Joe. Gatsby, of course, was born Jay Gatz and through the intervention of a wealthy benefactor achieves a new life. For Gatsby, the sponsor fulfills the role of both God and father. This help enables Gatsby to create a new identity for himself based on his understanding of what success and power mean in America. Fitzgerald writes, "The truth was that Jay Gatsby of West Egg, Long Island, sprang from his Platonic conception of himself. He was a son of God—a phrase which, if it means anything, means just that—and he must be about His Father's business, the service of a vast, vulgar, and meretricious beauty. So he invented just the sort of Jay Gatsby that a seventeen-year-old boy would be likely to invent, and to this conception he was faithful to the end." Similarly, Joe Paterson in *Loon Lake* achieves a new identity through the intervention of the industrialist Bennett who sees himself in certain ways as a mythic or God-like figure. Bennett adopts Joe. Joe in turn develops into the corporate, social, and political image of his new father. In a summary of his career at the end of the novel, Doctorow provides Joe with all the accoutrements of modern-day corporate and social success. His titles, organizations, positions, achievements, and memberships represent the things that Doctorow obviously detests about contemporary America. Joe's success, therefore, constitutes a political and moral failure. Along with all his achievements, including duty as "Deputy Assistant Director of the C.I.A." and an ambassadorship, Joe can call himself "Master of *Loon Lake*." The last title on the list indicates the ultimate betrayal in terms of the novel's values.

In *Loon Lake*, Doctorow continues to maintain a radical perspective on American culture. Imbued with the literary and mythic sensibility of an earlier radical generation, he still attacks corporate bureaucracy and capitalistic exploitation. However, like Daniel Isaacson, he embodies a new radical consciousness that reflects contemporary concerns and realities. For example, in his description of Disneyland in *The Book of Daniel*, Doctorow discusses the power that enables mass culture and the entertainment media to turn our great narratives into palliatives for complacency and conformity and to undermine the existential challenge of literature. As a writer, he wants to repossess the culture's natural resources of myth and narrative in order to restore the culture and to reaffirm the values of individual freedom and responsibility. Similarly, Doctorow uses psychology to develop a new radical perspective that can offer possible insights unavailable to traditional radical politics. Thus, early in the novel, he describes the sexual relations between Daniel and his wife, Phyllis, in a way that combines physical and political terms. The description implies that in a modern radical ideology the psychological roots of oppression may be as important as the economic. Portraying Phyllis as a "sex martyr" and Daniel as a "tormentor" who makes her suffer "yet another penetration," Doctorow plays with the idea of the sexual origins of political power as Daniel "explores the small geography of those distant island ranges, that geology of gland formation, Stalinites and Trotskyites, the Stalinites growing down from the top, the Trotskyites up from the bottom."

The different elements that form Doctorow's political and literary vision can be discerned from the figures he quotes at the beginning of *The Book of Daniel.* The quotations are from the Prophet Daniel, Walt Whitman, and Alien Ginsberg. All three indicate Doctorow's attraction to prophets who become aliens in their own lands partly because they often speak for the values and ideals of the very cultures that ostracize them and resist their messages. They are vital and distinct landmarks in Doctorow's moral and cultural consciousness and represent major aspects of his thought and his literary and political program—Jewish, American, and radical. Although important differences separate Daniel, Whitman, and Ginsberg, they are also related elements of one moral vision. They are like the various selves that comprise the one mythic American Self for both Whitman and Emerson. Their examples encourage Doctorow to continue his effort to meld together the literary, historic, and mythic to express the meaning of America. Taken together, the figures of Daniel, Whitman, and Ginsberg dramatize how well Doctorow propels the thrust of the New Covenant. As a Jewish writer and thinker, he contributes to the development of the American idea by being at once both the most conservative and the most radical of Americans. He is the most conservative because of his concern for preserving those institutions and values of democracy that constitute the American idea. At the same time, he is the most radical because he extends and modernizes the ideology and meaning of America to make it relevant to contemporary American life, thought, and needs. Like Daniel, he brings together the social visions of both the Isaacsons and Lewins into one unified whole. Thus, because of his purposes as a writer and thinker and his philosophy of the American idea Doctorow demonstrates that he holds a position of leadership in the New Covenant tradition in America.

GEOFFREY GALT HARPHAM

E. L. Doctorow and the Technology of Narrative

Readers of contemporary American fiction commonly divide the field into opposing groups: the postmodernists, led by such unpredictable demiurges as Nabokov, Pynchon, Barthelme, Barth, and Gaddis, and the post-Great Traditionalists who work the realistic vein, such as Bellow, Styron, Malamud, and Roth. One mark of the unusual interest of E. L. Doctorow is that he has contrived to be identified with both groups. He has done so by producing work that invokes both the real, in the radical form of historically verifiable fact, and the "experimental," chiefly through dislocations of identity and the breaking up of the narrative line. His work thus has a certain unclassifiability (a quality it shares with Thomas Berger's G, Pynchon's *Gravity's Rainbow*, Anthony Burgess' *Nothing like the Sun*, and Mailer's *The Executioner's Song*) that obscures the opposition between realism and experimentalism.

Doctorow's reviewers generally approach him by a gestalt switch, considering his "dazzling technique" or "technical virtuosity" as secondary to and largely independent of the real center of attention, his "vision of history" or his "view of the American character". But Doctorow and others emphasize that this way of reading is inadequate and call for an approach that can describe how issues of narrative technique interpenetrate and constitute the political, social, or historical subjects of narrative. Beyond the horizon of any particular meaning or device in Doctorow's work lies the abiding question of

From *PMLA* 100, no. 1 (January 1985): 81–95, ©1985 by The Modern Language Assocation of America.

the relation between thematics and technique. The goal of this discussion is to articulate the submerged but operative meditation on narrative that informs his most important novels. The evolution of this meditation can, in turn, articulate the shape of Doctorow's development as novelist and theoretician.

As a novelist, Doctorow usually does his thinking in his fiction, but he has written several essays, of which the most important is a 1977 discussion of "False Documents" where he argues that two kinds of power inhere in language. The first, "the power of the regime," is exemplified by a quotation from the *New York Times*, whose power resides in its unarguable attachment to the world. The second, exemplified by a paragraph from Nabokov, is "the power of freedom." This power resides in its reference to a nonverifiable ideal world and offers the writer "some additional usefulness," revealing not "what we are supposed to be" but "what we threaten to become."

Although Doctorow speaks of a "regime language" and a "language of freedom" and presents his examples as pure strains of each, he also discusses literature as a necessary mingling of two types of linguistic power. His analysis recalls the origins of narrative: "It is possible," he says "that there was a time in which the designative and evocative functions of language were one and the same." In ancient times the storyteller wielded social power "because the story he told defined the powers to which the listener was subject and suggested how to live with them. Literature . . . bound the present to the past, the visible with the invisible, and it helped to compose the community necessary for the continuing life of its members." In technologically developed countries, however, fact and fiction have become differentiated, and the privileges accorded imaginative literature now reflect, its ornamental status, its remoteness from, rather than its proximity to, the centers of social power. Real power in such societies is articulated in the regimes of science, law, business, government, or technology.

Whatever the merits of this argument as literary history, it has one possible advantage for Doctorow as novelist. In establishing literature's ancient double function of pleasing and of giving counsel, it implicitly validates his own project of treating historical fact in fictional terms. In the light of "False Documents," this project appears as a means both of reclaiming lost power and of realizing the full potentiality of fiction.

Doctorow describes as "false documents" novels written under a particular strategy of "creative disavowal" by which writers gain authority by distancing themselves from their texts, claiming that they were not or even that they could not have been the authors. Cervantes, Defoe, Conrad, and Nabokov acknowledge and try to combat the trivialization of literature by presenting their works as the "found" or transcribed inventions of others.

Doctorow's own protest in this essay is to declare that, as there is no meaning without the mediation of images, knowledge can never be grounded, and fiction actually lies at the heart of all factual records: "Facts are the images of history, just as images are the data of fiction."

Having settled the opposition of fact and fiction in favor of the latter, Doctorow abruptly abolishes the differences altogether, concluding that "there is no fiction or nonfiction as we commonly understand the distinction: there is only narrative." This "novelist's proposition" casts a curious light on the essay in which it occurs. If narrative is the single complex mode within which appearances of grounded knowledge and pure imaginative freedom arise, then why had the essay begun by arguing for the distinction between them, even arguing for two kinds of language? And if fiction subsumes fact, then how can the reader be persuaded to believe this as a fact? Indeed, given the conclusion, the forensic method of the essay is at odds with itself. Citing authorities, making distinctions, observing rules of evidence, the essays takes the objectivist position outside imaginative distortion to claim, first, that there are two kinds of power in language; second, that there are two kinds of language; third, that one of those kinds dominates and even constitutes the other; and, finally, that there is only one kind of language but that it is neither the first nor the second. The essay is itself an especially complicated kind of false document, as it seeks to persuade but becomes something we can neither believe nor disbelieve. Rather, it demonstrates its "point" by being a narrative of positions serially entertained by the author as well as an exposition of an argument.

This essay gives us a way of thinking about Doctorow: not as a formal innovator or as the author of fictionalized history but as a creator of texts whose ambivalences define his central continuing concern, narrative itself and its relation to power, imagination, and belief. Within the terms of this problem, Doctorow's career has taken shape. It has developed, I argue, from a critique of the coercive power of the textual and ideological regime to a celebration of the powers of imaginative freedom.

Time, Space, and the Textual Circuit

Doctorow's first important book, *The Book of Daniel*, is a meditation on the legacy of the Rosenberg trial, a public exercise of the power of the regime that foregrounded its dependency on the power of the imagination. For Doctorow, the criminal trial, and this one in particular, calls into question the fundamental issues of narrative, since it is a real event that can only be conceived in imaginative terms. "Consider those occasions," he says in "False Documents,"

> criminal trials in courts of law—when society arranges with all its investigative apparatus to apprehend factual reality. Using the tested rules of evidence and accrued wisdom of our system of laws we determine the guilt or innocence of defendants and come to judgment. Yet the most important trials in our history, those which reverberate in our lives and have most meaning for our future are those in which the judgment is called into question: Scopes, Sacco and Vanzetti, the Rosenbergs. Facts are buried, exhumed, deposed, contradicted, recanted. There is a decision by the jury and, when the historical and prejudicial context of the decision is examined, a subsequent judgment by history. And the trial shimmers forever with just that perplexing ambiguity of a true novel.

In this view, a trial is both a struggle and a temptation. A trial that "shimmers" marks the limits of the regime and of its underlying linguistic assumptions. The task ostensibly confronting juries is to decide whether the language of a given law adequately describes the act in question. Perhaps they can choose among several descriptions such as those that define first-degree murder, second-degree murder, and manslaughter. In either case, the assumption is that words acquire their meaning through correspondence to a nonlinguistic realm of events or objects. In most trials the linguistic element in guilt or innocence, the matching of word to deed, appears unproblematic. But in trials that shimmer, no single account adequately describes the "crime," which can be seen only through the more or less plausible accounts offered by opposing sides. The factor of plausibility introduces a fictional element into the description that confirms the novelistic enterprise. In redescribing the Rosenberg case, the novelist can feel that he is not violating an original factuality, for the event is already accessible only through fiction. The undecidability of such trials does not merely resemble a novel; it opens up a space that virtually produces the novel, a space in which narrativity takes precedence over referentiality.

The Book of Daniel does not just fictionalize the Rosenberg case as one of the Rosenbergs' children might have done. It equally concerns the difficulties of a would-be narrator trying to turn a real event into a narrated one. In focusing on this aspect of the text, we must be especially attentive to a number of marginal and essayistic passages in which the narrator, Daniel, records his thoughts on these difficulties. Groping for the facts in his parents' case, he confesses in one such passage, "I worry about images":

> Images are what things mean. Take the word image. It connotes soft, sheer flesh shimmering on the air, like the rainbowed slick of a bubble. Image connotes images, the multiplicity being an image. Images break with a small ping, their destruction is as wonderful as their being, they are essentially instruments of torture exploding through the individual's calloused capacity to feel powerful undifferentiated emotions full of longing and dissatisfaction and monumentality. They serve no social purpose.

This is a hard passage to explicate because it is itself an erratic explanation. We learn that images are delicate and murderous, that they are modes of liberation and of torture. Although they serve no social purpose, they are both weapons and victims. The singular "connotes" the plural, which, like bubbles merging, re-forms into a singular. Perhaps the only constant property of images is their utter potentiality: they can perform any function, acquire any characteristics. Unbound by discourse, the image is a potential anarchy, which may be why it is said to serve no social purpose and also why the radical Artie Sternlicht in *Daniel* can threaten to "overthrow the United States with images." Tightly bound images, however (images such as the swastika or the crucifix that "are what things mean"), tend to totalitarianism; they crystallize the thoughts and emotions repressed or dispersed over the course of a narrative, an argument, or a social process and concentrate them into a potent, complex, and undiscussable unity. Images serve equally freedom and the regime; any narrator concerned to write a factual account would worry about them.

Images are also cause for worry because they have an uncertain relation to the narrative that binds them. As the "data of fiction," images are the building blocks out of which the whole is constructed, a small unit of duration that can combine with other such units to produce a narrative representation of change over time. But curiously, the image can also encompass an entire narrative, washing it clean of temporality ("the multiplicity being an image"). This is the function Michael Riffaterre has in mind when he says that "A valid interpretation . . . must arrive at a stable picture of the text. This stability [is] the equivalent, in the reading act, of the immovable monumentality we expect in a work of art." So although the image is a subordinate unit of narrative, it is also the distillation of an entire narrative. At once slave and master, the image shimmers in irreducible paradox.

Narrative, which may appear in this context as a mere incident in the mitosis of images, owes to the image its ambivalent status as both a primary and secondary entity, as both a thing in itself and a representation, a kind of peeling off, of something else. Inasmuch as it is made of images narrative is a product of mediation, floating at a distance from the world it represents. But inasmuch as it resolves into an image, narrative can "stabilize" the world and articulate its meaning. The image is the permanently contradictory essence of narrative, and in writing fictional history, Doctorow is extending and recomposing *Daniel's* anxious insight into the image's powers.

Images may be what things mean, but they are neither really things nor meaning; they are, rather, a passage from one to the other, or, more precisely, a mediation from which things and meaning can be inferred. This passage enables the larger mediation of narrative, which is characterized by authoritative closure and formal coherence. In an illuminating discussion Hayden White describes these qualities as the basis of "narrativity" and argues that the sense of immanent structure and moral meaning imparted by closed or fully formed narrative gives to reality the odor of the ideal, making reality desirable even as it is falsified. Only narrativity can authenticate an account, making the narrated events "susceptible to being considered tokens of reality." What powers any narrative, White argues, is the need for an authoritative account of what really happened, and this means not only that some ruler or institution requires an account that justifies its claims to authority but also that the events themselves are problematical, their significance open to dispute. "In order to qualify as 'historical,'" White says, "an event must be susceptible to at least two versions of its occurrence." White points out how late medieval historians typically appealed to the authority of God, prince, patron, predecessor, or even parents in an attempt to sanction their versions of events. If the prince is potent the account may stand; if not, a shadow version that the first version sought to suppress may emerge under the sponsorship of some competitor.

Thus narrative, with its volatile images, is a political issue-perhaps the quintessentially political issue, since its truth status always depends on the power of the authorities that sanction it. And it is precisely the issue of *The Book of Daniel.* The agents of the political regime, the FBI, have composed one version of the Isaacsons' activities, "gradually perfect[ing] the scenario" with eight, then nine, and finally ten overt acts ("FRYING, a play in ten overt acts"). Contesting the FBI account, Daniel appeals to his biblical namesake, "a Beacon of Faith in a Time of Persecution," as the authority for an alternative account, the text before us. This desperately ironic appeal almost parodies the conventional relation between historians and their authority figures. The biblical Daniel is connected to Daniel only accidentally; moreover, he was himself a marginal and perhaps even nonexistent figure whose radically unauthoritative and disorderly text records both "some of the most familiar stories of the Bible" and "weird dreams and visions which have baffled readers for centuries." Such a shaky relation to authority helps account for what might otherwise be characterized as the technical aberrations of Daniel's text: its mingling of essay, diary, fiction, and dissertation; its abrupt shifts from first to third person; its jagged nonsequentiality; its inconclusiveness; its lack of overt acts. These aberrations betoken the absence of authority, or the resistance of instituted authority to Daniel's narrative. The degree of narrativity, the tightness of closure, is proportionate to the authoritativeness of the sanctioning authorities; Doctorow and his narrator are trying to discover what kind of narrative is possible when one stands not only outside but in opposition to the regime.

A number of passages in *Daniel* concern the bedrock issues of narrative: what is its cultural basis? what is it made of? who can make one? what kind of power does it require or reflect? Perhaps because Daniel stands in antagonistic relation to institutional authority, he sees narrative chiefly as a set of problems or contradictions. One of the most pressing is the discontinuity between the temporality of events and their atemporal meaning. Like the FBI's chronicler, Daniel seeks to establish not only the order of events but their significance, not only their sequence but their form, their pattern of repetitions. As he ponders his own writing, Daniel begins to realize that although meaning cannot be determined until sequence is established, sequence does not produce meaning but actually seems to struggle against it. At one point, Daniel describes "the novel as a sequence of analyses" but immediately turns his thoughts outside the novel: "But what of the executioner? A quiet respectable man, now retired. He is in the Yonkers phone book." Time has passed between the execution and a respectable retirement, but neutral sequence, fostering forgetfulness and deferring justice, has nothing to say against the passage. As the narrative sequence approaches the execution, Daniel interrupts his account to protest:

> What is most monstrous is sequence. When we are there why do we withdraw only in order to return? Is there nothing good to transfix us? If she is truly worth fucking why do I have to fuck her again? . . . I engorge with my mushroom head the mouth of the womb of Paul's mother. When we come why do we not come forever? The monstrous reader who goes on from one word to the next. The monstrous writer who places one word after another. The monstrous magician.

Sequence, the linearity of narrative, has the annalist's (though not the analyst's) claim of reality. But it is monstrous, pressing toward the electrocution, passing indifferently through it, and immediately relegating it to the past. It is magical, making things appear and disappear. And it creates a bond of monstrous complicity between the reader and writer.

Daniel is in the position of requiring an alternative account to establish his authority, even his identity, but of being betrayed by the very condition of all accounts. Fortunately, sequence is not the whole story. Even this passage exhibits a counterforce of repetition and metaphor, arranging images not simply by laying them end to end but by retrieving, reconstituting, and superimposing them. Take the middle sentence of the passage, "I engorge with my mushroom head the mouth of the womb of Paul's mother." "Paul's mother" is both Daniel's grandmother and his wife, just as Paul is both father and son. The sentence describes an oedipal cycle, or spiral, that transcends sequence in an ambiguous intimation of repetition. The figurality of language, its shimmeriness, enables the "head" to refer to both the penis and the cranium, so that the engorging suggests both fornication and birth, entrance and exit. The possible meanings are not strictly confined to the family romance, for the atomic aura of "mushroom" summons up the bomb with whose secrets the Isaacsons are supposedly so intimate. Thus the bomb in the womb implies a going-nowhere self-destructiveness that is a genetic inheritance of the Isaacson family, as well as a continually reenacted fate. As Susan, Daniel's sister, says, "They're still fucking us."

Susan's phrase directs us to a way of world making wholeheartedly endorsed by Daniel's parents, a way in which the sense of sequence is minimized in favor of the sense of repeatable structure. The epitome of nonsequentiality is Paul Isaacson's "famous remark": It's still going on. "In today's newspapers it's still going on. In this house." Artie Sternlicht names a collage—the characteristic radical art form—EVERYTHING THAT CAME BEFORE IS ALL THE SAME and inspires Daniel with an idea for an article:

> The idea is the dynamics of radical thinking. With each cycle of radical thought there is a stage of genuine creative excitement during which the connections are made. The radical discovers connections between available data and the root responsibility. Finally he connects everything. At this point he begins to lose his following. It is not that he has incorrectly connected everything, it is that he has connected everything. Nothing is left outside his connections. At this point society becomes bored with the radical.

As a corrective to the monstrousness of sequence, radical thought offers simultaneity, a system of conceptual connections among noncontiguous "data." Radical thought is predisposed to perceptions of complicity, perceptions that sequential thought obscures.

But, like sequence, the radical pole of narrative is ultimately self-canceling, working against the adequate representation it tries to establish. At the moment of fulfillment when everything is connected, the perfected system detaches itself from ongoing reality, losing its explanatory power. It becomes "boring."

The search for a narrative mode that will secure the truth has led Daniel to investigate the problematics of meaning in narrative and has brought him to the brink of a disabling conclusion: that the poles of narrative are, respectively, monstrous and boring, meaningless and all too meaningful, and that narrative is only a crossing of two types of misrepresentation. The juridical question of whether the Isaacsons were guilty or innocent has become tangled up with the technical question of whether there can be any reconciliation between sequence and repetition, temporality and structure, that will produce a genuine noncontradictory form of meaning.

It is the brutal paradox of *The Book of Daniel* that the technical solution to this problem is the thematic problem itself: electricity.

At one point Daniel recasts the question of the narrative transformation of experience into a question about education:

> I wish I knew how education works. I wish I knew the secret workings in the soul of education. It has nothing to do with time as we measure it. Small secret chemical switches are thrown in the dark. Tiny courses are hung through the electric passages of the tissues.

Electricity has stolen into this passage as a way of explaining the transformation of experience into significance, the irreducible basis of understanding. As a heuristic device it has several advantages over sequence and repetition. The problem with sequence is that it implies an indifference to the shape and closure of narrative. The problem with repetition is that it implies the abolition of linearity, an impossible stability of context, and a virtual stoppage of time. Electrical education unifies sequence and repetition by reducing them to a single elemental action—the throwing of a switch in the passages of the tissues. At this microlevel, we gain new knowledge and understanding through an action that is repeated constantly. This paradox will reappear in different forms in Doctorow's subsequent novels, and so I would like to dwell on it here. In this meditation on the secret soul of education, Daniel approaches the biochemical basis of narrative, which, incidentally, is etymologically linked with "knowledge," "known," "knowable," and so on. This basis can perform the same sanctioning and legitimizing function as that performed by authority figures for other historical narratives. In this passage we can glimpse a reconstitution of narrative under an epistemological rather than a political or cultural authority. Under this order narrative is not how institutions justify themselves; it is how we know. Perhaps the only disadvantage to conceiving of education in electrical terms is that the individual as an integrated entity is simply dissolved, for all the crucial steps occur through anonymous processes in "the tissues." Such dissolution is the price of clarity.

This aggressive reading of an obscure passage is supported by an entire network of references in the text. In another passage on education, for example, a ghoulish bit of quasi poetry, the California-mystical "om" is co-opted by "ohm," the measure of electrical resistance:

> what is it that you can't see but you can feel
> what is it that you can't taste and can't smell
>   and can't touch but can feel
> ohm ohm ohm ohm ohm . . .
> what makes you smell when you touch it, blacken
>   when you feel it, die when you taste it.
> ohm
> what is it that lightens the life of man and
>   comforts
> his winters and sings that he is the master of
> the universe; until he sits in it.
> ohm

Electricity filters into the concept of awareness or insight; it enters in disguise, revealing only its potent immateriality; it effects tiny changes in phrasing; it provides an illusion of mastery to those who appear to possess it; and then it suddenly unmasks itself as destroyer. This passage is more radical than the previous one, in which electricity appears to ground meaning and validate narrative by dissolving the individual. Electrical awareness, we can conclude, is a fatal enlightenment.

Among the numerous references to electricity scattered throughout the text (an imagined law firm of Voltani, Ampere, and Ohm; an "electric connection" to a thrown baseball; people "catching the current"; a mention of electricity as "the metaphor of fire" [and therefore a link to the biblical Daniel]; etc.), one pattern is constant, of electricity coming to inhabit ideas or places, making them appear safe and controlled, followed by an abrupt and terrifying turn.

This pattern is most manifest in mentions of the secure, enclosed place. The first of these is Paul Isaacson's radio repair shop, which Daniel recalls as "a place to feel safe. It was all enclosed." It was a refuge both from the outside world and from his father's ideological training, his pedagogy. When he was with his father in the shop, Daniel recalls, "History had no pattern" because his father was absorbed in the task at hand, tracking down the trouble in the "guts" of a "technology that was neutral and had no ideological significance." Several pages later Daniel mentions another sanctuary, occupied by Ben Cohen, who has "a really fine job" working in a subway change booth, where "You're underground in a stronghold that has barred windows, and a heavy steel door that locks from the inside. It's a very safe, secure place to be." The only trouble is that Ben never stays in one place; he's "always switching around." This switch activates a circuit that links these places—and perhaps even links them implicitly with the dentist's chair, with Mindish, finger man and family dentist, operating the drill. All these references contribute to a definition of the secure place of employment in terms of locks, bars, and electrical victimization—a definition, as Daniel puts it, of "The electric chair as methodology of capitalist economics."

Just as important, connections are being drawn among the peculiar powers and forces that organize the disparate elements of Daniel's experience, that make it narratable, impelling it toward the closure of the electrocution. Such references transform electricity from a figure of speech to a political and narratological force. These scattered electrical latencies, these dim signals, articulate the circuit of complicity that marks both the narrative or textual circuit and the political network that turns the switch on the Isaacsons.

Electricity in *The Book of Daniel* is a common principle of desire that gives the narrative cohesion and the odor of the ideal. In each significant reference to electricity, this narrative paradox is reinscribed: as the price for a desirable ideality and coherence, reality is deadened. In Susan's shock therapy, for example, a strong current induces "a rigid dance" whose curative processes resemble an attack. More dramatically, there is an occasion when the current enters a secure place, the Isaacson bedroom, to embrace the embracing couple:

> Flopping about, completely out of control, these people who control you. Grunting and gasping, who have told you to tie your shoelaces and drink your juice. . . . The world was arranging itself to suit my mother and father, like some mystical alignment of forces in the air; so that frictionless and in physical harmony, all bodies and objects were secreting the one sentiment that was their Passion, that would take them from me.

The Isaacsons are themselves "drinking their juice" as they anticipate their own execution and replicate Susan's rigid dance in which desire overlaps with annihilation. Their Passion, capitalized to recall Christ's, is both intrapersonal and universal. Individual "desire" is the ego's misnomer for the force that overcomes resistance, makes connections, and completes the circuit. Orgasm, "the little death," is an act of complicity.

Disneyland, scene of the terminal interview with Mindish, epitomizes the connection between desire and complicity. Sponsored by corporations promoting "YOUR CAREER IN ELECTRICITY," it functions chiefly, according to Daniel, to manipulate the masses. "What Disneyland proposes is a technique of abbreviated shorthand culture for the masses, a mindless thrill like an electric shock, that insists at the same time on the recipient's rich psychic relation to his country's history and language and literature." This is systemic desire: it appears in the guise of education and yet operates as a mindless thrill whose effect is crowd control. The individual ego is invoked and privileged but effectively bypassed, or short-circuited.

How to resist, when resistance constitutes the circuit itself? How to stand outside? If complicity is complicity and "Reform is complicity" and "It is complicity in the system to be appalled with the moral structure of the system," and even "Innocence is complicity," then there are no safe places, no neutral technologies, no gestures that escape connection. A strong resistance such as the Isaacsons made might slow the current but cannot intercept it; indeed it can only make it visible. After narrating the electrocution of his father, Daniel speculates that

> It perhaps occurred to the witnesses that what they had taken for the shuddering spasming movements of his life for God knows how many seconds was instead a portrait of electric current, normally invisible, moving through a field of resistance.

This passage has a powerful effect of inevitability, gathering up all the previous references to electricity and concentrating them into closure. At the same time, it distributes the force of an ending throughout the beginning and the middle, those safe textual places now revealed as having been complicitous—intimate with electricity—all along.

The electrocution is a "passage" in another sense, from life to death. The execution chamber, the ultimate enclosed space of desire, is the scene of transformation where, through the agency of electricity, Paul is transformed from the organic into the aesthetic. He becomes educational, textual, a "portrait" framed by the chamber itself. We read this portrait as we do any other, not as a representation of an essentially unknowable and private person, but as a manifestation of forces, a pattern of energy that moves through and defines the individual. This approach assumes a formal coherence, a readability; but it also implies, again, the elimination of the ego. To be legible, Paul must pass through electrical transformation and become an image. If, as Daniel recalls, Paul's entire life had been pedagogic, we must infer that in some ways he had desired precisely such transformation.

Closure has its benevolences. Daniel describes his text as "A Life Submitted in Partial Fulfillment" for a doctoral degree, reminding us that texts may be fulfilled, ongoing lives only partially so. Closure provides the consolation of narrative, without which we are trapped in an unmasterable flux, perpetual victims of sequence or of repetition. It is the desire to pass on, to situate events in a closed circuit to which access is gained only through the text, that motivates closure. Hayden White asks, "What else could narrative closure consist of than the passage from one moral order to another?" Susan's inability to close her parents' account is somehow responsible for her dying—a death, as Daniel puts it, "of a failure of analysis."

We could say that closure grounds the circuit, enabling author or reader to profit from its energies without being electrocuted. But the image of the circuit illuminates the cruelty as well as the protections of textuality. If Daniel would purchase the security of narrative, he must bring the account to closure and "do the electrocution." He must, as monstrous writer, desire to pass on, although this desire implicates him in the network of complicity no matter how he may resist. What is good for the narrative is bad for the Isaacsons. The text is not, after all, a mode of quarantine but, rather, a mode of mediation and ambivalence in which are mingled life and death, reality and fiction, freedom and the regime, past and present, even writer and reader. The monstrous reader is by no means outside the circuit. As Doctorow says at the beginning of "False Documents," "The novel is a printed circuit through which flows the force of a reader's own life." Some shocked readers, seeking refuge outside the circuit, might protest that this book is a mere fiction, a trivialized version of reality; but such a protest is self-abolishing, only constituting a resistance that, as Daniel teaches us, completes the circuit.

To recapitulate: In electricity, Doctorow has located a master principle of narrative that does not reside in cultural or political authority (although it is, of course, the ultimate weapon of that authority); it is a force that unifies all elements of theme and technique, and it is indigenous to the events themselves. Electricity serves as a principle of desire as well as the force that transforms experience into artifact. And in the circuit constituted by resistance, Doctorow has situated all actions by all characters, including the author and the reader. Resistance is a way of thinking about oppositions that structure narrative, such as sequence and repetition, fact and fiction, reality and image—perhaps even experimentalism and traditional realism. Conceive in this way, the entire novel—in fact, all novels, all narratives—could be said to be portraits of "electric currents . . . moving through a field of resistance."

A Ragtime Interlude

The Book of Daniel provides an intimate view of the narrator's mind and of an important historical event. *Ragtime*, by contrast, has no conventional angle of vision at all and no consistent or even possible narrative persona. The narration drifts in and out of characters' minds, recording private thoughts, conversations, actions, and historical generalizations in the same under punctuated history-primer mode. The text gives the extraordinary impression of being self-generated, privileging no character and producing itself independent of any narrator. Unfriendly reviewers have attacked the book on the grounds that this perspectiveless perspective yields no meaningful view, even that it "mocks the idea that a human life can become a coherent narrative." Refuting this charge is less important than understanding it, for it actually puts us in the vicinity of Doctorow's accomplishment. Writing a book with no meaning is not an easy thing, and we may well wonder why an author would go to the trouble. What is the urgent problem to which *Ragtime* is the solution?

We can approach this question by recognizing that *Ragtime* is a continuation of Doctorow's thinking on narrative. Whereas *The Book of Daniel* was concerned with the transformation of experience into story, *Ragtime* focuses on transformation as a universal phenomenon of which narrative is only a local instance. Doctorow does most of his ruminating through the character of the young boy, who is accorded a fitful privilege as the center of the migratory narrative voice. In chapter 15 the boy ponders his grandfather's reading from Ovid:

> They were stories of people who became animals or trees or statues. There were stories of transformation. . . . Grandfather's stories proposed to him that the forms of life were volatile and that everything in the world could easily become something else. . . . [The boy] knew the principles of photography but saw also that moving pictures depended on the capacity of humans, animals or objects to forfeit portions of themselves, residues of shadow and light which they left behind. He listened with fascination to the Victrola and played the same record over and

> over, whatever it happened to be, as if to test the endurance of a duplicated event. . . . he discovered the mirror as a means of self-duplication. He would gaze at himself until there were two selves facing one another, neither of which could claim to be the real one. The sensation was of being disembodied. He was no longer anything exact as a person. He had the dizzying feeling of separating from himself endlessly.

The boy compares his own dispersal to the volatilization of his father, so radically changed on his return from the polar expedition, and to aging, and to the greening of the bronze statue in the city park, as signs of universal and perpetual transformation: "It was evident to him that the world composed and recomposed itself constantly in an endless process of dissatisfaction."

This chain of related concepts—transformation, volatility, repetition, durability, replication—defines what might be called simply "the process," whose effects *Ragtime* traces everywhere, just as Daniel traced the secret circuitry of his world. The process achieves visibility in all the characters: in Evelyn Nesbit, a figure of pure replicability as a Floradora girl, a model for a statue, a media celebrity, and a movie star; in Tateh, who begins by making silhouettes, then develops flipbooks of primitive "animation," and ends as a motion picture director; in Emma Goldman, whose politics are based on collectivism and revolution—duplication and volatility; in Coalhouse Walker, who becomes a political force when his followers adopt the collective name "Coalhouse," becoming representations of him. The Model T on whose uniqueness he paradoxically insists is actually a case of duplication so utter that there cannot even be said to be an original. Even figures such as Mother and Father are figural, replicated by other mothers and fathers in the story. Everything that makes *Ragtime* unusual as a narrative—including the unplaceability of its narrative voice, its numerous replications and parallelisms of character and incident, its undefinable ontology, being at once diary, journalism, realistic novel, and history—contributes to a deemphasis of particularities and to a corresponding emphasis on the common destiny of the entire era. Everything is symptomatic of the process, an instance of it; everything is presented in miniature and has the curiously aesthetic quality of tiny things.

Miniaturization notwithstanding, *Ragtime* is a work of great aspiration, a sustained meditation in the form of a group conversation seen from above, on the subjects of mutability, human identity, the relation of the individual to the social and political collectivity. And, again and again, on the subject of technology. In a conversation with Henry Ford, J. P. Morgan suggests that the true brilliance of the assembly line is that it repeats and confirms "an organic truth," the principle that "the interchangeability of parts is a rule of nature." "Shared design," according to Morgan, "is what allows taxonomists to classify mammals as mammals. And within a species—man, for example—the rules of nature operate so that our individual differences occur on the basis of our similarity." Morgan is describing Doctorow's methods as well as Ford's, for *Ragtime* gives the appearance of having been produced by a narratological assembly line. Doctorow has said that his primary consideration while composing was "relentless pace"; and to maintain the pace he has not only eliminated most description, "setting," and "background" but also effaced the differences between the various elements of his narrative—between large and small, speech and thought, speech and description, historically real and fictional characters. These superfluities and inconvenient singularities have suffered the fate of the individuality of the assembly-line worker—they have been sacrificed in the interests of efficiency.

Continuing the project of *The Book of Daniel*, *Ragtime* posits a master principle—the process—uniting all elements of theme and technique, a principle so comprehensive that it even accounts for the production of the narrative itself. But *Ragtime* also marks a new sensitivity to what might be called the requirements for success. If compared to its predecessor the novel seems trivial and even vulgar, the reason may be that Doctorow's vision now has room for the happy ending, a fate most conspicuously enjoyed by Mother and Tateh. What segregates them from others is their "capacity to forfeit portions of themselves," to relinquish imaginative projections, to embrace the volatility of the world, and to control their lives by generating successive self-representations. In treating their selves as subject to recomposition, they achieve individuation by mastering the processes of replication.

Father, by contrast, is unable to end, and the boy describes him as a perpetual beginner, "the immigrant, as in every moment of his life, arriving eternally on the shore of his Self." The most poignant example of the incapacity to regard the self as subject to invention and reinvention is Houdini, for whom "the real world" is a stage for tricks "he couldn't touch." After his mother's death, his acts become all too real, and the crowds beg him to stop before he kills himself. "Every feat enacted Houdini's desire for his dead mother. He was buried and reborn, buried and reborn." One of a kind, Houdini is driven by a reverence for the uniqueness of his mother and for the reality of the world, but his insistence on these qualities constitutes a blindness to the force of replication in life. Fittingly, he is condemned to ceaseless repetition and to a rancid fictiveness, unable "to distinguish his life from his tricks." He epitomizes failure in *Ragtime* as an inability to forfeit a portion of oneself, to peel the image off and begin the composition anew.

The most successful character is, finally, the young boy, who materializes miraculously at the very end as an older narrator. He has mingled his memories with popular cliches, historical reconstructions, and invention in a narrative that simultaneously represents the era and falsifies it. This falsification is not, however, an avoidable betrayal of reality, as Fredric Jameson argues in a recent article; for as the text shows, the era was never fully present to itself: it constantly produced effects it could neither control nor predict and so was always becoming known and unknown to itself. This narrative does not render the essence of the era but arranges those parts of it that were forfeited or left behind. Including himself in his narrative, the narrator accepts the fact that falsification, distance, and "the process" affect self-knowledge as well as historical knowledge.

From Process to Processor

In the mid-seventies Doctorow became increasingly intrigued by the concept of the interchangeability of parts and by the general idea of a technology, of narrative. In *Loon Lake*, completed in 1979, he brings the technology up-to-date in a self-consciously state-of-the-art novel bearing the markings of the computer. The overt traces of the computer are most concentrated in intrusions on the narrative line—such as "Data comprising life F. W. Bennett undergoing review," the annotations to Penfield's poems, the notes the author has written to himself ("I have a comment here. I note the boy Warren Penfield's relentless faculty of composition")—and in the "reactions" of the program to itself ("Your register respectfully advises the need for additional countervailing data"). Apart from these signatures, the faculty of the computer most frequently exploited by the author is its capacity to transpose information, from one setting to another, the perfect mobility of its text. The computer liberates the writer from textual sequentially, augments the writer's powers of repetition, and encourages a view of textual units—and the things they represent—as interchangeable.

The "dehumanized" aspects, of computer authorship can be usefully compared with mythic modes of production, just as the transformations in *Ragtime* were anticipated by Ovid. For Lévi-Strauss, myth is constructed out of the ruins of previous narratives; it is not freely invented—indeed, it "has no author," it "speaks itself." The tale teller is not so much a creator as an arranger, a compiler, a juggler, or, to use Lévi-Strauss's term, a "bricoleur." The forms and effects of computer bricolage are everywhere in *Loon Lake*, and everywhere strange, but they do make a species of metareferential sense. Take, for example, the first interruption of Joe's first-person narrative at the beginning of the book. The narrative voice has been distinctively "human"—hectic, sensuous, gorgeous—in describing a young boy's experiences, including an encounter with "a great chunky big-bellied soft-assed flop-titted" woman for whom the boy imagines "composing a fuck." As if somehow snagged, the narrative detaches itself from the narrator and, responding to the intimation of a pun, yields:

> Come with me
> Compose with me
> Coming she is coming is she

It is impossible that the first narrator, "Joe," has written this, and yet the narrative resumes, spinning out Joe-like prose until another snag:

> Come with me
> Compute with me
> Computerized she prints out me
>
> Commingling with me she becomes me
> Coming she is coming is she
> Coming she is a comrade of mine

Such doggerel variations give the impression of the voiceless meditations of a printout, a computer version of oral-formulaic poetry. They fracture, pluralize, mechanize the narrative voice, threatening to break down into nonsense. But they do point to a half-articulated intuition about the complicity, signaled by the prefix "com," between desire and invention, coming and composition. The second passage discovers that the computer itself participates in this complicity and that printing out is analogous to giving birth. In the second triplet of this passage the pool is widened to include volatility, identity, and political collectivism. In a "data linkage escape" near the end of the book these passages are recalled and reconstituted—"Come with me compute with me / Coupling with me she becomes a couplet"—so as to extend the associations to poetic composition.

By alienating the narrative voice and introducing the computer into the domains of sexuality and poetic creation, the text appears to be following the program announced for the "human sciences" by Lévi-Strauss at the conclusion of *The Savage Mind*: not to constitute human character but to dissolve it. In fact, at one point this prescription is nearly quoted:

Computer nukes come pray with me
Before the war, the war, after the war
Before the war the war after the war the war
  before the war
Disestablishes human character.

This passage suggests that the computer—which can, in addition to its other feats, launch and direct nuclear weapons—"disestablishes human character." But the extension and retraction of time in the middle two lines imply that human character was already disestablished even before the war and that the computer merely disestablished it once again. This idea is retrieved in a later passage that speaks of Warren Penfield's visit to a Bunraku performance in Japan in which each puppet was manipulated by "three black shadows" standing behind it "and to further disintegrate the human idea the voices of the puppets their growling thrilling anguish was delivered from the side of the stage by a reader." Like myth, Bunraku is virtually founded on the corruption of human identity.

Human identity in *Loon Lake* is corrupted in two ways. One is an affliction epitomized by genealogy. The very first words of the text describe Joe's parents: "They were hateful presences in me," unwelcome shadows produced not by his desire but by theirs, so that he is in effect their puppet. This affliction finds its paradigmatic figure in Clara, who also suffers from overcrowding, her life determined by others: "their presence moved in her their wills directed her even insofar as she created opposition she had been crowded by them their wills their voices their appearance directing her . . . " The massive blocks of unpunctuated prose that record this suffocation stand in sharp visual contrast to other "molecularly reassembled widely spaced" passages, as the young Joe and Clara contrast with other, more widely spaced characters. These figures include Red James, who had cultivated a "union self" and an "espionage self"; the Buddha, thousands of images of whom Penfield sees at tourist shops and shrines-signifying, Penfield reflects, the Buddha's "godlike propensity for self-division, the endless fractioning of himself into every perceivable aspect"; and finally F. W. Bennett, whose wealth purchases "isolation, its greatest achievement is isolation, its godliness is in its isolation." Bennett is himself "spread out and made into a corporation." All these figures accomplish themselves through an "impersonal force," by willed acts of self-representation or self-dispersal that have the effect not of restoring an original integrity of the self but of clearing out unwanted presences within, so that disestablishment is chosen and directed rather than merely suffered.

Thus a distinction may be drawn between identities corrupted by overcrowding and those corrupted by fractioning and partitioning, between those who are controlled and those who control. The most conspicuous sign of control in this text is the manipulation by the narrator (with the aid of the computer) and others of the effects of repetition. Susan Stewart clarifies this dimension of repetition, describing it as the token of "an aesthetic world, a world where the ongoingness of space and time is substituted for by a parallel reality. . . . The illusion of repetition is an illusion of holding context still, of 'taking place' without breaking into the time and space of the 'real' world." Warren Penfield betrays an aesthetic capacity to hold context still when in speaking to Lucinda Bailey Bennett he twice uses the phrase "I have in my life just three times seen a face" or when he tells her that he has loved three times in his life, "Always the same person."

Repetition is not just an "aesthetic" flourish but an event in a narrative that, broadly, describes Joe's growth from a young boy with only one skill, a gift for impersonation, to the Master of *Loon Lake*, heir of F. W. Bennett, deputy assistant director of the CIA, and inventor of this text. The young Joe defines the project of the narrative at the beginning, vowing that he would never

> lose the look in my eye of the living spirit, or give up till that silent secret presence grew out to the edges of me and I was the same as he, imposed upon myself in full completion, the same man with all men, the one man in all events—

At the end, Joe, having decided to "save [Bennett] from wasting away" and to "extend his reign," has put the power of the aesthetic to work in his life; he has imposed himself on Bennett, filling himself to the edges. He not only has become a "repetition" of Bennett but has become one with his representation of himself:

> I stand poised on the edge and dive into the water. With powerful strokes learned in the filth of industrial rivers Joe swims a great circle crawl in the sweet clear cold mountain lake. He pulls himself up on the float and stands panting in the sun. . . . Up on the hill Bennett stands on his terrace, a tiny man totally attentive. He has seen the whole thing, as I knew he would. He waves at me. I smile my white teeth. I wave back.

If *Loon Lake* is viewed as a narrative of self-accomplishment, two events assume special importance as alternative models or myths of the self, corresponding roughly to the two types of corruption of identity. The first occurs in the Jacksontown police station, when the chief of police, interrogating Joe in the death of Red James, says, "You don't like my story, maybe you have a better one." By a sudden illumination, Joe realizes that narrative is survival and improvises a story that accounts for the crime, demonstrates his innocence, asserts that he is Bennett's son, and, incidentally, prevents the police from checking the story's veracity. The story itself is, to its inventor, "a kind of industrial manufacture of my own," an assembly-line product of "a factory of lies, driven by Paterson Autobody doing its days' work. I was going to make it. This was survival at its secret source, and no amount of time on the road or sentimental education could have brought me to it if the suicidal boom of my stunned heart didn't threaten my extinction." Narrative self-invention does not require literary models (such as Kerouac or Flaubert) so much as it requires simple threat. Invention is the mother of necessity, for what Joe has created is his own genealogy, replacing hateful presences with a more truly protective parent. Joe's "autobody" reinscribes the central myth of capitalism, the Horatio Alger notion of the "self-made man," a product of "industrial" rather than genetic necessity.

The other central event of the text describes not the birth of narrative but rather its umbilicus back to its predecessors, the raw material of industrial manufacture. I am speaking of Warren Penfield's bequeathal to Joe of "all my papers, copies of chapbooks, letters, pensées, journals, night thoughts—all that is left of me." There is no further explanation of this gift, but this is what *Loon Lake* is: Penfield's papers, annotated, commented on, arranged, rewritten, and filled out with text composed by Joe, using some original material and some of Penfield's and often making it impossible to draw lines of demarcation. Penfield had articulated the basis for a very different model of self-accomplishment, telling him, "My pain is your pain. My life is your life," and, in the letter bequeathing his papers, "You are what I would want my son to be. More's the pity. But who can tell, perhaps we all reappear, perhaps all our lives are impositions one on another." Penfield suggests an alternative myth of self-reproduction according to which the self that co-opts is already co-opted and the "central intelligence agency" that directs the imposition of self on self is already constituted by multiple impositions beyond its control or desire. In this account, Joe is already a "reappearance" of others, and his youthful talent for impersonation reflects the fact that he is from birth "im-personated," inhabiting and inhabited by alien presences.

Both myths are ultimately self-abolishing. On the one hand, the myth of self-production militates against desire, love, propagation; with isolation as its greatest achievement, it provides its own dead end. The myth of self-reproduction, on the other hand, leads to death on different terms. At the end of *Loon Lake*, with Joe imposing his form on Bennett's and Penfield's story twisting in and out of Joe's, a final "data linkage escape" notes that as "human lovers commonly resemble each other," love works to eliminate differences:

> Given wars before wars after wars genocides
> and competition for markets cloning will eliminate
> all chance
> and love will be one hundred percent efficient
> No *Sturm und Drang* German phrase no
> disynchronicity
> but everyone having seen everyone else somewhere
> before
> we will have realized serenity of perfect universal love
> univerself love uniself love unilove
> until the race withers and blows away like the dried
> husks
> of moths but who's complaining

The text itself is a qualified complaint, for although it is the product of multiple voices, it is imperfectly "efficient" in reconciling those voices. The "register apologizes for rendering nonlinear thinking in linear language," but there is no other kind. In language as in life, repetition is an illusion. Joe's career demonstrates that it is often a potent and useful illusion, but the very mastery it enables him to attain resists it, insisting on its own uniqueness, its own power. In fact, the computer itself provides the most comprehensive model for this resistance. As its memory is multiple, atemporal, and "universal" but its text is singular, linear, and differential, the computer negotiates between the myths of the self as production and the self as reproduction. In *Loon Lake* the force of the personal arises in the dialectic of these two models of impersonal force. It is, in short, the computer that "personalizes" the myths rather than the other way around.

The concept of resistance brings us back to the problematic of *The Book of Daniel*, a problematic from which Doctorow has never departed. The dialectic of *Loon Lake* is inhabited by the dialectic of sequence and repetition in *Daniel* and of replication and uniqueness in *Ragtime*—and even that of freedom and the regime in "False Documents." Earlier I said that Doctorow's central continuing concern was narrative, but it seems equally just to say that he has always been concerned with the conditions of the self. In recent essays Doctorow has spoken of his dissatisfaction with traditional notions of "the psychologized ego" ("Language of Theater") and of "Private Life," the subject of most contemporary fiction, which appears to him "lacking in social reverberations" ("House of Fiction"). His response has always been not to write an even more traditional narrative dominated by social or political concerns but to represent the narrative subject itself as "social," reverberating with the voices of others. In this way Doctorow has tried to liberate the self from the restrictions of the ego: the self is finally—or perhaps originarily—defined by the limits and shape, the formal integrity, of the story it generates with the materials at hand. Dramatizing this notion, Doctorow has made a striking contribution to the neo-Joycean representation of the self. This contribution is most striking in its suggestion that the self is as historically contingent and inconstant as the technologies it appropriates.

In his last three books Doctorow has retold the same story, about a boy who finds himself in an unacceptable narrative determined by the wills of others and who gradually acquires the skills to form his own narrative. But Doctorow's career is noteworthy less for its consistency than for its leaps, which can be variously characterized. The narratological center of attention in *The Book of Daniel* is on the self tentatively producing a narrative; in *Ragtime*, on an oddly self-producing narrative; and in *Loon Lake*, on narrative producing the self. Or we could say that in *The Book of Daniel* the impositions made on the individual by the political system create mostly victims; in *Ragtime* the system—or "the process"—indifferently creates victims and victors; while in *Loon Lake*, which Doctorow has described as "about success" ("Writer's World"), the imposition of self on self opens up creative opportunities. The "secret soul" of education in Daniel is complicitous with the system that kills the Isaacsons, while the "secret source" of survival in *Loon Lake* enables the hero to create himself. As Doctorow becomes more alive to the possibilities for self-invention, he has begun to conceive of his art in nearly capitalistic terms, confessing his enthusiasm for "the American entrepreneurial sense of novel writing" ("Creators"). He has even spoken in ambivalent approbation of Ronald Reagan in 1980 as a "dream candidate" with "a peculiar affinity for simulated life" ("Ronald Reagan").

In a 1980 interview Doctorow described the "connecting themes" in his work as follows: "I find myself extremely sensitive to the idea of injustice. The idea that something is not fair really gives me energy in writing. The idea of the imposition of people on each other—whether in their personal relationships or in large historical terms—seems to intrigue me" ("Creators"). In these three sentences Doctorow has inadvertently described not only the continuities between his books but, more interestingly, their differences, as he modulates from political outrage to a more neutral "energy" and concludes with an apolitical-sounding epistemological "intrigue."

One word whose meaning is undeflected throughout Doctorow's work is "dissatisfaction," which he uses in connection with the power of the image in *The Book of Daniel*, with mutability in *Ragtime*, and, consistently, with his attitude toward his own work. So radical is this dissatisfaction that it appears to attach itself to anything already known, already achieved. The writer, he says, "writes to find out what it is he's writing" ("House of Fiction"), aware that "the sound of a particular language . . . can control any intention" he may have ("*Ragtime*"). Doctorow seems in such statements to situate himself in the systems he has represented, systems that transcend the psychologized ego. From the beginning he has set himself the task of articulating and documenting the changes wrought in human identity by the linguistic, social, and technological systems in which the self participates and tries to manipulate. He has approached the position that there is no such thing as a uniquely human character, that the self is both the cause and effect of processes and elements generally thought of as external to the self. If the novel can survive such a position—and it can, it has—then it can survive anything.

PAUL LEVINE

Politics and Imagination

> The principle which interests me . . . is that reality isn't something outside. It's something we compose every moment. The presumption of the interpenetration of fact and fiction is that it is what everybody does—lawyers, social scientists, policemen. So why should it be denied to novelists?

Writers and critics do not agree on many things but there appears to be a consensus that American literature has undergone a crisis in the past two decades. Philip Roth's famous lament, expressed in 1961, that contemporary reality was constantly outstripping the novelist's imagination has been echoed in many quarters. John Barth spoke of 'The Literature of Exhaustion' while Ronald Sukenick complained that 'What we think of as the novel has lost its credibility—it no longer tells what we feel to be the truth as we try to keep track of ourselves. There's no point in pushing ahead with fiction: we might as well write autobiography and documentary, or social criticism and other how-to books.'

Beginning in the 1960s the American writer faced the kind of imaginative crisis identified by Doris Lessing as 'the thinning of language against the density of our experience'. The result was a literature pulling in

From *E. L. Doctorow*, ©1985 by Paul Levine, Methuen & Co. Ltd, New York.

opposite directions towards a greater concern for objective reality and a deeper obsession with literary self-reflexiveness. Under pressure from the density of contemporary experience some writers moved to the hybrid forms of the 'non-fiction novel' and the New Journalism. I'm thinking of such works as Truman Capote's *In Cold Blood*, Norman Mailer's *The Armies of the Night*, Joan Didion's *Slouching Towards Bethlehem* and James Baldwin's *The Fire Next Time*. Feeling the thinning of language, others turned to black humour, paranoid visions and a kind of linguistic guerrilla warfare—for instance, Joseph Heller's *Catch-22*, Thomas Pynchon's *The Crying of Lot 49*, Ken Kesey's *One Flew Over the Cuckoo's Nest* and William Burroughs's *Nova Express*. Aware of the exhaustion of literary forms, still others like John Barth, John Hawkes, Robert Coover and Kurt Vonnegut explored the vein of reflexive and fabulistic writing we now call post-modernist. Perhaps Vonnegut spoke for them all when he wrote in *Slaughterhouse-Five*: 'everything there was to know about life was in *The Brothers Karamazov*, by Feodor Dostoevsky. "But that isn't *enough* any more." '

But about the same time that writers like Barth and Sukenick were advising their contemporaries to leave realism to the social scientists, semiologists and historians were beginning to question the traditional distinctions between history and fiction. In different ways, Roland Barthes and Hayden White attacked the special status of history as representation of reality by noting the similarity between the linguistic structures and rhetorical strategies of historical and imaginative writing. It seemed that there was no privileged view of the past. History did not hold up a mirror to reality any more than fiction did. Both were constructed by a particular narrative vision in which facts never spoke for themselves.

Recently, the social historian Herbert Guttman pointed to yet another crisis in the contemporary writing of American history: the failure of scholars to reach an audience beyond their own limited professional membership. Guttman attributed this to the inability to create a viable alternative to the discredited old Progressive synthesis which dominated the writing of history until the 1950s. In recent years, he pointed out, exciting new areas have been opened up in the history of previously 'silent' groups like blacks, women and the working class. But an emphasis on quantitative research and microhistorical studies has tended to fragment our understanding of American history and reduce its intelligibility. Thus, while aspects of the American past look different, 'American history itself does not look different. And that is the problem.' So, Guttman concluded: 'A new synthesis is needed, one that incorporates and then transcends the new history.'

These gloomy thoughts were stimulated by Guttman's participation in a panel discussion at the American Writers Conference in 1981 of the question 'Have Writers Discarded History?' Interestingly enough, another panel member was E. L. Doctorow, a novelist who certainly has not discarded history. Indeed, in a 1978 interview, Doctorow explained why history had once again become important to writers of fiction:

> Well, first of all, history as written by historians is clearly insufficient. And the historians are the first to express skepticism over the 'objectivity' of the discipline. A lot of people discovered after World War II and in the fifties that much of what was taken by the younger generations as history was highly interpreted history. And just as through the guidance and wisdom of magazines like *Time*, we were able to laugh at the Russians' manipulation of their own history—in which they claimed credit for technological advances that had clearly originated in other countries, and in which leaders who had fallen out of favor were suddenly absent from their texts—just around that time, we began to wonder about our own history texts and our own school books. And it turned out that there were not only individuals but whole peoples whom we had simply written out of our history—black people, Chinese people, Indians. At the same time, there is so little a country this size has in the way of cohesive, identifying marks that we can all refer to and recognize each other from. It turns out that history, as insufficient and poorly accommodated as it may be, is one of the few things we have in common here. I happen to think that there's enormous pressure on us all to become as faceless and peculiarly indistinct and compliant as possible. In that case, you see, the need to find color or definition becomes very, very strong. For all of us to read about what happened to us fifty or a hundred years ago suddenly becomes an act of community. And the person who represented what happened fifty or a hundred years ago has a chance to say things about us now. I think that has something to do with the discovery of writers that this is possible.

Doctorow was calling attention to one of the most remarkable developments in recent fiction: the creation of a new kind of historical novel. The renewed interest in history, in part a reaction against the excessive privatization of fiction in the 1950s and in part a response to the political and cultural events of the 1960s, grew during the 1960s with the publication of such varied works as John Barth's *The Sot-Weed Factor*, Thomas Berger's *Little Big Man*, Bernard Malamud's *The Fixer* and William Styron's *The Confessions of Nat Turner*. If fiction was moving in the opposite directions of a greater emphasis on both reality and imagination, then for many writers history became a vehicle for mediating between the two. This concern for historical recreation was shared by a wide spectrum of writers, from orthodox modernists like Styron, Mailer and Gore Vidal to orthodox post-modernists like Barth, Pynchon and William Gass. It may be too much to argue that history has become the organizing principle of recent fiction, like Marxism in the 1930s and Existentialism in the 1950s. But it is not too much to suggest that novelists are providing the new synthesis that Herbert Guttman found missing in contemporary historiography.

This new historicizing fiction appears to be an international phenomenon. One thinks of established figures like Grass, Márquez and Solzhenitsyn as well as younger ones like Thomas Kenneally, Timothy Findley and D. M. Thomas. Indeed, Martin Green has called this international movement 'the most promising development of the last decade or more'. According to Green, novelists like John Fowles, John Berger and Doctorow combine historical perceptions with modernist methods to recreate an epoch from a contemporary viewpoint. The result challenges not only our traditional view of history but the conventional notion of the historical novel as well. 'This is an aesthetic kind of historical fiction,' Green noted; 'the writing is notably elegant, and the writer's most necessary qualifications are taste, tact, and erudition.'

Yet not all contemporary novelists approach history from the same perspective: modernists and post-modernists exploit the past in radically different ways. Both Doctorow and Robert Coover, for instance, have written 'revisionist' texts about the trial and execution of the Rosenbergs. In Doctorow's *The Book of Daniel* and Coover's *The Public Burning* the Rosenbergs are treated similarly as pathetic but complicit scapegoats in some anthropological ritual. But whereas Coover invents outrageous situations for actual figures in order to portray the hysteria of the McCarthy era, Doctorow creates his own characters and immerses them in history to suggest something larger about American radicalism in the twentieth century. Thus in Coover's novel, the public burning itself—the execution of the Rosenbergs—takes place in Times Square, the Mecca of hype and entertainment. For Coover, politics in America is packaged as show business and the execution is depicted as an orgiastic celebration of the corrupt national character. In dealing with post-war America, *The Public Burning* transforms history into myth. Similarly, the climactic scene of *The Book of Daniel* takes place in that other symbol of debased mass culture, Disneyland. But Doctorow's exploration is more resonant historically because the final attempt to retrieve the past occurs in the place which has already abolished history and translated it into popular mythology. This opposition between a critical and a corrupted historical perspective runs through the novel and becomes its main theme. At the end of *The Book of Daniel* we are released from history only by embracing it.

We can see how history operates in Doctorow's work by turning to his most popular novel. In *Ragtime* there is a wonderful description of Sigmund Freud's visit to the United States in 1909. The purpose of Freud's visit was to accept an honorary degree from Clark University—the first official recognition of his endeavours. As Doctorow recounts it, the trip was a fiasco. Freud's disciples took him to see the sights of New York but the great man was not impressed. 'What oppressed him about the New World was its noise. The terrible clatter of horses and wagons, the clanking and screeching of streetcars, the horns of automobiles.' They drove to the Lower East Side, the centre of Jewish immigrant life in America, where Freud could not find the toilet he so desperately needed. 'They all had to enter a dairy restaurant and order sour cream with vegetables so that Freud could go to the bathroom.' Finally, the party went to the amusement park at Coney Island where Freud and Jung took a boat trip together through the Tunnel of Love. 'The day came to a close only when Freud tired and had one of the fainting fits that had lately plagued him when in Jung's presence.' But the worst was yet to come:

> A few days later the entire party journeyed to Worcester for Freud's lectures. When the lectures were completed Freud was persuaded to make an expedition to the great natural wonder of Niagara Falls. They arrived at the falls on an overcast day. Thousands of newly married couples stood, in pairs, watching the great cascades. Mist like an inverted rain rose from the falls. There was a high wire strung from one shore to the other and some maniac in ballet slippers and tights was walking the wire, keeping his balance with a parasol. Freud shook his head. Later the party went to the Cave of Winds. There, at an underground footbridge, a guide motioned the others back and took Freud's elbow. Let the old fellow go first, the guide said. The great doctor, age fifty-three, decided at this moment that he had had enough of America. With his disciples he sailed back to Germany on the *Kaiser Wilhelm der Grosse*. He had not really gotten used to the food or the scarcity of American public facilities. He believed the trip had ruined both his stomach and his bladder. The entire population seemed to him overpowered, brash and

> rude. The vulgar wholesale appropriation of European art and architecture regardless of period or country he found appalling. He had seen in our careless commingling of great wealth and great poverty the chaos of an entropic European civilization. He sat in his quiet cozy study in Vienna, glad to be back. He said to Ernest Jones, America is a mistake, a gigantic mistake.

This passage from *Ragtime* provides a convenient point to enter Doctorow's work because it contains three essential characteristics that we shall find in all his writing. First of all, Doctorow's fiction is rooted in history. Each of his major novels deals with a significant moment in the American past: the settling of the West in *Welcome to Hard Times;* the transformation of American life at the turn of this century in *Ragtime*; the trauma of the Great Depression in *Loon Lake*; and the legacy of political radicalism and repression in post-war America in *The Book of Daniel*. Taken together, these books form a mosaic of American society from the closing of the frontier to the end of the Vietnam war.

Yet each of these novels is not simply a faithful recreation of a historical event but rather an imaginative revisioning of a historical epoch. *Welcome to Hard Times* imagines the life and death of an archetypal Western town; *Ragtime* weaves real and imaginary figures into a tapestry of modern American culture; *Loon Lake* explores the American myth of success at the critical moment when its assumptions were being tested by the Depression; *The Book of Daniel* transforms an actual event—the trial and execution of the Rosenbergs—into a meditation on post-war American radicalism. In each case, Doctorow is more concerned with imaginative truth than with historical accuracy. That is, he is concerned with what *truly* happened rather than with what *really* happened. Thus it does not matter whether Freud and Jung did, in fact, take a boat trip through the Tunnel of Love at Coney Island in 1909. Doctorow's description reveals in a witty image a psychological truth about their relationship. Private persons and facts are transformed in their essence when they enter the public realm. In this connection, Doctorow observed in an interview:

> I'm under the illusion that all my inventions are quite true. As, for instance, in *Ragtime* I'm satisfied that everything I made up about Morgan, for instance, or Ford, is true, whether it happened or not. Perhaps truer because it didn't happen. And I don't make any distinction any more and can't even remember what of the events or circumstances in *Ragtime* are historically verifiable and what are not.

Second, Doctorow's revisioning of history reveals a concern with form as well. What was new about *Ragtime*, he once suggested, was not that it used historical figures as fictional characters but that it created a narrative distance that was somewhere between the intimacy of fiction and the remoteness of history: 'a voice that was mock historical—pedantic'. This search for a narrative voice appropriate to each novel is part of the quest for the right fictive form: the process whereby the artist distances himself from his material. 'I don't write autobiography or autobiographical fiction,' Doctorow has insisted. 'I don't take characters directly from my own life or experience. I put them through several prisms.' These prisms are necessary 'to filter myself from my imagination in order to write'.

Doctorow's concern for form has led him to fracture both chronology and narration in order to create the necessary energy for his fiction.

> Beginning with *Daniel*, I gave up trying to write with the concern for transition characteristic of the nineteenth-century novel. Other writers may be able to, but I can't accept the conventions of realism any more. It doesn't interest me as I write. I'm not speaking now of a manifesto—but of the experience of the writer, or at least this writer. You do what works. Obviously, the rhythms of perception in me, as in most people who read today, have been transformed immensely by films and television.

These experiments with discontinuous narrative and multiple narrators might suggest a connection with self-reflexive post-modernist writing but Doctorow rejects the identification. 'I'm opposed to that view,' he has insisted. 'I think art and life make each other. Henry Miller said, "We should give literature back to life." I believe that. I believe more than that.'

Third, each of Doctorow's novels is political in that it addresses in some significant way Freud's judgement that America is a 'gigantic mistake'. By this I do not mean that Doctorow shares Freud's judgement but rather that his fiction describes the gap in American life between its ideals and its reality. He has said of American society:

> It seems to me we are, at least on paper, supposed to be different from, or better than, we are. And that kind of irritation confronts us all the time and has from the very beginning. The Constitution was a precipitate of all the best Enlightenment thinking of Europe, and it's really quite a remarkable document. That we don't manage to live up to it is the source of all our self-analysis.

Consequently, it is not surprising to find in Doctorow's fiction an obsession with the idea of justice.

> There is a presumption of universality to the ideal of justice—social justice, economic justice. It cannot exist for a part or class of society; it must exist for all. And it's a Platonic ideal, too—that everyone be able to live as he or she is endowed to live; that if a person is in his genes a poet, he be able to practice his poetry. Plato defined justice as the fulfillment of a person's truest self. That's good for starters.

Yet in his fiction the pursuit of justice is never resolved: those who try to redress an injustice by an act of vengeance are often destroyed. Apparently, the idea of justice, like the idea of truth, lies beyond human grasp. 'Of one thing we are sure,' concludes the narrator of *The Book of Daniel*. 'Everything is elusive. God is elusive. Revolutionary morality is elusive. Justice is elusive. Human character.' It is tempting to trace Doctorow's social and aesthetic concerns back to his upbringing and education. He was born into a Jewish family in New York City in 1931 and 'grew up in a lower middle-class environment of generally enlightened, socialist sensibility.' After graduating from the prestigious Bronx High School of Science, he attended Kenyon College where he majored in philosophy and studied literature with the famous critic, John Crowe Ransom. After a year of graduate work in drama at Columbia University and two years in the army, he returned to New York to begin his writing career. During the early lean years he worked at a variety of editorial jobs. By the time he quit to write full-time he had become a top executive at the Dial Press.

Clearly, Doctorow's family background has deeply influenced his development as a writer but in ways which are more complicated than they seem at first glance. His grandfather and father were secular Jews committed to ideas of progress and socialism. But his grandmother and mother were both politically and religiously conservative. Consequently, 'there's always been this tension in the family which is, I think, quite reflected in what I've done.' Yet Doctorow sees these conflicting positions not as contradictory but rather as complementary. Thus his identification with radical Jewish humanism is broad: it embraces both the political progressivism of Emma Goldman and the cultural conservatism of Sigmund Freud. 'Whether they were radical or not, there was some sort of system of thought—a humanist critique, a social or political skepticism, whatever you want to call it—that had to come from their inability to be complacent or self-congratulatory.' This 'humanist critique' is fundamental in everything he has ever written.

But there is another source for his radical scepticism. Coming of age in the early 1950s, Doctorow is part of what has been called the silent generation. Irving Howe once described them as 'the generation that did not show up', meaning that they fell between the political radicalism of the 1930s and the cultural radicalism of the 1960s. Doctorow would agree. 'My generation has known, without having to go through the experience of the Thirties, the dangers of ideology as they are applied to fiction and poetry,' he observed. 'We have learned that lesson. We were taught that lesson.' But the lesson has had its costs in the lack of a shared set of convictions. 'It's the fate of my generation that we've never shared a monumental experience. We think of ourselves as loners.' The effect of this detachment is reflected in the isolation experienced by his protagonists and in the genuine ambivalence expressed in his novels. 'In every work I've ever done,' Doctorow has remarked, 'I've always heard the answers to whatever assertions are made by anybody.'

Because he has chosen to deal with explicitly political issues in his fiction, Doctorow has sometimes been labelled an ideologue. But, as I have already suggested, he is aware of the dangers of ideology for art. He knows that the artist's political convictions 'cannot be brought into the writing. They must come out of the writing.' Moreover, his own scepticism about the efficacy of simple political solutions is evident in each of his novels. 'But surely the sense we have to have now of twentieth-century political alternatives is a kind of exhaustion of them all,' he has explained. 'No system, whether it's religious or anti-religious or economic or materialistic, seems to be invulnerable to human venery and greed and insanity.'

Doctorow's ideas about the nature of literature and the role of the artist were perhaps best stated in an essay he published in 1977 entitled 'False Documents'. The essay begins with a comparison of two sentences, one from a newspaper article and one from a novel, which stem from the different realms of fact and fiction and represent the conflicting powers of '*the regime*' and of '*freedom*'. By '*the power of the regime*' Doctorow means our acquiescence to the authority of brute facts which goes by the name of realism; by '*the power of freedom*' he means the ability of the imagination to subvert that authority. 'There is a regime of language that derives its strength from what we are supposed to be and a language of freedom whose power consists in what we threaten to become. And I'm justified in giving a political character to the nonfictive and fictive uses of language because there is a conflict between them.'

But '*the power of the regime*' is like the emperor's new clothes. It is a product of our perception of reality and not reality itself. As such, it may be changed as our consciousness is transformed. 'What we proclaim as the discovered factual world can be challenged as the questionable world we ourselves have painted—the cultural museum of our values, dogmas, assumptions, that prescribes for us not only what we may like and dislike, believe and disbelieve, but also what we may be permitted to see and not see.' Thus reality is something that we invent and the notion that fact and fiction belong to separate realms is itself an invention.

This interpenetration of fact and fiction undermines the distinction between scientific and imaginative writing. Historians and sociologists borrow the techniques of fiction in the name of the regime of language. The characteristic devices of historical narrative turn out to be closely linked to the fictive conventions of realism. So Doctorow is 'led to the proposition that there is no fiction or nonfiction as we commonly understand the distinction: there is only narrative.'

The discovery that the boundary between fact and fiction was itself fictional was made by the first novelists, by Cervantes and Defoe, who presented their own inventions as factual accounts. Doctorow adopts Kenneth Rexroth's phrase 'false documents' to describe these fictions. In American literature a similar strategy was used by Hawthorne and Melville. Hawthorne described his own work as romance which attempted to connect past history and present reality through an act of imagination. He claimed that his romances occupied 'a neutral territory, somewhere between the real world and fairyland, where the Actual and the Imaginary may meet, and each imbue itself with the nature of the other'.

The qualities that Hawthorne imputed to the romance come down to us in the mainstream of American literature from Hawthorne and Melville through Faulkner and Fitzgerald to the fabulators of the present day. But a contemporary practitioner like Doctorow, with his abiding political interests, has more in common with such writers as Grass and Márquez than he does with most other American post-modernists. What this international group of writers shares, in addition to a belief that all history is contemporary history, is a faith in the subversive significance of the imaginative act. In 'False Documents' Doctorow put his position this way:

> Novelists know explicitly that the world in which we live is still to be formed and that reality is amenable to any construction that is placed upon it. It is a world made for liars and we are born liars. But we are to be trusted because ours is the only profession forced to admit that it lies—and that bestows upon us the mantle of honesty.

CUSHING STROUT

Twain, Doctorow, and the Anachronistic Adventures of the Arms Mechanic and the Jazz Pianist

"The locus of fiction is the unruly jostling of all the objects of culture," as Avrom Fleishman has said, "—of the real with the illusory, the found with the imagined, the irreducible with the artificial." He notes that "it is a paradox of our time, in which "the 'fictionality' of fiction has become a watchword of literary pundits, that many currently approved fictional works have incorporated pieces of the real world in an increasingly self-assured way." Indeed, one vivid literary sign of our times is the breaking down of any *boundary between novelists and historians. On the theoretical level, it is reflected in the work of Hayden White, who has insisted that written histories presuppose certain narrative forms, derived from literature, and these are held to be built on a few basic figurative forms of language, or tropes. Among journalists, the same tendency is evident in Norman Mailer's strategy in* The Armies of the Night *(1968), his account of the March on the Pentagon in 1967, which is subtitled "History as a Novel/The Novel as History." Among novelists, John Barth in* The Sot-weed Factor *(1960) characteristically mixes real and invented documents, borrowing his title, hero, and diction from a real person, who in 1731 published a verse satire in Maryland. Barth's novel deliberately blurs the line so that "we cannot be sure when we arc in touch with facts, as opposed to fictionalized versions of facts."*

The novelist who captured the popular imagination by this tendency to collapse history and fiction together is E. L. Doctorow. The traditional historical novel tends to keep historical persons on the margin of the fictional

From *Making American Tradition: Visions and Revisions from Ben Franklin to Alice Walker.* ©1990 by Cushing Strout.

scene, but *Ragtime* (1975), a best-seller made into a popular movie, freely intersects the lives of historical characters with each other as well as with fictional characters. Its intention is to suppress in the reader's mind any question about "what actually happened" as a matter of detail, but at the same time to suggest to the reader something pertinent in contemporary terms about the meaning of the past. The author himself told a reporter: "If you ask me whether some things in the book 'really' happened, I can only say, 'they have now.'"

Ragtime was advertised in its jacket copy as a sport: "You will never have read anything like *Ragtime* before. Nothing quite like it has ever been written before." But, in some important respects, it has at least one unnoticed classic American precursor as a speculative and satirical history: Mark Twain's *The Connecticut Yankee in King Arthur's Court* (1889). Like Twain's romance (three times made into a movie), *Ragtime* is also a time-travel story with a deliberate anachronism built into its structure, with a magician playing an important part in the plot, and with an ironic and violent climax involving military technology.

The analogy between these two comic historical romances may seem implausible. Twain's story, unlike Doctorow's, which is told by an imitation of an impersonal historian's narrating voice, is a vernacular, first-person narrative, and its material is legendary, the Arthurian Camelot, far removed from the author's own time and country, unlike Doctorow's prewar period of America. Moreover, the plot of *Ragtime* turns centrally on racial conflict, which is absent from Twain's sixth-century Britain. Yet, the more each text is read over the shoulder of the other, the more interesting correspondences do appear. Are they accidental or was Doctorow, at some level of his mind, aware of Twain's story, which he never mentions in connection with *Ragtime*? At any rate, the audience for *Ragtime* eagerly assimilated its deceptively simple declarative sentences without paying any attention to its epigraph, a warning by Scott Joplin: "It is never right to play *Ragtime* fast." A good way to play it slowly is to read the novel side by side with Twain's story. If *The Connecticut Yankee* is not a close relative of *Ragtime*, it is surely at least a first cousin once removed.

It is clear that Doctorow was self-consciously rewriting (though few of his readers know it) another precursor text; his hero Coalhouse Walker is an updating of the hero in Heinrich von Kleist's *Michael Kohlhaas* (1810) which is set in the time of Martin Luther but is based on an earlier medieval document. The American hero's first name, overlapping with the German hero's last name, is Doctorow's only offered clue (as he has confessed) to this "intertextual" aspect of the story. He has changed Kohlhaas's horses to an automobile, but the hero's retaliatory and escalating violent acts, done to avenge the unjust loss of his vehicle, is the pattern in both stories.

Twain's romance also has its self-conscious reference to a precursor—Sir Thomas Malory's fifteenth-century version in *Morte d'Arthur* of the sixth-century Arthurian legend, a text Twain read in 1884 when George Washington Cable gave it to him while they were on tour, doing public readings on stage. Another classic, *Don Quixote*, which Twain echoed earlier in his pairing of Huck Finn and Tom Sawyer, can also be heard as a presence in the Yankee's recreation of the Quixote project to laugh away the chivalric tradition, which he believed Sir Walter Scott's *Ivanhoe* had romantically restored in antebellum Southern imaginations as a prop for slavery. The usual Cervantes polarities are reversed by the Yankee's time travel: "The past is made vividly present and the present is relegated to a visionary future." It is possible that Twain knew of even another precursor for some of the ingredients of his story. Marcus Cunliffe has noted that Edward Bulwer Lytton's *The Last of the Barons* (1843), a book in Twain's library, involves three characters who are literary relatives of Twain's cast: the fifteenth-century Earl of Warwick, an inventor of a kind of steam engine, and a villain who is a friar. Twain's story opens in Warwick Castle and the Warwick Arms Hotel. The point of my method, however, is not to accumulate evidence for all the possible influences on the making of a book; it is rather to put texts side by side, or back to back, to see how they illuminate each other. From this point of view, a comparison of *Ragtime* with *A Connecticut Yankee in King Arthur's Court* will have to carry its own evidence of its value.

Twain's Hank Morgan, a superintendent of a Hartford arms factory in 1879, is obviously anachronistic in Arthurian England, and he can only get there by a kind of magical time travel. The hero speaks mysteriously about the transposition of epochs and bodies. (J. P. Morgan in *Ragtime* believes in reincarnation.) He claims to have been responsible for a bullet hole in a suit of armor, on display at Warwick Castle, the costume once worn by a knight of the Round Table. From reading Malory in the Warwick Arms, the narrator turns to reading Morgan's own bizarre story of his time travel (the result of a blow on the head) to Camelot. At the end of Morgan's account, called "The Tale of the Lost Land," we learn from a postscript that Merlin, disguised as an old woman, has magically put his rival to sleep for thirteen centuries. (In *Ragtime*, Houdini disguises himself as a veiled gray-haired widow while attending seances.)

Twain's narrative technique has not only licensed his extravagant departures from realistic historical standards, but also alienated his hero. In a second postscript, this time by "M. T.," we learn how he has finished reading Morgan's manuscript and finds him in a last delerium in his bed. Twain's additional spin to the time-travel idea is to have the dying man imagine that he is back in Camelot. He speaks, in fact, as if his real home were in ancient Britain, while his nightmare is that he has been set down thirteen centuries later in the England of 1879, which "M. T." inhabits. Morgan's time-travel experience has dislocated him from both time periods so that he is a stranger when he is in Camelot and a stranger when he is in the Warwick Arms.

This ending connects with a precedent in Twain's own work, his short account of his war experience in "A Campaign That Failed," written four years earlier. In it a stranger in civilian clothes, fatally shot by Twain's band of rangers, looks at him reproachfully and mumbles, "like a dreamer in his sleep," about his wife and child; and the situation is partly replicated when "M. T." bends over another stranger, Hank Morgan, and hears him make precisely the same kind of murmur. As Justin Kaplan has pointed out about the Civil War story, "the victim is related to all the other 'strangers' who populate Mark Twain's fiction," and the biographer could have cited Hank Morgan as a highly charged example.

Doctorow's narrative strategy is similar in its effect. His hero, the black jazz pianist, Coalhouse Walker, is anachronistic because he engages in confrontational violence against the establishment in a way that was characteristic of the 1960s and quite unthinkable for blacks in the *Ragtime* era before the First World War. Moreover, *Ragtime*'s plot also begins with a magical element, a premonition that is fantastic rather than historical: a small boy mysteriously tells a magician, Harry Houdini, to "warn the Duke," and many years (and pages) later it will be the Archduke Ferdinand's assassination that triggers the First World War. Houdini is notoriously effective in exposing fraudulent mediums, and his own magic is entirely naturalistic. But *Ragtime* links him to the paranormal by portraying his love for his dead mother as a motive that drives him to visit seances in the hope of finding a genuine medium who can put him in touch with his mother.

Morgan's final homelessness is paralleled by Coalhouse Walker's displacement from the 1960s to the *Ragtime* era. Doctorow subtly acknowledges his hero's unhistorical presence by telling us that there is no information about his parentage, no school records, no explanation for his vocabularly and manner of speaking-except perhaps "an act of will." (That act, of course, is the author's decision to put him into the *Ragtime* era.) In the end, his wife having been fatally wounded by a militia man and a Secret Service man at a public appearance of the Vice-President, the bereft Walker is suicidally prepared to be shot down when he leaves the Morgan Library, after successfully negotiating the rebuilding of his car and the escape of his terrorist band of supporters. No more than Hank Morgan does Walker have any secure place in the earlier era to which he too brings the outlook of a later one.

The climax of both stories shows an embattled hero, surrounded by a small band of youthful supporters, using modern firepower in a showdown with armed authorities. To carry the analogy even further, there is a final stroke of irony in the use of weaponry. Hank Morgan in the Battle of the Sand-belt, aided by a small band of fifty-two young boys, confronts the massed might of the Arthurian establishment and defeats the enemy by the effectiveness of his electric fence, Gatling guns, and an artificially created flood. Nevertheless, the poisonous air bred by the dead puts the victors in a trap of their own making. Similarly, one of Doctorow's major characters, Father, a flag manufacturer, goes to London on the *Lusitania* with a shipment of grenades, depth charges, and puttied nitro invented by his son, Younger Brother, and thus inadvertently contributes to the explosion that kills him when the ship is torpedoed by a German submarine.

Both Twain and Doctorow by their technique of deliberate anachronism put two eras into juxtaposition. In both books, the later one judges the earlier one. Twain's preface tips his hand, signaling his critique of the Arthurian era, by explaining that if he refers to any laws or customs that did not actually exist in the sixth century, "one is quite justified in inferring that whatever one of these laws or customs was lacking in that remote time, its place was competently filled by a worse one." Doctorow is moved by a similar political indignation to subvert any sentimental nostalgia for the earlier era. He begins with the mock-historical tone of a social historian: "Patriotism was a reliable sentiment in the early 1900's." Then he shifts gears: "There were no Negroes. There were no immigrants. . . . Across America sex and death were barely distinguishable." The mention of Emma Goldman, the revolutionary anarchist, an immigrant Jew, leads him to this second thought: "Apparently there *were* Negroes. There *were* immigrants." The end of chapter 6 coldly enumerates with cumulative force the oppressions suffered by miners, child workers, immigrants, and blacks, while trusts proliferate and the rich entertain themselves by playing at being poor.

Both authors underline the continuity as well as the differences in their comparison of earlier with later times. Twain's treatment of serfdom explicitly insists on its continuity with slavery in the Old South and the old regime in France. By dramatizing the racial conflict of the *Ragtime* era through the takeover of the Morgan Library, a tactic characteristic of radical politics in the 1960s, Doctorow underlines the persistence of racial injustice. More subtly, when the conservative black leader Booker T. Washington encounters the militant Coalhouse Walker in the library, the narrator notes on the wall portraits of Martin Luther, and Washington prays that the Lord may lead his people to the promised land—a strong echo of Martin Luther King, Jr., with Walker playing the role of the radical Malcolm X. Walker's supporters speak in revolutionary terms of setting up a provisional American government. At the same time the story dramatizes another aspect of the 1960s, the reluctance of the authorities to enter into, or respect, negotiations with the rebels.

What saves both books from historical smugness is their refusal to follow a traditional Whig interpretation of history with its idea of progress that congratulates the past for having led to the present. Twain judges the British past by his endorsement of the American and French revolutions. But from this point of view, his present is also criticized. When the Round Table becomes a stock exchange, wildcat manipulations (with which Twain as a heavy investor in the market was familiar) lead to warfare among the knights and the end of the Boss's new deal. He may think that his anomalous position in the kingdom makes him "a giant among pygmies, a man among children, a master intelligence among intellectual moles; by all rational measurement the one and only actually great man in that whole British world." But the reader is made increasingly aware of the dark side of the Boss's project with its complacency about his own assumption of power and his addiction to a technocratic "progress" that depends heavily on weapons of destruction. His political and cultural imperialism is the other side of his role as the democratic reformer.

Similarly, Doctorow is aware of the comic absurdity in some of the radicals' 1960s-style gestures. The small isolated band of terrorist blacks speak ideologically about being "a nation," and neurotic Younger Brother, in his disgust with his father his identification with the rebels, and his obsession with violence, corks his face black the better to be one of them in their occupation of the library. He ends up, as a *villista* in Mexico, wearing cartridge belts crossed over his chest, making bombs, and leading reckless guerrilla raids for the *zapatistas*. Emma Goldman sees that this "poor dangerous boy" is like the assassin of President McKinley, Leon Czolgosz. (He had heard her lecture on anarchy, and when she was falsely arrested as a coconspirator, she had insisted that he was a troubled homeless man who had acted alone. The reader of the novel in 1975 would probably think of Lee Harvey Oswald.)

Doctorow's hero is locked into an escalating confrontation with the bigoted firechief Willie Conklin, who trashed Walker's car, because each man is as intractable as the other, and their violent methods become virtually indistinguishable. Eventually, with eight people dead by his hand, Walker transforms Pierpont Morgan into his enemy, substituting for an ordinary bigot one of the most influential people of his era, and captures his library as a symbol of the white world. Struck by the arrogance of the avenger, the narrator's mock-historical voice speculates: "Or is injustice, once suffered, a mirror universe, with laws of logic and principles of reason the opposite of civilization's?"

The other Morgan—Hank, not Pierpont—in his own way mirrors his rival Merlin, who exploits the credulity of the public. When the Yankee is first captured by a knight on horseback, Morgan assumes that he is someone from the circus; and Morgan later virtuously contrasts his "new deal" program of education with a violent revolution that would appeal to "the circus side" of his own nature. It constantly erupts, nevertheless, with comic effect in his various stunts to impress the populace culminating in the liberation of the imprisoned king by five hundred knights on bicycles, "one of the gaudiest effects" Morgan ever instigated. In his duel with Sagramor on behalf of "common sense and reason" the Yankee incongruously appears in flesh-colored tights and uses a lasso like a cowboy in a circus Wild West Show. It is quite in the Boss's style, foreshadowed in Dan Beard's sketch, introducing "The Tale of the Lost Land," that shows a check-suited man in a derby, looking like a carnival barker or pitchman, tickling the nose of the British lion with a straw.

Ragtime has its own strong link to show business. Evelyn Nesbit's testimony in the murder trial of Harry K. Thaw "created the first sex goddess in American history," an inspiration for "the concept of the movie star system." The Jewish immigrant Tateh's upward mobility carries him out of the labor movement into making drawings that move by flipping the pages and on to the new movie industry and a made-up identity as Baron Ashkenazy, who acquires a WASP wife and a new career as a director of popular comedies. Doctorow's impersonal historian's voice interprets this development: "Thus did the artist point his life along the lines of flow of American energy. . . . The value of the duplicatable event was everywhere perceived."

Its corollary in business is Henry Ford's Model T automobile, and Doctorow pictures Ford regarding his first car on the moving assembly line: "His derby was tilted back on his head. He chewed on a piece of straw." It is uncannily like the image, sketched by Dan Beard for Twain's book, of the Yankee mechanic tickling the British lion with a straw. Ford in *Ragtime* is an evil genius because he establishes not only that the parts be interchangeable, "but that the men who build the products be themselves interchangeable parts." It is the reverse of Twain's idea of the Yankee's "man-factories," where he is going "to turn groping and grubbing automata into *men*." Twain himself, however, is aware that the factory has its own automatism, and he burlesques the process of mass production in a scene where Simon Stylites, praying on his pillar, is hitched up to a sewing machine in order to use his energy to produce cheap shirts for the masses. The Yankee also shrewdly understands that the creation of wants by advertising is necessary to the economy of popular consumption, and he uses knights to advertise stove polish before there are any stoves.

Both writers are joined as well by an amusing, American talent for using vernacular culture to poke fun at more pretentious or foolish high-mindedness. They both use baseball for that purpose. The Yankee replaces the chivalric ritual of a tournament with a baseball game, in which all the players are kings, to preserve the spirit of emulation without the violence of jousting. Doctorow shows Father's disdainful surprise at finding out that ballplayers are not Yale boys, but immigrants; and he portrays J. P. Morgan's even greater disdain and surprise when, after spending a chilly, itchy night, fruitlessly awaiting revelation from Osiris, in service to his obsession with a religious belief in reincarnation, he emerges from Egypt's Great Pyramid and is stunned to see the New York Giants baseball team scrambling over the Great Sphinx. Both Twain and Doctorow see the comic possibilities in the American reversal of the profane and the sacred.

Both writers, for all their demystifying spirit, do not escape, however, some sentimentality. Twain's Yankee improbably describes his marriage with Alesande ("Sandy") in Camelot as "the dearest and perfectest comradeship that ever was," and when he is dying, he yearns for Arthurian England again because it contains "all that is dear" to him, "all that could make life worth the living!" Doctorow's story is more tough-minded and sexually explicit, in the modern manner, but it sentimentalizes Walker's beautiful wife Sarah, who is portrayed as a pure innocent "who understood nothing but goodness." Nevertheless, she attempts to kill her newborn child.

The time-travel idea poses a problem for Hank Morgan's republicanism as it does for Coalhouse Walker's insistence on equality of respect, because both are obviously utopian in eras totally unprepared for them. Even the Yankee realizes that his educational work is cut out for him, and he sometimes doubts its value because "no people in the world ever did achieve their freedom by goody-goody talk and moral suasion: it being immutable law that all revolutions that will succeed must *begin* in blood, whatever may answer afterward. If history teaches anything, it teaches that." He believes that a reign of terror would be necessary, as in the French Revolution, but he thinks that he is "the wrong man" for that role.

If training is everything, how can it be reversed? In the end, he discovers that it cannot be done: "The mass of the nation had swung their caps and shouted for the republic for about one day, and there an end!" When the church, the nobles, and the gentry frowned upon them, the masses like sheep had begun "to gather to the fold." The Boss can only use his technological superiority to tip the balance in his favor, but it is only snatching defeat from the jaws of victory because of the ironic result of his success in extermination. Doctorow's Houdini does not have Merlin's triumph, but *Ragtime* does return to the magician after Walker, doomed by the scale of his own resistance to injustice, has been shot. On the day that the Archduke Ferdinand is assassinated, the magician, hanging upside down in a strait-jacket during one of his daring escapes, remembers the boy, who had warned him about the event.

If we raise the question about the meaning of history in these two historical romances, we are faced with problematic answers in both cases. In the chapter "The Beginnings of Civilization," the Yankee brags that he has with his hidden program conspired to have "the civilization of the nineteenth century booming" under the nose of the kingdom, but he also calls it "as substantial a fact as any serene volcano, standing innocent with its smokeless summit in the blue sky and giving no sign of the rising hell in its bowels." Morgan speaks here as if he has condemned his own project before he has accomplished it. He sounds as if he were both a character and the author's mouthpiece, though the two outlooks are not the same. Morgan's bragging is characteristic; his metaphor of the volcano is not; it registers the profound unstable ambivalence of Twain's own relation to the nineteenth-century civilization that is the Boss's goal. Twain's uneasiness was accentuated by his frustrating investment in the Paige typesetting machine that was too fiendishly complicated ever to function properly, "a sublime magician" that bankrupted him soon after he finished his novel.

Twain does not entirely explode the idea of progress—at least not yet for himself, whatever the modern reader may think. The American and French revolutions still make sense out of history for him in 1889, as his letters show, even after he finished the book. Dan Beard, Twain's illustrator, whose work much pleased the author, read the novel as a "great missionary work to bring Americans back to the safe honest and manly position, intended for them to occupy, by their ancestors when they signed the declaration of independence." Twain told Howells, who edited the novel and liked its references to the French Revolution, that "next to the 4th of July & its results, it was the noblest and the holiest thing and the most precious that ever happened in this earth. And its gracious work is not done yet—nor anywhere in the remote neighborhood of it." Twain shared Howell's lament that "an aristocracy-loving oligarchy" had replaced "the American Republic."

Yet, either Twain's hold on the Yankee as a republican slips badly at some points or else he is trying to trace a change that modifies the Yankee's outlook by Arthurian influences. Morgan falls into a didactic reformer's meditation about the power of training over originality and then incongruously adds that all he thinks about in "this prodding sad pilgrimage, this pathetic drift between the eternities, is to look out and humbly live a pure and high and blameless life." It is as if he were a monk, more influenced by the sixth century than by the nineteenth. At another point Morgan seems to lose his republican identity when he sees the crowd doing homage to the king and reflects that "really there is something peculiarly grand about the gait and bearing of a king, after all." When the Yankee learns of the king's death, he is surprised because he did not think "that any wound could be mortal to him"; he seems to have succumbed to the idea, which he has always scorned, of the divinity of kings. These changes would be appropriate if Twain were bent on doing an international novel, in the mode of Henry James, with the European milieu having its forbidden attractions for the New World American, as it certainly did for Morgan's creator, who eventually resided in Vienna as if he were the American literary ambassador to Europe. Twain's Yankee has some of the same charm and naiveté of James's Christopher Newman as a fellow innocent abroad. Yet the novel cannot consistently be read in this way, even though it would make its ending more appropriate. The ending is problematic for both republicanism and feudalism. With Hank Morgan's "redoubled homelessness," as Walter Reed has called it, he becomes "exiled from the past that had previously exiled him from the present, and neither time nor place retains its identity."

Morgan's showmanship is replicated in his creator's performance as a comic writer, and Morgan's conflict between Camelot and Hartford replicates his creator's life as an exile from the South, a deserter from the Confederacy, who became an admirer of General Grant, whose memoirs he published, and then an independent Republican Mugwump, who voted in 1884 for the Democrat Grover Cleveland. Dualism is built into Clemens's choice of a pen name. In a notebook entry for 1897, appropriately made while he was living in Freud's Vienna, Twain expressed his interest in Stevenson's *Dr. Jekyll and Mr. Hyde* as an attempt to account for "the presence in us of another *person*." Twain went on to argue that experiments with hypnotism show that the two persons are not known to each other. He elaborated the idea into "a dream self" who can make "immense excursions" in the role of one's "spiritualized person." He humorously called his other self "Watson," rather than Mr. Hyde, but surely one of those "immense excursions" of his dream self was Hank Morgan's journey to Camelot.

Doctorow ends his story with the historical facts of the First World War and the deportation of Emma Goldman. But he also suggests the circularity of history by his last line, which refers to the murderer Harry K. Thaw, marching in the annual Armistice Day Parade, after obtaining his release from an asylum. This last note brings the music of time back to its beginning, as if none of the author's changes in the mosaic of the past has changed time's repetitious tune. Doctorow makes it explicit: "The era of *Ragtime* had run out, with the heavy breath of the machine, as if history were no more than a tune on a player piano."

Doctorow's point of view is hard to elicit from *Ragtime* because at one point he devotes a chapter to the meditations of the boy in Father's family as a theme for the novel. The boy seems to be a mouthpiece for the author in expressing thoughts too metaphysical for a child. Listening to his grandfather, the boy learns that "the forms of life were volatile and that everything in the world could as easily be something else." The boy finds proof of this in his own experience of "the instability of both things and people," and his own self-duplication in the mirror gives him a sense of having two selves "neither of which could claim to be the real one." (Mark Twain would have no trouble understanding him.) His conclusion is simple: "It was evident to him that the world composed and recomposed itself constantly in an endless process of dissatisfaction."

From this point of view, the world is pure contingency; nothing is necessary; time has no meaningful direction, and there is no place to stand from which judgments can be made. Twain himself did move towards this nihilism. With Doctorow, however, the boy's strange meditation is perhaps a rationalization for Doctorow's own playful rearrangements of history—anything might be anything else in the historical past. He has elsewhere cited the structuralist critic Roland Barthes on behalf of the proposition that historical discourse is itself "a particular form of fiction," and Doctorow concluded that fiction itself is "a kind of speculative history, perhaps a superhistory, by which the available data for the composition is seen to be greater and more various in its sources than the historian supposes."

This erosion of any difference between fiction and history is too facile. It is even contradictory. The idea of a "superhistory" itself suggests some kind of referentiality, not explained by "fiction," yet it is not at all clear what constraints would discipline this new kind of history. Doctorow's byplay with historical characters, however, is not as fancy-free as it might appear at first, for it is controlled by his own considerable historical knowledge. To take what seems to be a bizarre example: Emma Goldman's orgasm-inducing massage of Evelyn Nesbit. The event never took place, but Goldman's criticisms of Nesbit's life in that scene are entirely authentic ideologically, and the erotic aspect of the moment connects with an historical fact: Goldman admitted that her friendship with Margaret Anderson, editor of the *Little Review*, had stirred feelings expressive of a "previous theoretic interest in sex variation."

Doctorow himself is not prepared to question that "some facts, for instance the Nazi extermination of the Jews, are so monstrous as to seem to stand alone." His example is revealing. His earlier novel *The Book of Daniel*, the strongest expression of Doctorow's historical consciousness, fictionalizes the story of the electrocuted Rosenbergs, as seen from the point of view of their children, to dramatize a larger theme involving three generations of Jewish-Americans and the defeat of their hopes for America. The only non-Jew in the novel is a black janitor.

Doctorow's Jewishness is not just a fact; it is the key to his personal interpretation of the history he has fictionalized, for he orients himself in it by his concern for the Jewish immigrants, whether they be Houdini, Tateh, or Emma Goldman. His views of the three cases are pertinent: Houdini "never developed what we think of as a political consciousness" because he could not "reason from his own hurt feelings." His obsession with escapes speaks to the immigrant experience of repression and to the function of show business as an opiate of the people. Tateh's upward mobility sacrifices his solidarity with the workers and compromises his artistic aspirations when he achieves affluence in making escapist movies. Emma Goldman, when arrested and asked for her views about Coalhouse Walker, simply says, "Wealth is the oppressor. Coalhouse Walker did not need Red Emma to learn that. He needed only to suffer." It is a radical perspective, married (in contrast to the usual socialist realism) to a modernist interest in technique, one that calls attention to its own fictionalizing.

In an interview, Doctorow has spoken of his admiration for Goldman's prophetic kind of Jewishness and of his growing up in "a lower-middle class environment of generally enlightened, socialist sensibility," stemming from his Russian grandfather's radical humanism. Indeed, *Ragtime*'s image of what historians used to call "the Progressive era" is notable for the conspicuous absence in it of persons drawn from the large, ideologically mixed group of non-immigrant native reformers, who were active in the period. Teddy Roosevelt appears in *Ragtime* only as a greedy big-game hunter, and Woodrow Wilson is seen only as a man "who wore rimless glasses and held moral views. When the Great War came he would wage it with the fury of the affronted."

Ragtime's image of the past is vulnerable to John Lukacs's criticism that Doctorow's interest in America is in "*things* American—altogether on a different level from his knowledge of Jewish-American *thoughts*." His remoteness from the non-Jewish characters is indicated by the fact that (except for Walker) they have no particularizing names. What is most American about *Ragtime*, Lukacs suggests, is its pictorial imagination and a rapidly moving clipped style, like the comics and the movies. Doctorow himself has spoken of his experiments in narrative discontinuity as being "akin to television-discontinuous and mind-blowing." It is curious that this experimental vanguardism in technique and this radicalism in political ideology should be akin to the mode of a mass medium. It testifies to the extent to which the 1960s marked the process in which, as Gerald Graft has pointed out, "the antinomian disparagement of 'bourgeois values' is celebrated by the agencies of publicity, exploited by the manipulators of cultural fashion, and emulated in personal conduct—an additional reason why the ante of provocation and radical experiment must continually be raised if the arts are to justify their vanguard credentials. . . . The point seems to have been reached at which artistic intransigence is indistinguishable from celebration of the dynamisms of mass society." *Ragtime*'s immense popularity illustrates his point.

Doctorow's sense of having a particular place to stand in Jewish-American radicalism, as a resource for his art, does not square with the boy's nihilistic metaphysical meditations in *Ragtime*. They may serve to rationalize Doctorow's fictionalizing of the historical material, but the material itself is viewed from the standpoint of the political sympathies that he acknowledges in the interview. The tension between the boy's meditations and his creator's responses in the interview defines the ambiguous quality of *Ragtime*'s point of view. It has led one perceptive critic to say that his art is "committed yet unconvinced," written out of a Jewish biblical view that "history is redemptive-and also out of Modernist doubt."

Twain's conflict is analogous to Doctorow's because of the tension between his view of history as redeemed by the American and French revolutions and his despair of majority human nature on whose good judgment democratic republicanism depends. The Yankee can assure the reader at one point that "there is plenty good enough material for a republic in the most degraded people that ever existed . . . if one could but force it out of its timid and suspicious privacy," but in the end he finds that the Arthurian masses are sheep. That disappointment could be explained, however, by the immense historical gap between his project and the society in which he is a stranger. But Morgan's ideological conflict intersected with his creator's self-division, the sense of having a separate "dream self." The artistic result for his novel was a lack of control reflected in its loose, rambling, repetitive, and anecdotal structure in contrast to the controlled and skillful braiding of historical and fictional lives in Doctorow's tale.

The competing elements in Hank Morgan are significant, however, because they are not just the author's. His sympathy for the oppressed majority and his deep suspicion of its judgment and ability would be competing themes as well in the Progressive movement itself, which often joined indignation against the trust, the political boss, and the sweatshop with a passion for organized efficiency. Hank Morgan has the artistic burden of having to carry more meanings than Doctorow's stylized characters. The Yankee contains a multitude, incorporating the showman, inventor, rationalist, entrepreneur, democratic reformer, dictatorial imperialist, and disenchanted romantic in his identity. This amplitude of meaning, however, is also what gives a modern resonance to Twain's fantastic version of history, which might otherwise simply have been reduced to what it is in its worst stretches—a heavy-handed tedious assault on monarchy and aristocracy. It is Hank Morgan's complexity that makes it possible for a contemporary reader to think of Twain's story as the precursor of a more sophisticated and more disenchanted form of black humor.

Twain needed a successor to go beyond his own speculative history. His literary sense of America, for all its close familiarity with a rich variety of American experience, lacked any appreciation for the immense process of immigration. It is historically symbolic that the year in which Twain began writing his story about the Yankee was the year that Emma Goldman emigrated from Russia to America, her romantic imagination stirred by anarchist literature and history. When the novel was published, she was moving to New York to join the anarchist movement. One of the important literary consequences of immigration was the development after the Second World War of many influential and highly accomplished Jewish-American novelists. Doctorow's *Ragtime* is one sign of that coming-of-age; and, among the historical figures in his book, Emma Goldman is the heroine. *Ragtime* is also a sign of the extent to which a Jewish grandchild of the immigrants can become what Mark Twain was, a popular interpreter of America to itself. Hank Morgan, meet Coalhouse Walker and Emma Goldman.

Doctorow in *Ragtime* cites Freud's remark that "America is a mistake, a gigantic mistake." Another Jewish-American novelist, Saul Bellow, referred to the remark in a speech, given shortly after the publication of *Ragtime*, to the Anti-Defamation League when accepting its America's Democratic Legacy Award. (Curiously enough, Bellow's *Henderson the Rain King* seems also to be partly inspired by Twain's fable: a Connecticut pig-farmer journeys to a fabulous Africa, encounters a primitive society, and becomes involved with a king.) Bellow used the occasion to counter Freud's judgment with the philosopher Morris Cohen's belief that "the future of liberal civilization was bound up with America's survival and its ability to make use of the heritage of human rights formulated by Jefferson and Lincoln." If this stirring confidence is missing from both Twain and Doctorow, it is partly explained by the difficulty in the late 1880s or in the Nixon years of hearing any trumpets sounding in the corridors of power for that great tradition. The final despair of Hank Morgan and Coalhouse Walker draws on that silence.

JOHN G. PARKS

Art and Memory: Lives of the Poets *and* World's Fair

In *Lives of the Poets* (1984) and *World's Fair* (1985)—written and published within a year of each other—Doctorow, in part, appears to be engaging in a kind of midcareer stocktaking of the novelistic enterprise. In his previous fiction, Doctorow's highly imaginative and perceptive narrators seek a narrative solution to the problem of unavoidable historical repetition, on the one hand, and unpredictable sequence, on the other. They are by no means unalloyed in their success. In *Lives of the Poets* and *World's Fair*, the writer appears to make a much more direct artistic use of memory to explore the role and commitment of the artist in today's world. The *Lives of the Poets* is focused upon a contemporary writer's struggles with his vocation, while *World's Fair* returns to the past, the 1930s, to portray a writer's meditation upon his childhood in a rich and elegiac tone.

Lives of the Poets

This book is, in many respects, a change of pace or a midcareer shifting of gears for Doctorow. In the four years after the publication of *Loon Lake*, Doctorow did some nonfiction collaboration. He also worked closely with the director Sidney Lumet on the film version of *The Book of Daniel*, which came out in 1983 as *Daniel.* He also rented an apartment in Greenwich Village for purposes of his collaboration and teaching commitments. This studio apartment serves as the setting for the narrator of *Lives of the Poets.* One of the most self-reflexive and self-referential of all of Doctorow's works, the book is a kind of portrait of the artist at fifty. While the making or composing of narrative is the major task, if not the major problem, of all of Doctorow's protagonists, his work is not just about itself. The world outside is never abandoned, the incursions of historical forces never denied. The dialectic in Doctorow is never only between the writer and his work, but always between the writer and his relation to the world.

The book consists of six stories and a novella, which Doctorow says are unified.

> I found myself writing them in sequence as they appear in the book. As I read the stories over, I discovered a connection, like a mind looking for its own geography. I found that I was creating the character of the person creating them. So I wrote the novella to give him a voice. I saw the possibility of presenting a writer's mind in both formal stories and then in a confessional mode. The novella is the story of the stories.

The six stories are the imaginative transmutations of memory and experience of the artist-narrator of the novella *Lives of the Poets*. The novella is about the struggles of a writer with his work and his world. The stories are, in part, analogues to the shifting emotional situation or condition of the writer of the novella. In the novella are echoes of the stories. As a whole, the work conveys the predicament of a writer today. As Benjamin DeMott puts it, the work is "an account of one man's search for seriousness—and for human connection and truth." For Doctorow, "the key image of the book is the idea of migration—the stories migrate. Today, what is teasing and what is perplexing is our relationship to the national culture."

Doctorow acknowledges the influence of Hawthorne's fiction on his work. This influence is both direct and indirect in this present book. In the strange piece entitled, "The Leather Man," an incident is told about a missing husband named Morris Wakefield. A Peeping Tom is caught outside the Wakefield residence who turns out to be the missing husband Morris Wakefield. This incident is a direct borrowing of Hawthorne's haunting story "Wakefield," which in turn was based on an actual case in England. The story is about an apparently happily married man who decides one day to leave his home. He does not go far; in fact, he takes up residence in disguise a few blocks away. He spends his time snooping around and watching people live. Hawthorne refers to Wakefield as an outcast, a self-alienated exile, and tells him to go home. The spirit of Wakefield permeates the *Lives of the Poets*. It is a fitting image for Doctorow's writer—he leaves home to see life more clearly. To go inside he must go outside. The artist is a derelict and his book is a study in dereliction.

The idea of dereliction permeates all of Doctorow's fiction. The word *derelict* or *dereliction* appears at least six times in *Lives of the Poets* and appears frequently in Doctorow's other work as well. The word *derelict* refers to something or someone given up or abandoned by its owner. A derelict is unfaithful and neglectful. A derelict also denotes a person outside the pale of respectable society. To be derelict is to be guilty of a neglect of some duty. An artist, it appears, is a Wakefield, a derelict by choice, who puts his life at risk for his vision. It is dereliction that Jonathan, the narrator of the novella, risks in his move to his loft in the Village. But it is a move he feels compelled to make in order to recover his artistic sensibility, his commitment. His story (told in first-person confessional mode) is about that struggle: the "Lives of the Poets" and their derelict lives. Like Joe of *Loon Lake*, Jonathan is a man telling on himself and others. Dereliction is the inevitable condition of an artist, for not to leave home, not to go outside, is to be derelict to one's art. As one of the voices in the story "The Leather Man" says: "What is the essential act of the Leather Man? He makes the world foreign. He distances it. He is estranged. Our perceptions are sharpest when we are estranged. We can see the shape of things." To the authorities of the regime, such dereliction appears incomprehensible and hence potentially politically subversive. The artist as derelict sees the world as it is and tells the truth about it—an act of transgression.

The connections between the six stories are not readily apparent as one reads through them. They share in a mood or tone of forlornness, even of melancholy and longing. It is not until one reads the novella that the stories begin to reverberate in the mind and begin to connect with the voice of the narrator. As Christopher Lehmann-Haupt writes: "The stories constitute an autobiography of the writer's imagination. In mood and style and imagery, they are a history of the times and places in which their creator has lived." One might refer to the stories as "subjective correlatives" of the narrator of the novella—products of the artist in his derelict condition.

Jonathan, the narrator of the novella, feeling oppressed by his successes at writing, abandons his wife, Angel, and his nice Connecticut home to take occupancy of a studio apartment in Greenwich Village in order to recover his flagging artistic vocation. Reminded constantly by Angel of tales of male perfidy, Jonathan knows there is a fine line between the necessary artistic estrangement and outright dereliction. Various migrations characterize the times. Marriages fall apart. Older men seek younger women. Jonathan writes for the return of his young lover—really a symbol of the Muse—traveling in Greece, Egypt, and India. She sends him postcards, one of which breaks off their relationship. Riddled with guilt, uncertainty, fearing physical breakdown, Jonathan sits at his typewriter recording his angst. "So my discovery at fifty is that this mortal rush to solitude is pandemic, that is the news I bring. It is not that everyone I know is fucked up, incomplete, unrealized. On the whole we are quite game. It's life itself that seems to be wanting."

He cannot evade the world, however. It comes to him through the windows—the shots, the sirens, the sounds of urban life. It comes to him through the mail slot—appeals for contributions to various programs for world salvation. The world comes to him in the form of the many dark-eyed peoples choking the subway cars, the new immigrants fleeing their homes "because we have made their lands unlivable. They have come here to save themselves from us. They have brought their hot politics with them." What kind of fiction can come from such a desolate man?

To begin to answer the question of how he got to where he is, Jonathan's first story is a tale recalling an important first discovery about being a writer, "The Writer in the Family." In 1955, after his father dies, Jonathan is called on by his aunts to compose letters to his father's ancient mother in a rest home. The aunts want Jonathan to write as if the family has moved to Arizona. Jonathan's letters get rave reviews from his aunts and he is quite flattered. Jonathan's brother makes him feel his complicity with an unnecessary lie and he begins to resist his aunts' charade. Impersonating his own father, Jonathan discovers something about his father and about writing. Jonathan comes to see that his father was a failure only because he led the wrong life. And Jonathan, as a composer of lives, must compose the truth, no matter what the consequences. It is this that the elder writer of the novella must reaffirm or be lost in his dereliction. He must never lose his faith in the power of the imagination.

Jonathan's father was nearly a sailor. His favorite books were tales of voyage and adventure. But life imposed a very different destiny upon him, not one he might have chosen. Jonathan's second tale, "The Water Works," is a tale of a drowning, the death of a child while sailing his toy boat. The tone is dark, suggesting Poe or Kafka, a kind of nightmare. The narrator watches a man who watches a child sailing a boat. The narrator follows the man into the water works where the child's body is recovered by the indifferent workers. The man takes the body away in a carriage. The narrator writes: "I went back in and felt the oppression of a universe of water, inside and out, over the dead and the living." Vivid in its own right, the story is a fitting metaphor for the struggling writer in the novella, and an emblem of a life not lived.

As Jonathan observes and ruminates upon the lives of his fellow poets, their failing marriages, their betrayals of their talents, upon his own squandering of his gifts, he conjures a story of human betrayal full of rich ambiguity. Recalling the terrible fights between his parents as a child and his desperate attempts to make peace—"I didn't know who to believe, whom to love, whom to defend, whom to attack"—Jonathan creates "Willi," a tale set in Galicia in 1910 and told by a narrator many years later. The narrator was thirteen at the time and his feeling of a mystical oneness with a regenerative nature is destroyed when he witnesses his mother coupling with his tutor in the barn. This Oedipal betrayal is unbearable for him to live with and he betrays his mother to his father, knowing that it will utterly undermine his father's authority and confidence. When his father is beating his mother, he flies to her defense. As a kind of rationalizing afterthought, the narrator concludes: "All of it was to be destroyed anyway, even without me." Perhaps the roots of human estrangement, the creation of the "criminal of perception," lay in scenes of Oedipal betrayal, real or imagined.

A longing of a different sort characterizes the next three tales—a longing for clarity, an end to frustration and confusion. In this respect also, the stories are imaginative projections of Jonathan's life as he gropes toward some understanding of his life, his work, his loves, his mortality. Loneliness, frustration, the waste of an unlived life take a female shape in the story "The Hunter." Perhaps an imagining of Jonathan's young lover, the story tells of the anguish and frustration of a young teacher stuck in a dying mill town. On one of her restless nights, she walks down "Mechanic Street," the street Joe of Paterson, in *Loon Lake*, fled from in his quest for fame. But the teacher of "The Hunter" appears to be locked in, imprisoned by a gray fate. Her only emotional attachment is with her students whom she deliberately tries to make love her. Hiking to an old, deserted mansion, the teacher looks out a window and sees a hunter come out of the woods. She wonders whether he can see her. The hunter raises his rifle and shoots, hitting the side of the house, before disappearing into the woods again. Perhaps to fight the threat of invisibility, the teacher calls in a photographer to photograph her and the children at school. The photographer balks, saying the children are not properly dressed. The teacher says: "Take it, she says in a fierce whisper. Take it as we are. We are looking at you. Take it." A sad ending to a disturbing story of a love-starved human being. But her command to the photographer is the command Jonathan, the writer, must follow as he perceives a volatile world.

It is Jonathan's guilt and unease about that volatile world that gets treatment in the story "The Foreign Legation." Like Jonathan, Morgan is a kind of derelict, abandoned by his wife and children. Trying to create a life for himself alone, Morgan is into jogging and waiting and watching other people's lives and coping with fantasies of violence and destruction. At one point Morgan thinks: "I suffer a vision of the incessant migrations of mankind lapping the earth prehistorically, historically, and to the present moment." This vision bursts into fleshy reality when he jogs by a foreign legation one morning as a bomb explodes and he finds a sock with a child's leg in it. "Did I do this?" he asks. Such a question reflects the probing moral consciousness of Jonathan the writer. The claims of human history cannot be avoided-one cannot run by them; they might explode in your face.

There are outsiders in our midst. Some are the result of the new waves of human migration. Some are the derelict—rejects of an ominvorous system, the flotsam and jetsam of history. Some are derelict by choice, dropouts of the American Dream Machine. How can that be? Why are there people like Melville's Bartleby or Hawthorne's Wakefield? Whose business is it to know or care? Jonathan's sixth story, "The Leather Man," is a kind of paranoid fantasy of some faceless government agents—CIA, FBI, whatever—who are investigating the dropouts and their potential political threat. What if these isolatoes should come together? As one of the voices asks: "So the question is, why?" Wherever dropouts gather, these agents are there, watching, taking pictures. One of them speculates on the theory of the oscillating universe and its applicability to human history. In an expanding and contracting universe, the crucial thing is direction: "If things come apart enough, they will have started to come together." The agents are worried about any "coming together" that might constitute a challenge to the existing order. The agents of the regime worry about any act of defamiliarization—the act of the Leather Man, who makes the world foreign so people can see the true shape of things. Which is to say, the Leather Man is a metaphor of the artist, the writer as derelict. Can one get anything important from artists, the agents wonder? Can they tell us anything we need to know? The story echoes in Jonathan's great desire to matter, to "sit once more in the councils of state," to be taken seriously.

Near the end of the novella, Jonathan quotes the poet Rilke: "*Here there is no place that does not see you. You must change your life.*" In Jonathan's observations of the lives of the poets, he sees that many of them have gone too far in their dereliction, succumbing to the malaise of urban life, undone by success, by a world filled with narcissistic strategies of self-fulfillment. Artistic commitment flags like their sexual potency. One of Jonathan's colleagues comes up to him at a party: "Tell me, he says, looking me in the eye, is there a writer here who really believes in what he's doing? Does any one of us have a true conviction for what he's writing? Do I? Do you?" Jonathan cannot answer him. He had believed that his young lover, his Muse, would return and restore his life and revive his artistic energies. When she leaves him, he must face his life anew. Recalling Rilke, he knows he must change his life, but how? In the "immigrated universe" where he is "strangled in history," Jonathan faces the demands of the world. After learning of the needs of political refugees, Jonathan agrees to house a Central American family in his Village flat. "Look, my country, what you've done to me, what I have to do to live with myself." For Jonathan, a writer cannot, must not, forsake the claims of human history. An art that does so is truly derelict.

World's Fair

There is Jonathan, narrator of *Lives of the Poets*, contemplating the forms of dereliction that comprise his age. "What has happened to *my* life!" he asks. How have I gotten to this point, how have I become what I am? And where am I going? The answers to these great midlife questions lay in his past, in his childhood. The novel *World's Fair* represents an artist's return to his roots to recover his sense of vocation. Like *Loon Lake*, *World's Fair* is set in the 1930s but in a very different setting from *Loon Lake*. Where Joe wanders picaresquely across the Depression landscape, Edgar, of *World's Fair*, travels widely only about the Bronx. It is a lush narrative giving the reader a portrait of the artist as a child. The novel is reminiscent of James Joyce's poignant story "Araby." Both stories are Bildungsromans and both end in a youth going to an exotic fair. But Edgar, unlike the protagonist of "Araby," comes away not so much disillusioned as wizened about the ways of the world. Despite some painful experiences and familial setbacks, Edgar comes out of his childhood in love with the great multivariousness of life. This knowingness comes through because of the double vision of the narrative. The novel is the memoir of a mature man of his childhood, just as *Loon Lake* was Joe's attempt to write an autobiography of his youth. Joe, master of Loon Lake, looks back upon his youth as a moment of great loss; Edgar, of the Bronx, looks back upon his childhood as a time of great discovery.

The title of the novel refers to the 1939 World's Fair held at Flushing Meadow, New York. The fair offered images of a brilliant technological future. It was symbolized by the Trylon obelisk and the Perisphere, male and female images. Going to the fair becomes Edgar's most intense ambition and goal, which he realizes twice, once with his girlfriend and once with his family. The title also suggests Edgar's attitude toward, or feeling about, life—it is a fair world and it is a great joy to be alive in it. Edgar's memoir refers both to a place and a time and to a condition. At the end, Edgar and a friend put together several of their precious objects to go into a time capsule made from a cardboard mailing tube and tinfoil. This is a fitting image of the novel—a time capsule comprised of the human memory. And Edgar remembers well; his prose is stunningly evocative of the sights, sounds, and smells of the Bronx in the 1930s—the fish markets, the butcher shops, the bakeries, the dairy, the clothing stores, the cafeterias, the streets. Like so many of Doctorow's narrators, Edgar sees clearly and intensely. In an interview, Doctorow comments on the novel:

> I wrote the book on the presumption—which I realized after I started—that a child's life is morally complex, and that a child is a perception machine. A child's job is to perceive, that's his business. So the novel is the sentimental education of a kid, a *Bildungsroman*, if you will, that simply stops at the age of 10.

As Edgar informs us in the novel: "In my own consciousness I was not a child. When I was alone, not subject to the demands of the world, I had the opportunity to be the aware sentient being I knew myself to be." In fact, the novel is about the growth and development of that perceptiveness, the major skill of a writer.

Despite mixed reviews, the novel won the American Book Award for fiction in 1986. Like *Loon Lake*, *World's Fair* possesses multiple voices—the narrator's and seven "recorded" narratives by three members of his family that are interspersed throughout the novel. The novel is thus a combination memoir and oral history (à la Studs Terkel). While the major events of history impinge upon Edgar and his family, Edgar's memoir is mostly and essentially an inner-history. Significantly, the author quotes from Wordsworth's great autobiographical poem "The Prelude" as an epigraph to the novel: "A raree-show is here, / With children gathered round." Edgar's narrative consists of intensely and beautifully recounted "spots of time" of Edgar's childhood. The memoir is also a family history—of Edgar's parents, brother, his grandparents, his aunts and uncles. We have seen this family before in other Doctorow works. Edgar's family resembles the Isaacsons of *The Book of Daniel* and Jonathan's family in *Lives of the Poets*. What Edgar's memoir captures so well is the passion for life of this family. Such a passion for life seems often to run counter to the world. As Daniel's immigrant grandmother says in *The Book of Daniel*: "That excess of passion, that shimmering fullness of stored life which always marks the victim. What we have, too much life in each of us, is what the world hates most. We offend. We stink with life. Our hearts make love to the world not gently." In *World's Fair*, however, Edgar is no victim, nor is his life a failure. His memoir is his "making love to the world." In a sense, Doctorow in this novel uses *his* past to show the coming of age of his artist, as he has used our past in other novels, most notably *Ragtime*, to show America's coming of age.

Like *Ragtime*, *World's Fair* is a coming of age novel that ends positively for its narrator. Both novels end with the coming of a war. Like *The Book of Daniel*, *World's Fair* climaxes when the protagonist attends an amusement park. Both Daniel and Edgar learn important truths about life in an artificial environment, the ever-elusive "tomorrow land." Both Daniel and Edgar return to history from the bogus constructs of the technophiles, trusting in their own instincts and powers of self-composition. Doctorow has often said that he writes to find out what he is writing. Similarly, in *World's Fair*, he appears to be remembering in order to see what he knows, to see what his experience means to him, what he has learned from it, what he might make of it, to see what treasures it might hold for him. The act of remembering is an act of composition, of interpretation. The accumulating insights of the memoir are the discoveries of the mature writer as he works his way through his childhood years. Like Wordsworth, Edgar regains and comprehends his experience through the process of recollection and contemplation in tranquillity.

For anyone born before World War II, the book is provocative of nostalgia for a world that is no more. The novel captures lovingly what life was like in the 1930s for most Americans—a veritable time capsule of daily life. Here are the street vendors, the vegetable wagon, Joe the Sweet Potato Man, the itinerant photographer and his pony, radio programs, Saturday movie serials, the comic books, all the individual shops that are now part of the supermarket. Edgar mentions the radio programs he listened to: *Gang Busters*, *The Kraft Music Hall*, *Easy Aces*, the *Chase and Sanborn Hour*, the *Green Hornet*, *The Shadow*, *Jack Benny*, *Eddie Cantor*, *Information Please*, and many other. His father listens to the commentators Gabriel Heatter and Walter Winchell, but hates the right-wing commentators Father Coughlin and Fulton Lewis. Curiously, perhaps, the novel does not mention President Roosevelt's "Fireside Chats" or Orson Welles's famous Halloween broadcast of *The War of the Worlds* in 1938. In any event, the imagination in a radio world had to function on the basis of sound, to create pictures from auditory images—perhaps the last stages of an oral culture, now supplanted by the visual culture of television.

If *Loon Lake* is a study in discontinuity, *World's Fair* is a study in continuity, of a multigenerational family seeking to sustain itself in an ever-changing world. As a memoir of his childhood, Edgar recounts the ways people belong to families, to things, to places, how they connect, how they move from their little worlds to the world outside their homes. It is a portrayal of the development, finally, of an historical consciousness, of our connection to history. This connection or consciousness is especially crucial to being Jewish. Dave's rather rebellious younger sister, Molly, says at the annual Seder: "The Jews are the only people in the world who give you a history course before they let you eat." It is this development of a vital historical consciousness that keeps the novel from being merely an indulgence in nostalgia for a vanished world.

Edgar's memoir is not only a "remembrance of things past," but a bearing witness and a paying homage to those who were the witnesses of his life, especially his father. *World's Fair* is another variation of the tale of the missing or derelict father so prominent in Doctorow's fiction. At the time of compiling his "memoir," Edgar's father is dead. Yet his voice, his presence, pervades Edgar's narrative. To help Edgar remember this time are the "recorded remembrances" of his mother. Rose, his brother, Donald, and Aunt Frances, his father's sister. Rose's voice, appropriately, begins Edgar's memoir and appears three more times, following after two three-chapter sequences and one four-chapter sequence. Then the reader gets one excerpt of Donald's narrative, followed by one by Aunt Frances. The last is by Donald about three-fourths of the way through the novel. Dave, as brother-husband-father, is the family enigma that needs explaining, the problem that needs solving, the failure that needs justification. Each oral history, in addition to giving its remembered version of the family in the 1930s, tries to give Edgar an answer to his questions about his father—this bright but shadowy figure who lived and died of the wrong life. Edgar's memoir represents a double quest—one, to recover a nurturing relationship to his past, and second, to redeem his father's life, to show, in effect, that he is, indeed, his father's son. He succeeds at both.

The novel shows Edgar successfully making the challenging passage from the inner circles of his family to the expanding perimeters of the world. His first and continuing task is to come to grips with the colossal beings of his mother and father, whose troublesome relationship plagues him throughout his childhood. The mother and father are a study in contrasts. Rose is Apollonian, all order and efficiency and common sense: "My mother ran our home and our lives with a kind of tactless administration. . . . She construed the world in vivid judgments. . . . Everything she did was a declarative act. Her mastery of our realm was worth my study." Dave is the free spirit, the Dionysian, the impulsive, dreamy but passionate: "My father was not a reliable associate, I was to gather. Too many things he said would come to pass did not. He was always late. . . . He created suspense. He was full of errant enthusiasms and was easily diverted by them. . . . I knew he was unreliable, but he was fun to be with. He was a child's ideal companion, full of surprises and happy animal energy." Rose worries about the world's dangers, its diseases and threats. Dave delights in the world's crazy possibilities: "My father loved tricks, gentle practical jokes. . . . He loved word games, riddles. . . . He loved puns and limericks. . . . He relished the lore of the trickster in song or story." Edgar comes to see that his father was teaching him something about an age-old conflict between the male and the female: "He was teaching me the available recourses in a universe run by humorless women." Where Rose seeks to control the world, Dave seeks to defy it, elude it. Rose's realm is the home and the markets, Dave's realm is the multitudinous city—there is where Dave finds his order: "It was a place of accommodation for human desire, it supported the diverse intentions of millions of people simultaneously, and he knew that and gave me the confidence to understand it and not be afraid." While Edgar often depicts these contrasts rather starkly, he knows, and his memoir shows, that the reality is more complex. In one of her recorded remembrances, Rose concludes: "Only now do I see that our lives could have gone in an entirely different direction."

The novel captures well Edgar's struggle as a child to negotiate his acceptance and position in an adult world. Children, he learns, must endure indignities—only children had to change out of their wet bathing suits on the beach; only children had to get their pictures taken on ponies. Edgar feels the disproportion of things—adult freedoms and privileges, child restraints and weaknesses. Adults do not always tell the truth and, hence, cannot be trusted, as Edgar learns when his parents take their dog Pinky away. Some adults had to be carefully observed and worried over. A child, Edgar sees, is never certain about how to move into the adult world: "All around me was the example of passionate survival, but I could never be sure, as I held in me the conflicting arguments of how it was done, what was the margin for error, the tolerance for wrong moves." As a child, Edgar wants only to be taken seriously, as someone useful. He gains some of this when he tells his brother about a kid faking his ability to play a saxophone during an audition. Receiving lots of praise, Edgar learns something important: "There was also a new awareness in me that size wasn't everything, that wit was a strength in the world, the exercise of one's brain." Edgar will make good use of this skill on the streets to survive.

Certain nursery rhymes lead Edgar to think about death, another of life's deep, dark secrets he needs to learn. A number of experiences bring Edgar face to face with death. It is Edgar who discovers that his old grandma has died. In an art book, Edgar finds prints of famous paintings depicting "pale, unhealthy looking yellowish men with the nails in them," images that make him queasy. At school one day, Edgar and the other children see the body of a woman who had been hit by a car lying in the school yard. Edgar, watching from the window, recalls: "I had felt not fear but enlightenment." On May 6, 1937, Edgar sees the great air-ship *Hindenburg* fly over the Bronx. Later he learns of the terrible fire that engulfed the *Hindenburg* and killed so many over Lakehurst, New Jersey. This leads Edgar to feel terror about falling things: "Everything around me was going up and down, up and down." He has a nightmare about his father crashing to the ground. The world, he learns, is not invulnerable. Death makes the world uncertain. Edgar tries to protect himself by some "magical thinking": he has a theory about death, that if he thinks about a certain form of death, it will not happen to him—"mental inoculation," he calls it. However, he is soon afflicted with a ruptured appendix and almost dies of it, a condition he had not thought about, but which does not cause him to forsake his theory.

Another of life's deep, dark secrets Edgar must learn, of course, is sex. He often wonders about the "dark mysterious things" his parents did in private. But his real education comes from his friend Meg and her attractive mother, Norma. In Meg, Edgar sees a lovely girl possessing "a quality of inner certitude," which evokes a similar feeling in him: "I felt as if I were looking ahead down a still corridor into my calm and resolute manhood." Norma, with no husband in her life, is like no other mother he knows, a free spirit. Of course, Rose disapproves of her, feels she is disreputable, calls her a "ten-cents-a-dance" woman, which makes her all the more attractive to Edgar. Because Norma works at the *World's Fair*, Edgar is invited to attend with Meg. When Meg invites him, she says, "Edgar, we could see everything!" And "see everything" is exactly what Edgar does. Norma's job is "to wrestle with Oscar the Amorous Octopus in a tank of water," which involves the removal of Norma's swimsuit, a sight that stuns Edgar deeply. Later, he reflects that he should not have seen what he did. Nevertheless, "Norma's freedom made life more thrilling and more dangerous. I felt the danger now. Meg had been born to thrilling freedom that I only now suspected was possible." Edgar recalls that moment as an epiphany:

> I knew everything now, the crucial secret, so carelessly vouchsafed. After all, I had not intended this, it had come to me without my bidding, without any planning or calculation on my part, presented, in fact, as an accident of the adventure. It was not my fault. I had worried before, all the time in the enormous effort to catch up to life, to find it, to feel it, comprehend it; but all I had to do was be in it and it would instruct me and give me everything I needed.

Knowledge of death and sex, Edgar learns, comes as a kind of gratuity in life—all you have to do was "be in it."

Edgar is a kind of anthropologist of his own consciousness as it lay buried under and within layers and sediments of memory. One of his earliest and most vivid moments occurs at Far Rockaway beach in the summer of 1936. There he learns the "enlightening fear of the planet," a revelatory moment where he gains "some quiet revelation in me of unutterable life." He recalls this experience in lush Whitmanesque terms:

> I felt through my fingers the sand pour of bones, like some futile archaeologist of a ground-up mineral past. I recognized the heat in the sand as some invisible power of distant light. And from the glittering blue water I took its endless motion and unimaginably frigid depth. All of this astonishingly was; and I on my knees in my bodying perception, worldlessly primeval, at home, fearful, joyous.

This virtually mystical "at-homeness" is the beginnings of Edgar's self-consciousness, a discovery of his separateness and his belongingness. It is the source, finally, of his confidence as a human being in the world.

The story of childhood, as Edgar depicts it, is the story of the discovery of the world, of history. Edgar moves from the micro to the macro level in his development. From his most immediate family, he discovers his extended family—his mother's side, his father's side—the family's complexity, its conflicts and contrasts, which often produce pain and insult as well as love. Edgar's development corresponds with his father's decline—the loss of his store, the move to a smaller apartment, his going to work for someone else. The outside world intrudes in other ways as well. Edgar hears about anti-Semitism as the Nazis come to power in Germany. The *Hindenburg* disaster breaks into his sense of security. The radio and the newspapers are filled with the stories of war in Europe and in the Far East. At Madison Square Garden, Charles Lindbergh and Father Coughlin are the featured speakers at an American Nazi party rally.

That the world poses a threat to Edgar comes to a focus in his unexpected encounter with two youthful thugs on the way home from the library. With a knife against his belly, Edgar is asked if he is Jewish, which Edgar denies. He saves himself—not unlike Joe in *Loon Lake*—by his wit, by a convincing lie. Claiming that his father is a cop deters the thugs from harming Edgar further. Nevertheless, Edgar is ashamed of his cowardice; he feels humiliated and enraged.

Partly to atone for his dishonor, Edgar writes an essay sponsored by the World's Fair committee on "The Typical American Boy." In many respects, the essay reflects what Edgar has learned as a child. "The typical American Boy" he writes, "is not fearful of Dangers." Moreover, "if he is Jewish he should say so. If he is anything he should say what it is when challenged." He appreciates music and all women. And finally: "He looks death in the face." Edgar sends the essay in without his parents' knowledge. His essay wins an Honorable Mention, which his father reads about in the paper. The prize is a free visit to the fair for the boy and his family. This incident is a high moment for the family, both parents deeply proud. His father "opened his arms and pulled me to him and he held me." This draws them all together, at least briefly, despite the other hardships of their lives. They go out to celebrate. "My father strode along as he did when he felt good, his shoulders moving from side to side, it was almost a dance. His head bobbed. 'Shoulders back,' he said to me, 'chin up, eyes straight ahead. That's it. Look the world in the eye.'" Edgar's composition recomposed his family—an important discovery about the power of art to create a community.

Significantly, it is Edgar, the child, who is the guide for his family's visit to the World's Fair. Edgar had "seen it all" before, and now he can lead his family, to show them what he knew, to show them a vision of the future, a future he will live in much more than they. The fair is an imaginative construct, a composition in which Edgar feels at home. "We stood in the shadow of the Trylon and Perisphere, and I felt these familiar forms, huge and white, granted me some sort of beneficence to my shoulders. It was hard to articulate, but it was as if I were in some invisible field of their guardianship." Edgar knows, intuitively at least that the World's Fair is a noble human attempt to create a vision of a future at a time of great economic dislocation and gathering clouds of world war. Certainly, the elder Edgar, looking back upon this movement from the 1980s, sees the fair as an act of imagination that runs counter to the historical forces of dissolution. But he can also see its flaws. In a sense, the fair is not so much an image of hope as an illusion based upon a false optimism, a faith in a technology that is blind to history. Edgar feels responsible for the fair as he leads his family from exhibit to exhibit. He sees paint peeling and other signs of decay, and hopes his family will not notice. His father's "commentary" on the things put into the Time Capsule—not to be opened until 6939—serves as a reminder of America's social and political blindness. "He asked my brother and me why we thought there was nothing in the capsule about the great immigrations that had brought Jewish and Italian and Irish people to America or nothing to represent the point of view of the workingman. 'There is no hint from the stuff they included that America has a serious intellectual life, or Indians on reservations or Negroes who suffer from race prejudice. Why is that?'" Similarly, after the General Motors' sponsored Futurama exhibit—"an intricate marvel of miniaturization"—Dave cannot help commenting that this is what General Motors wants the future to be: highways built by our tax money for its cars. Later, on the electric bumper cars, Donald shouts to Edgar: "*This* is the Futurama!"

Edgar, the writer-in-the-making, is always impressed by individual acts that compose a believable illusion. As a child, he watches his brother and friends build an igloo out of snow in their backyard. Edgar comments that it was "almost as if my brother and his friends had used the magic of an ethereal idea as something to hand-like the most skillful magician." He overhears his mother's friend, Mae, refer to him as an "acrobat" because of his breech birth. At the circus, Edgar takes "profound instruction" from a clown-acrobat who fools the audience by disguising his real identity and ability. "There was art in the thing, the power of illusion, the mightier power of the reality behind it. What was first true was then false, a man was born from himself." What is most keen to his understanding is that there are ways to dramatize your inner-truth to an unsuspecting world. Similarly, listening to the amateur hour on the radio, Edgar's favorite performers are the "one-man bands" that produced not real music but the semblance of it. All of these images comprise Edgar's notion of the artist. But perhaps the key metaphor for the artist-writer is ventriloquism, an image that closes the book. In the summer before his second visit to the fair, Edgar finds the Little Blue Book no. 1278, *Ventriloquism Self-Taught*, which he had sent for some time before. He recalls: "I had always been attracted to ventriloquism. It was a powerful magic, throwing your voice and fooling people." Later, in preparing his own time capsule, he puts that book in it, but then changes his mind—it is too valuable to waste. Returning home, Edgar "practiced the ventriloquial drone." A ventriloquist does not so much "throw" his voice as imitate other sounds, other voices. So, too, does the novelist—as Edgar portrays him in his memoir of the many voices, the many witnesses of his life.

Edgar's birthday is January 6, the day traditionally used to celebrate the Epiphany, the gifts of the Magi to a child in a manger. *World's Fair* is a gift from a contemporary magus. It is a rich time capsule that does not bury its mementoes for some indeterminant future, but rather offers its gifts to the present.

CHRISTOPHER D. MORRIS

Illusions of Demystification in Ragtime

Ragtime recounts and intertwines three main stories: of an upper middle-class family identified only as Father, Mother, Mother's Younger Brother, and the little boy; of Tateh, a Jewish Latvian immigrant; and of Coalhouse Walker, a black pianist. The unnamed family is outwardly happy and prosperous, but over the course of the novel the three adults become estranged. Tateh begins as an impoverished socialist but becomes an entrepreneur and successful film-maker. Coalhouse Walker is humiliated by Irish firemen; when his fiance dies as an indirect result of Walker's search for justice, he and a few confederates avenge themselves in acts of violence that eventually lead to his death. In addition to these three connected plots, the novel contains a number of characters and incidents from the years 1906 to 1914, the chief temporal setting.

Ragtime is the first of a series of works in which Doctorow experiments with narration; more specifically, in this novel, *Loon Lake*, *Lives of the Poets*, and *World's Fair*, the principal narrator cannot finally be determined, either as "omniscient" or as an identifiable character. By detaching discourse from any ultimately determinable source, this series of experiments may attest to the severity of previously explored narrative predicaments; it shows in new ways the delusion of the self as the autonomous manipulator of language; it shows the writer orphaned by writing. At the same time, these narrational

---

innovations explore alternatives to the specter of eternal return. Of course, from the existence of experiment, no sure motive and no sure author can be deduced; indeed such an impossibility becomes a subject of these later works, perhaps because *Ragtime*'s experimental quest for alternatives is in the end disappointed.

The undecidability of the narrator of *Ragtime* is the result of the generic names assigned to the primary family: Father, Mother, Mother's Younger Brother, and the little boy. The first three names appear to imply that the narrator is the little boy, the only child in the family. However, throughout the novel the little boy is referred to in the third, not the first person, as though he is not the narrator. The anonymous narrative voice of *Ragtime* appears to be the voice of an American writing in about the year 1975, a person familiar with American cultural history and one who is given to both irony and rhetorical flourish. With one exception, this narrative voice refers to itself as the editorial "we" when generalizing about history ("This was the time in our history"). The exception to this practice occurs near the end of the novel, when Father's death at sea, in the sinking of the *Lusitania*, is recounted: "Poor father, I see his final exploration. He arrives at the new place, his hair risen in astonishment, his mouth and eyes dumb. His toe scuffs a soft storm of sand, he kneels and his arms spread in pantomimic celebration, the immigrant, as in every moment of his life, arriving eternally on the shore of his Self."

Some critics conclude, on the basis of this passage, that the narrator is the little boy grown up. This inference can be supported by other internal evidence; for example, the narrator's knowledge of a visit from Houdini comes from "the family archives." The full implications of this inference will be analyzed later; for now it is important to emphasize that the identification remains only inference: nowhere is the "I" explicitly identified as the little boy. Because the reader acquiesces to the convention of an anonymous narrator telling a story about characters known as Father, Mother, Mother's Younger Brother, and the little boy, the introduction of "I" instead of "we" does not remove the mystery. As other critics have maintained, the exceptional use of "I" can still refer to an anonymous narrator who names only an object of his narrative, not necessarily a relative.

The ambiguity does not end there, for a third possibility is that the narrator is the little girl, Tateh's daughter Sha. Since the Yiddish words for father and mother are Tateh and Mameh, she occupies a position in the narrative equivalent to that of the little boy. If Sha is the narrator, then the scene in which she and Jung mutually experience a moment of recognition or telepathy makes more comprehensible the narrator's otherwise inexplicable condemnation of Freud. Also, if Sha is the narrator, then the vivid detail in her recollection of a chance meeting with the little boy becomes more comprehensible. There is yet fourth possibility, that the editorial "we" refers to both Sha and the little boy speaking together. At the end of the novel, in Atlantic City, the two children are depicted as ideal, telepathic playmates, in the spirit of Goethe's "elective affinities" or Shelley's complementary lovers. Although this possibility cannot be dismissed, it obviously creates new problems in examining the exceptional use of "I."

Geoffrey Galt Harpham captures the radical quality of Doctorow's experiment when he refers to "the unplaceability of [the novel's] narrative voice." In fact, the narrational uncertainty is an enigma that forces the reader to concentrate on the issue of pronoun references. The identity of the narrator can be decided only by the conferral of equivocal referents to the pronouns "I" and "we," linguistic shifters without inherent meaning. Four different interpretations of the novel can flow from the four different identifications of the narrator; at the same time, each ends in contradiction, for to adopt one is to exclude others equally plausible: male pronouns exclude the female; singular pronouns exclude the plural; the three specific attributions (the boy, the girl, both) exclude the anonymous narrator; and vice versa in each case. This wholesale indeterminacy, which mandates error in interpretation, forces the reader to entertain the possibility that the whole concept of a narrator may be only the fabrication of novels.

In order to read the novel, however, ultimate uncertainty cannot be tolerated; some attribution of a source to the words must be made. One act of naming that respects the enigma is to consider the narrator "double," that is *simultaneously* two different entities, a specific attribution and a separate, anonymous voice. In fact, such a practice could find some support in the novel's many images of duplication, especially in this description of the little boy's gazing at himself in the mirror: "He would gaze at himself until there were two selves facing one another, neither which could claim to be the real one." If no determinable source for this sentence (or for others in *Ragtime*) can be settled upon, then it embodies the very doubleness it describes. It suggests that an integral Cartesian self is not the originator of discourse but that, instead, a story can be told by *two equally unreal entities*. In this way, the novel's two unreal sources seem to demystify the illusion of a single consciousness as narrator.

Nevertheless, the demystification is only *seeming*, since in any practical reading it is next to impossible to posit unreal, plural sources. In the next few paragraphs, the awkward "narrator(s)" and "they" are used to refer to the narrative voice. (It is understood that this procedure is already in error. In this state of indeterminacy, to name at all is already to err; any "insight" afforded by the problem of the novel's narrator(s) is made possible, after all, only by a prior blindness.) The reader is falsely demystified in the attempt to interpret characters as well as narrator(s), but that delusion is anticipated in the narrator(s). For example, the very first pages of the novel try to represent the ragtime era: "Everyone wore white in summer. Tennis racquets were hefty and the racquet faces elliptical. There was a lot of sexual fainting. There were no Negroes. There were no immigrants."

After one page of further description, centering on the murder of Stanford White by Harry K. Thaw, the narrator(s) write: "Evelyn fainted. She had been a well-known artist's model at the age of fifteen. Her underclothes were white. Her husband habitually whipped her. She happened once to meet Emma Goldman, the revolutionary. Goldman lashed her with her tongue. Apparently there *were* Negroes. There *were* immigrants."

The narrator(s) now speak from the vantage point of a completed narration, from knowledge supposedly derived from the tale, because they refer to the meeting between Evelyn and Emma, which has not yet been narrated. At the same time, the futility of their own "learning process" is obvious in the irony and self-mockery that accompanies their supposed demystification. Paul de Man's two-stage process is evident here: first, the reader believes in a demystification; next, that demystification is perceived as only a construct. What will be the value of narrating (or reading) *Ragtime* if the illusions it depicts can be destroyed only by new illusions?

In fact the narrator(s)—whether anonymous or specific—never learn; illusions persist until the end. Consider first the case of the anonymous narrator, whose continuing blindness is brought home to the reader on the last page, in the description of the origin and nature of Tateh's new films. Tateh gets his idea for the films one day while watching the three children (his daughter, his stepson, and Coalhouse Walker III) playing together in his California backyard. The narrator(s) endorse the films' sentimental depiction of a "society of ragamuffins, like all of us, a gang, getting into trouble and getting out again." Of course, the "vision" of these new films is a gross misrepresentation of the bulk of the action of *Ragtime*, which tells of violent, incurable racial and ethnic conflict, but the narrator(s) identify themselves with the gang of ragamuffins, thereby accepting Tateh's Pollyannaish vision and revealing a blindness to the events of their own completed narration.

Now suppose the narrators are identified specifically, that is, as the boy, the girl, or both. In this alternative, either or both specific narrators, in their California backyard, serve as the very model for the cinematic misrepresentation that Tateh, in ignorance, perpetuates. There is no retrospective denunciation of this irony. If error is generated and perpetuated in this way, then narrating is misrepresenting, learning is illusory, and the circularity of error is inescapable.

Illusory demystifications also afflict the major characters in the three principal plots. Within the New Rochelle family, Father is at first depicted as the embodiment of the unexamined pieties of his day, benign capitalism and patriotism, which—as we seem to learn—mask exploitation, racism, and sexism. He is a manufacturer of the signifier of these illusions, the American flag, which draws credulous immigrants in ships to New York Harbor. Over the course of the novel, Father undergoes two seeming transformations. The first occurs during his trip to the Pole with Peary, when his adultery with an Esquimo woman appears to teach him a new knowledge of female sexuality, but despite this knowledge, he quickly becomes emotionally and sexually estranged from Mother. A second false lesson grows out of his contact with Coalhouse Walker, which seems to teach him American racism, but despite this knowledge, Father commits himself even more faithfully to the patriotic dimension of his business; eventually his firm supplies the government with advanced munitions. In both cases Father's supposed demystification is only apparent; he remains in thrall to the false values symbolized by the now-discredited flag he manufactures.

Mother also undergoes a seeming demystification. After she is forced to assist in the management of Father's flag-making company, Mother no longer holds the world of business in awe. As critics have noted, Mother seems to become, simply through practical experience, a working example of the abstract doctrines of women's liberation espoused by Emma Goldman, but this supposed learning process does not lead to her independence and autonomy. Instead, Mother's liberation from Father's sexism is finally accomplished through her enchantment with another man, another manufacturer of (and believer in) illusions, Tateh. Tateh's new false identity, as Baron Ashkenazy, adds to the sense in which she is again seduced as soon as she flees from Father's demystified values. It is as if one set of illusions can be exposed only when they are exchanged for the new.

Such empty learning is obvious in Mother's Younger Brother, whose life first has meaning for him when he is dazzled by the glitz of Evelyn Nesbit. The memorable scene in which Mother's Younger Brother observes her from a closet recalls the story of the intrusion of Actaeon into the bath of Diana, an allusion suggested by other details as well. For this intrusion, Actaeon is punished by being transformed into a stag that is later hounded to death by his own dogs; like him, Mother's Younger Brother becomes a kind of prey, possessed by self-destructive delusions. First the spell of Evelyn herself victimizes him, but he recovers from this mystification with the aid of a new belief system, Emma Goldman's anarchism, which propels him into the causes of Coalhouse Walker and Emiliano Zapata. Mother's Younger Brother believes that in adopting Goldman's anarchism he has demystified the American political system. But the self-contradiction in anarchism is made clear by Goldman's highly organized, very unanarchic way of life: a small but telling example is her habit of having a change of clothes and a book ready in case of imprisonment on short notice. A *purely* "anarchic way of life" may not be possible. In order to help Coalhouse Walker, Mother's Younger Brother and Walker's anarchic confederates must be highly disciplined. As a munitions expert, Mother's Younger Brother has sophisticated technical skills; moreover, this intellectual prowess appears in blueprints later put to use in maintaining American state power—the opposite of anarchy. In any case, Mother's Younger Brother's false belief in his demystification of politics becomes clear in the suicidal final stages of his career when he loses his hearing just before dying in Zapata's cause.

Insofar as the boy may be considered solely as a character, his education follows a familiar literary path of imaginative and sexual awakening which holds forth the prospect of exchanging innocence for reliable knowledge. From his beginnings in a nearly solipsistic absorption in his own small world, the boy becomes aware of the world through examining its detritus—the oil-stained letter from Father, the silhouettes of Evelyn Nesbit discarded by his despondent uncle. He passes through moments of usual childhood belief in the omnipotence of thought. He becomes aware of his mother's sexuality. By the end of the novel, the boy experiences a relationship of ideal intersubjectivity with Tateh's daughter Sha. So outlined, the boy's maturation is an apparent demystification, a movement from innocent illusions, through engagement with the world, to love, and yet this demystification vanishes whenever the reader recalls the possibility that the boy alone narrates the events. When this thought obtrudes, a whole series of new considerations rapidly destroys confidence in his learning. As a sixty-year-old cultural historian, the grown boy endows himself, in retrospect, with preternatural powers concerning the assassination of Archduke Franz Ferdinand (II). He reconstructs his parents' sexual relations with detail bordering on the obsessive or voyeuristic; he blandly narrates Tateh's erotic attraction to his mother while his Father sleeps. On other occasions he is ironic; by kidnapping young men, he writes, Harry K. Thaw was "beginning to work out his problems." He inserts dogmatic opinions about cultural history, makes generalizations about history without supplying evidence, and concludes by imagining himself as part of a happy "society of ragamuffins." In short, study of the boy as narrator suggests that he has shed the illusions of youth only to acquire new ones in maturity.

If the experiences of the New Rochelle family suggest deceit in the idea of learning, they are no more its victims than are Tateh or Coalhouse Walker. Some of the illusions have already been noted which change Tateh from a starving Jewish socialist—one who adheres strictly to Hebraic codes governing adultery—into a pseudonymous, seducing director of films that misrepresent his country and his past. Although Tateh sees his progress as a movement away from the mystifications of politics and class conflict, the reader sees that he gains success only by renouncing his heritage and accepting a vision of America that contradicts his own suffering. Tateh does not regress from an earlier, authentic perception to later illusion; on the contrary, nothing in the novel suggests that his treatment of Mameh, his denunciation of Evelyn Nesbit, his flight from the strike of Lawrence, or his work on flip-books represents either progress or regress. Indeed, critics believe that these episodes, too, can be interpreted as symptoms of blindness in Tateh. Thus his life may be regarded as a series of false demystifications, the shift from one illusion to another.

Of all of the major characters, only Coalhouse Walker seems a probable candidate to embody an authentic demystification. The music he plays gives the novel its presiding metaphor and principle of organization; it recalls the nonverbal alternatives to delusion tested in Red Bloom's jazz and Billy Bathgate's songs. Walker's belated courtship of Sarah seems a direct expression of human dignity. His revolt against racial humiliation appears to be designed to demystify, to expose contradictions in the heart of the political and economic systems. His insistence on the particular—his car and Willie Conklin—seems to give the lie to other characters' absorption in theory and fantasy. As long as readers concentrate on the Coalhouse plot by itself, the novel provides a seeming anchor by which to judge the circularity of its other characters' behavior: whatever the excesses of his revolt, it is a response that at least confronts a world that other characters avoid or flee. The novel's movement toward climax proceeds inexorably. The precipitation of an ultimate disclosure is promised in the still tableau of Coalhouse bending over the plunger wired to blow up the Morgan Library, to explode the decadent repository of Western metaphysics. The considerable intellectual recourses of the novel—its critiques of enlightenment, of capitalism, of the melting pot, of America itself—are evidently at stake in the moment of Coalhouse's silent surrender. If the lives of other characters remain mystified, then this moment may bring truth. Such is the expectation wrought.

The story of Walker is drained of this potential for signification, however, the moment the reader sees it intertextually, as the adaptation of Heinrich von Kleist's "Michael Kohlhaas." Coalhouse now appears not a representation of an authentic mode of existence but of only another representation. As a sign his putative referent—racial or human justice, the dignity of man—is replaced by another sign, Kleist's Michael Kohlhaas. Likewise Sarah now recalls Kohlhaas's wife Lisbeth, Booker T. Washington,

Luther, Conklin, Junker von Tronka. Since Kleist's story, in turn, is based on a previous text (a medieval chronicle of incidents in history befalling one Hans Kohlhasen), there is now the prospect of even further regress. As recent studies suggest, interpreting Kleist is no simple matter. The famous "deadpan" narrator of "Michael Kohlhaas" provides a foretaste of this difficulty in his initial remark that Michael Kohlhaas was "one of the most upright and at the same time one of the most terrible men of his day." If Coalhouse is derived from a Michael Kohlhaas who is undecidable from the outset, then contemporary interpretation will only commit once more, in modern trappings, the necessary error of interpretation exposed in the execution of Kohlhaas. Instead of escaping the circularity afflicting other characters' phony learning, Coalhouse Walker, too, becomes a manifestation of Nietzsche's "eternal reiteration of the same thing."

Once this moment of intertextuality occurs, the problem of narration becomes a new morass. Whether Coalhouse's story is being told by an anonymous or nonanonymous narrator, the narration now loses its once-supposed anchor in the real. If the story of Coalhouse/Kohlhaas is told by the boy or the girl grown old, or both, the novel's credibility collapses: earlier suspicions of their illusions are confirmed; they become palpable fiction writers. Even if the Coalhouse/Kohlhaas story is told by an anonymous narrator, its meaning in *Ragtime* now depends on a prior interpretation of Kleist's story; but that story's narrator, like its critical history, warns that secure interpretation may be impossible. Once again, the very moment that insight into *Ragtime* appears to be approachable, blindness is evident. The reader sees in fleeting moments of demystification only phantasm.

Inducing this momentary illusion of learning is one of the exertions of art. In *Ragtime* the perils of that effort are dramatized in Houdini, who has been analyzed as a figure for the artist. Houdini follows in the tradition of the artist-as-performer, which was begun with the image of the clown in "The Songs of Billy Bathgate." In addition, he continues the depiction of the artist as struggling with the representation of death in ways observable in Blue and Daniel. Like his predecessors, he strives to demystify but only spellbinds and, in so doing, shows the limitations of art in the crucial test case of representation, death.

Even before the death of his mother, Houdini's feats are geared to defy mortality. After escaping from sealed milk cans and chains, Houdini asks to be buried alive but finds he cannot escape. Nevertheless he continues to be fascinated by events that seem to defy death; he pays homage to a sandhog who somehow survived an explosion during the construction of a tunnel under the East River. After the death of his mother, Houdini's acts become frightening as he risks death with even greater intensity. Houdini's art raises the Heideggerian issue of the fallacy in representations of death. In this way,

Houdini also resembles Blue: death is the end point and origin of their quests. And like Daniel, Houdini feels driven to display his artistry in the composition of a death scene. In retrospect these representational efforts were doomed from the outset. In Houdini's case, it becomes obvious that death cannot be truly represented by artifice (if only because no successful performance could be iterable). Thus, even in his harrowing performances, Houdini can only repeat an artifice that can never "more closely approximate."

This futility also haunts other representations. After his mother dies, Houdini arranges framed photographs of his mother in his New York brownstone "to suggest her continuing presence." He puts a picture of his mother on the very chair in which she posed for it. He hangs a picture of her entering the house inside his door. This futility is not confined to visual representations. A delusion of presence is induced by the music-box songs his mother once loved and "the redolence of her wardrobe." These are pathetic models of misrepresentation.

In this delusion Houdini nevertheless tries both to perfect his own art and to find a "genuine medium" to make the absent present. Even as he persists in this delusion, he works to demystify the artifice of others, his colleagues or competitors in the art of deathly illusionism. Desperate to make contact with his deceased mother, Houdini hires a detective agency to investigate the claims of spiritual mediums; he casts about for some scientific means of reaching his mother. Like his performances, these efforts at enlightenment cannot succeed, because they assume that the absent can be represented. For the reader of Houdini (as of Blue and Daniel), death uncovers the dysfunction of language.

Whatever its dysfunction, there seems to be no alternative to the artifice, whether the illusions of Houdini or such fiction as *Ragtime*, to which they allude. This sense of the absolute necessity for illusion-making and illusion-believing is conveyed by the narrator's comment that today "nearly fifty years since [Houdini's] death, the audience for escapes is even larger." In this famous aside the narrator makes self-canceling statements about illusions; audiences, like readers, are gullible, but the narrator—the fiction-writer of the Coalhouse/Kohlhaas story, for example—is busy writing the "escape." What Miller calls "varnishing"—the authorial assertion of a center that reveals, instead, its own incipient collapse—is once again disclosed. Like Houdini, the narrator demonstrates that both writer and reader, performer and audience, are escape artists. It is as if the attempt to represent must necessarily delude with the false promise of escape, in the face of a necessity.

If escape from delusion is impossible, the events of human history become repetitions, duplications of attempted escapes and failures. This is, again, the "burdensome thought" of Nietzsche's eternal return, which haunted Doctorow's earlier work. In *Ragtime* the eternal return is "the duplicable event," a phrase that links reiteration in history with narration.

The phrase first appears in an account of the ragtime era: "All across the continent merchants pressed the large round keys of their registers. The value of the duplicable event was everywhere perceived. Every town had its ice-cream soda fountain of Belgian marble. Painless Parker the Dentist everywhere offered to remove your toothache. At Highland Park, Michigan, the first Model T automobile built on a moving assembly line lurched down a ramp and came to rest in the grass under a clear sky."

The duplicable event is here associated with a seemingly inexorable loss of individuation—a kind of cultural entropy of the sort depicted in the novels of Thomas Pynchon. The imminent homogenization of America will be accompanied by an equivalence of people and of things mandated by Henry Ford's application of the principle to industry: "not only that the parts of the finished product be interchangeable, but that the men who build the products be themselves interchangeable parts." Both passages suggest that behind the apparent diversity of men, of machines, and of environment lie only the monotonous repetitions of history.

Of course, repetition is a structural principle of the plot. Harry K. Thaw has two trials. Evelyn Nesbit bathes Tateh's daughter, Sha; then Emma Goldman, in turn, ministers to Evelyn's body. Theodore Dreiser repeatedly tries to find the perfect alignment in his room. Admiral Peary searches for the precise position of the North Pole. To win back Sarah, Coalhouse repeats his Sunday visits. Tateh cries twice for his daughter and makes numerous silhouettes of Evelyn Nesbit. J. P. Morgan finds evidence of the same doctrine of reincarnation in Rosicrucianism, in Giordano Bruno, in the Hermetica. Scott Joplin rags are heard in New Rochelle and Atlantic City. The first explosion at a fire station is followed by a second. These explosions are framed by the tunnel blast that nearly kills a sandhog and by Younger Brother's detonations in Mexico. Booker T. Washington's mediation is followed by Father's. Coalhouse Walker's ruined Model-T is replaced by a rebuilt one. Tateh's films are made in series, as sequels. This list only begins to suggests the extent of repetition in the novel. The futility and monotony of such repetition suggest that history signifies nothing at all.

This suggestion is supported by the novel's many scenes of imprisonment and false liberation. Houdini's numerous escape attempts result only in the persistence of his delusion that human effort may produce some correct understanding of death. The futility of Houdini's imprisonments and escapes is repeated in the imprisonment and eventual release of Harry K. Thaw, events that purport to distinguish madness from sanity but obviously do not. Like the incarceration of Susan in *The Book of*

Daniel, the institutional distinction between madness and sanity in *Ragtime* is shown to be fictional. The saddest example of phony freedom is the experience of immigrants, who are first "arranged on benches in waiting pens" after landing in New York. The presumed further liberation of the immigrant can be tracked in Tateh; the novel's imagery suggests that Tateh's life in New York is also a kind of prison from which he makes several escapes—first to Lawrence, Massachusetts, then to Philadelphia, Atlantic City, and California. However, each of his attempts at human or spiritual liberation lands him in a new mirage world: the "Hollywood ending" of *Ragtime* repeats the Disneyland climax of *The Book of Daniel* and anticipates the dream pavilions of *World's Fair*. In *Ragtime* the duplicable event means the movement from one imprisoning illusion to another. Each promise of demystification turns out to be false, a model of misrepresentation.

A similar effect is created by the many empty coincidences in the novel. Readers agree that the novel teems with them. For example, Tateh got his start on a career in film-making by designing flip-books for the Franklin Novelty Company in Philadelphia. The same company manufactured a cheap pamphlet that taught Henry Ford the doctrine of reincarnation. Stanford White planned the home of Mrs. Stuyvestant Fish, who hired Houdini to entertain guests at her party; White's assistant, Charles McKim, designed the Morgan Library. In Egypt, J. P. Morgan sees the same New York Giants baseball team that Father took the little boy to see at the home ballpark. Such intersections of independent plot lines seem portentous, but in the end they reveal nothing. Equally teasing are the accounts of Freud's visit to America to lecture at Clark University in Worcester, Massachusetts, and of Theodore Dreiser's artistic depression following the publication of *Sister Carrie*. Such coincidences seem to invite interpretation; indeed, critical discourse about the novel, including the one now in progress, has been drawn to them as loci of meaning, but Arthur Saltzman aptly summarizes the mystifying effect of this lure: "If we are gratified by the connections our narrator makes for us . . . we are still disheartened by how seemingly fruitless those connections are." By themselves, coincidences express nothing other than their existence; the impulse to make them represent creates new error.

This de Manian delusion in reading is underscored by a second reference to the duplicable event, one that further links the repetitions and coincidences of history to narration. It occurs as the boy perceives the "instability of both things and people." In a kind of radical solipsism, he acknowledges no permanent reality separate from his own perception. The movies and his grandfather's stories are images of an importance equal to his hairbrush or his window, which seem to conform to his will. He listens to the Victrola and plays "the same record over and over, whatever it happened to be, as if to test the endurance of a duplicated event." In this passage the boy—one of the putative narrators—occupies himself in a *double* repetition: the recorded song is of course a "duplication," and the repeated playing duplicates it. Whatever the narrator's identity, narration and reading may resemble the repeated playing of the recorded song; both are double duplications that have the effect of testing art's "endurance." The open-ended "playing" of the song is like the potentially infinite, repetitive sequence of reading and interpretation. Only in this logical necessity can it be said that the duplicated event of art endures.

The novel seems to endorse the boy's version of the eternal return, as meaningless redundancy, especially when that idea is contrasted with more obviously mystified versions, such as J. P. Morgan's belief in reincarnation. According to Morgan's doctrine, divinely inspired leaders reappear throughout history to lead people and to inaugurate new epochs. In a secret room in his Library, Morgan propounds this theory to Henry Ford. He finds evidence for it in Rosicrucianism, Giordano Bruno, and the Hermetica. The first such leaders, Morgan confides, were the Egyptian pharaohs. In the belief that he and Ford are modern avatars of those demigods, Morgan invites the industrialist to accompany him on a trip to the Pyramids. In the end, Ford subscribes to the theory, with some ironic detachment; and though Morgan travels to Egypt alone, the two become sole members of "The Pyramid."

In this famous fictional meeting, Morgan and Ford accept a theory of history as the eternal return which resembles the Nietzschean doctrines of the *Übermensch* and cyclical history set forth in *Thus Spake Zarathustra*. That Morgan sees himself as an *Übermensch* is suggested by echoes of the Nietzschean hero: "He knew as no one else the cold and barren reaches of unlimited success. The ordinary operations of his intelligence and instinct over the past fifty years had made him preeminent in the affairs of nations and he thought this said little for mankind . . . . I have no peers, Morgan said . . . . It seemed an indisputable truth. Somehow he had catapulted himself beyond the world's value system."

Morgan's philosophy of the eternal return is formidable indeed. Like Emma Goldman's anarchism, it has the potential—if endorsed by the novel—to justify such radical actions as the revolt of Coalhouse Walker or Mother's Younger Brother's terrorism. In addition, Morgan's version of the *Übermensch* could provide intellectual sanction for Harry K. Thaw's murder of Stanford White or for Tateh's abandonment of his earlier Hebraic code. In short, Morgan's Nietzscheanism proposes a transvaluation of values by which any individual action could be justified. With so much at stake for interpretation, the novel's treatment of Morgan's theory must be carefully evaluated.

The contradiction in Morgan's "practical Nietzscheanism" is made apparent in his meeting with Ford and in his trip to Egypt. In the meeting, Morgan says he suspected Ford might be an embodiment of a divine mission when he noticed a resemblance between Ford's features and the mask on the sarcophagus of Seti the First. In other words, an underlying belief in representation is a condition of Morgan's Nietzscheanism: an *Übermensch* must be discernible. The shakiness of this assumption is evident enough in the resemblance Morgan claims to have found. Ford's deflating reply—that the doctrine of transmigration may be apprehended without the trappings of Morgan's intellectualism—further gives the lie to the existence of the necessary signs, from manuscripts, pamphlets, or physiognomy, that Morgan valorizes.

Morgan's historical Nietzscheanism is undermined in the laughable account of his trip to Egypt. There, he spends the night in the King's Chamber of the Great Pyramid, hoping to learn the disposition by Osiris of his ka, or soul, and his ba, or physical vitality. These lofty aspirations are brought up short when the experience yields only two results: he dreams of a former life as a peddler, and he is bitten by bedbugs. Confused, Morgan reasons as follows: "He decided one must in such circumstances make a distinction between false signs and true signs. The dream of the peddler in the bazaar was a false sign. The bedbugs were a false sign. A true sign would be the glorious sight of small red birds with human heads flying lazily in the chamber, lighting it with their own incandescence. These would be ba birds, which he had seen portrayed in Egyptian wall paintings. But as the night wore on, the ba birds failed to materialize."

Morgan's pathetic distinction between true signs and false signs recalls Blue's wish, in *Welcome to Hard Times*, for the "good signs" of spring that keep life going, and as with Blue, the wish is circular. Notice that Morgan's desultory gropings for meaning are prompted by previous representations, the ba birds in the Egyptian wall paintings. Of course, the fallacy that human destiny in history is readable in resemblances and recurrent signs is fundamental to many doctrines other than Nietzsche's; it is evident in Calvinist "signs of election" or the historiography of Thomas Carlyle, for example. Thus in the character of Morgan, the novel exposes the impoverishment of this tradition, that an "eternal return" can be read in history.

By contrast, the little boy's version seems less mystified; he is content to register the empty repetitions of the world without conferring meaning on them. In this aloofness—a kind of refusal to read—boy separates himself from all of the other characters, not simply Morgan, who cannot tolerate a condition of uninterpreted redundancy. The boy resists the hermeneutic need to assign a meaning to repetition, preferring instead to see himself and the universe as part of history's dumb metamorphosis: "It was evident to him that the world composed and recomposed itself constantly in an endless process of dissatisfaction . . . the boy's eyes saw only the tracks made by the skaters, traces quickly erased of moments past, journeys taken."

This cold, ontologically neutral view of change is also expressed in the boy's fascination with the eternal return in baseball: "[Father] turned to his son. What is it you like about this game, he said. The boy did not remove his gaze from the diamond. The same thing happens over and over, he said. The pitcher throws the ball so as to fool the batter into thinking he can hit it. But sometimes the batter does hit it, the father said. Then the pitcher is the one who is fooled, the boy said."

The boy's acceptance of deception and pure repetition seems to fit the plot of *Ragtime*. Moments of insight, supposed climaxes, and turning points are revealed, in retrospect, to be hollow: Evelyn Nesbit seems to galvanize the lives of Tateh and Mother's Younger Brother, then runs off with a dance-hall musician; Coalhouse Walker brings official New York to a crisis, then dies, his confederates and Mother's Younger Brother dispersed to other causes; the marriage of Mother and Father gradually deteriorates; the obsession behind Houdini's quest to pierce the veil of death recedes, and he is last seen repeating old escape tricks; the sensational murderer, Harry K. Thaw, returns to march in an Armistice Day parade. Far from ratifying the idea that history has a meaning, the inconclusive action of *Ragtime* makes time appear random and open-ended, in keeping with the tradition of *Big as Life* and Doctorow's other novels.

But this conclusion is also incorrect, confounding character-narrator and author. Recall that as character in his California backyard, the boy served as a model for Tateh's misrepresentation, and that as narrator, the boy never learned. So the false impression of insight must be amended again. The boy's view of time, history, and change is no loftier than that of the other characters; it is only another illusion that reading, afterwards, discovers.

DOUGLAS FOWLER

Billy Bathgate

"The Americans are certainly great hero worshippers, and always take their heroes from the criminal classes," wrote Oscar Wilde from St. Joseph, Missouri, in 1882, in the midst of the New World tour that would seal his fame. "Outside my window about a quarter mile to the west stands a little yellow house and a crowd of people are pulling it down. It is the house of the great train robber and murderer, Jesse James, who was shot by his pal last week, and the people are relic hunters. . . . His doorknocker is to be offered for sale this afternoon, the reserve price being about the income of an English bishop."

Billy Bathgate is a novel about the criminal classes. Its animating energy is indeed a species of hero worship, and the "disreputable genre materials" Doctorow says he likes to start from may well have derived from the comic book and the Depression-era pulp thriller. Doctorow seems to have tried to give his novel the joyful velocity and preposterousness of what the literary establishment would call "subliterature." *Billy Bathgate* is an attempt to elevate crime-thriller subliterature into art, just as *Lolita: Or the Confessions of a White Widowed Male* is an attempt to raise pornography to art. To try to make its origins respectable is to miss the point. Some of America's best novelists admit that they never got over the Great Bad Books, the Hollywood B-movies, the three-color Sunday funnies.

From *Understanding E. L. Doctorow*.

Doctorow has declared that "a novelist is a person who lives in other people's skins," and for his eighth novel he has gotten inside the skin of a fatherless Bronx kid who calls himself Billy Bathgate and happens to fall in with one of the Depression's most ruthless and fascinating gangsters, Arthur Flegenheimer, known as Dutch Schultz. The novel begins with Billy's presence at a gangland killing out in the midnight waters of New York Harbor, a scene spellbinding and preposterous in about equal measure. It is a comic-book opening, a pulp-thriller opening, the best moment in the novel. Recall that when Doctorow described finding the narrative formula that would allow him to go forward with *The Book of Daniel*, he spoke of his discovery of a tone and method that were "reckless" and "irresponsible"; in *Billy Bathgate* we sense the same sort of abandon.

"Nobody said not to so I jumped aboard and stood at the rail," Billy, a fifteen-year-old lackey for the gang, tells the reader many years after the event. As usual, Doctorow has taken pains to amplify a naive intelligence with his own, and Billy does not speak to the reader as an uneducated fifteen-year-old, but as a mature and cultivated sensibility recalling the experiences of his youth. And so the Billy of middle years goes on to recount the killing of Dutch's henchman Bo Weinberg, a classic crime rub-out right down to the tub of cement around the man's feet, with the crime czar coldly making the murdered man's girlfriend watch. It is a scene that is not actually completed until much later in the book, when the last grisly details of Bo's destruction are recounted in what Peter S. Prescott of *Newsweek* calls "all its marvelous, hair-raising detail." Doctorow has saved the particulars for a second climax. Bo's cement overshoes quickly harden, and the little tub in which he is standing imprisoned is fitted out with a rubber-wheeled dolly to roll the gangster over the side. But of course he is made to wait for his own death, tormented by his humiliation as well as his fear, and the Billy of 1935 abetted by the Billy of 1989 is there to record every nuance:

> Later he whispers to me take care of my girl don't let him do it to her get her away before he does her too, do I have your promise? I promise, I tell him in the first act of mercy in my life. . . . [But soon] Mr. Schultz in his shirtsleeves and suspenders appeared and came up behind him and lifted one stockinged foot and shoved it in the small of Bo's back, and the hands broken from their grasp and the body's longing lunge for balance where there was none, careening leaning backward he went over into the sea and the last thing I saw were the arms which had gone up, and the shot white cuffs and the pale hands reaching for heaven.

As in *Loon Lake*, a Horatio Alger miracle allows Billy the underage nobody to get himself initiated into the most dangerous, glamorous gang in New York. Dutch sees Billy juggling near one of his Bronx illegal beer barns and is charmed enough by the lad's discipline and cool to take him on as an amusement and an apprentice. Millionaire adopts guttersnipe, just as Dan Cody takes in Jay Gatsby.

Billy is led by degrees into the inner sanctum of the Schultz gang, with its "purveyed lawless might and military self-sufficiency . . . so thrilling to boys," a lad useful to Dutch and his men because, like any captain of industry, the gangster needs eyes and ears and a face the police don't know to run errands, to tail people, to report back: a spy. Thus the novel has its privileged narrator, privy to secrets but distanced enough for his voice to lend a moral and intellectual dimension to the raw action. The United States is the country of the creation of the self, and the crime novel is one of the truest variants of the American national *Bildungsroman*. From *The Great Gatsby* to William Kennedy's *Legs*, the romance of high crime has engaged some of America's best writers. There is the sheer escapism of the thing. As Billy puts it, he risks his life to join the Dutch Schultz gang and live in a "thrilling state of three-dimensional danger." Doctorow has written his novel so the reader can do the same.

New York, 1935. As with *Loon Lake*, the novel of Doctorow's which it most closely resembles, *Billy Bathgate* is set in the era of Doctorow's own childhood, and to its atmosphere he has devoted many pages of his best descriptive prose. Stephen Schiff remarked in *Vanity Fair* that Doctorow is "a masterly stylist of the Lush, Gorgeous Prose school (no Raymond Carver minimalism here, thank you)." Certainly it is a vivid, precise, anachronistic New York, like a stereopticon slide. Apples are five cents each, and since October 1929 you might even get to buy one from a former Wall Street stockbroker. Peaches on the Bronx's Bathgate Avenue, "this bazaar of life," are eight cents a pound. There are breadlines, hobos, Hoovervilles. What we call "soul music" is known as "race music" in 1935, and Tammany Hall is the name for a vast spiderwork of favors and patronage and bribery just beneath the surface of New York political life. A boy can save carfare by clinging to the backside of an electric trolley, and the basketball sneakers that help him hold on might well be autographed by Nat Holman, just as Billy's are. It has been said that God lives in details, and Doctorow has provided them in delicious prodigality. As for his plot, it is pure and defiant daydream, as essentially unreal as a James Bond novel. After the cautious and appealing fidelity to life of *World's Fair*, Doctorow has gone to the other extreme, and his crime novel bears only the sketchiest relationship to observed reality. In consequence, the reader never really believes in Billy or Dutch or the others, and we never for a moment fear *for* them. This is a heavy price for a writer to pay for creating daydream thrills.

Perhaps sensing this deficiency, Doctorow has attempted to heighten his prose, and instead of the understated precision that marked *Ragtime* and *World's Fair*, *Billy Bathgate* is written with a sort of Faulknerian excess, with some of its sentences running half a page and the vocabulary charged with overkill. The book is never boring, but we are never *involved* in it in as we are with Doctorow's best work. As George Orwell said of the characters in some of Dickens's novels, "They start off as magic-lantern slides and they end by getting mixed up in a third-rate movie."

Bo Weinberg dead, the girl Drew Preston becomes Dutch's prize, and Billy is assigned to watch her. He accompanies her back to her sumptuous Manhattan apartment, the likes of which he has seen before only on the silver screen and the sophistication of which allows Doctorow the same sort of ironic leverage for comic description that Twain derived from Huck Finn gawking at the Grangerford decor. For example, urns in the foyer are decorated with "Greek philosophers holding wrapped sheets around themselves." Even more Greek is the spectacle of Drew's husband, Harvey, in an embrace with a nameless young male, but the men are hardly disconcerted. When Harvey languidly asks his wife what became of Bo Weinberg ("you were so gaga about him"), her reply is a classic instance of aristocratic understatement: "Well if you must know, he died." Doctorow manufactures this sort of fun from the social gulf between the cafe-society world from which Drew Preston springs and the guttersnipe world of the East Bronx, which is in many instances a grotesque parody of its upper-class analogue. When he is not being melodramatic, Doctorow generates some familiar but amusing social satire.

Dutch's gang is composed of underworld denizens as colorful as the cast of a comic book. There is a hood called Lulu Rosenkrantz of the garlic breath and Mickey the driver who says nothing ("his intelligence was all in his meaty hands") and the faithful foot soldier Irving who does whatever he is told. Most successful of all in the supporting cast is Otto "Abbadabba" Berman, the dapper, hunchbacked mathematical genius who serves as the brains of the gang, a "deviously instructive" presence of perfect reserve and solemn wisdom. Since Billy is fatherless and his laundress mother is as disconnected from reality as Daniel Isaacson's grandmother, the gang becomes his new family. Once again Doctorow's fascination with the family asserts itself.

Strange family. Billy watches Dutch kill a greedy fire inspector with his bare hands and stuff his corpse into a garbage can. Troublesome window washers trying to establish their own union are allowed to fall to their deaths from scaffolding fifteen stories high right before Billy's eyes. Dutch tells Billy about cutting the throat of a rival numbers- racket boss in a barbershop, a piece of clever professional work with chloroform and razorblade of which the crime boss is extremely proud and a passage on which Doctorow has lavished his most craftsmanlike attention. Billy's gift for juggling a few stray objects in the air has led the boy into a dark, thrilling realm just behind the facade of the reasonable world, and he will never submit to the commonplace existence again. "Life held no grandeur for a simple thief." Billy's "enlistment" is not only an education; it is an identity.

The scene shifts to upstate New York, just as it did in *Loon Lake*, where Dutch is preparing the jury for his upcoming trial for tax evasion by injecting large doses of cash into the local economy. This is the first pastoral scene Billy has ever encountered, so very different from the teeming, dirty avenues of the slums, "where the natural world was visible only in globules of horse manure ressed flat by passing tires." Billy learns the magic that lives in guns when he learns to shoot, watches a disloyal union boss assassinated, and hears Dutch cheerfully reminisce about blinding a rival. Daydreams being daydreams, he even gets to sleep with Drew Preston while he is supposedly chaperoning her at the Saratoga racetrack, a far cry from the two-for-a-dollar rooftop sex he has experienced back in the East Bronx with his small "witchy" orphan friend, Rebecca.

But Dutch's career and life are on the down curve. Billy had juggled "in adoration of our great gangster of the Bronx," but now *Götterdämerung* is at hand. "He had risen and he was falling." Special prosecutor Thomas E. Dewey is closing in on Dutch's tax predicament, and when Dutch discovers that even his bribery money has turned unacceptable in the city, he retreats to New Jersey to perfect a scheme for assassinating Dewey. This is a mortal mistake. Other gang bosses want anything but an open assassination, for even Depression-era America is not quite lost to the cynicism of a banana republic just yet, and these bosses protect the destruction of their system with an assassination of their own. Dutch's gang is attacked at the Palace Chophouse in Newark on 23 October 1935, and of course Billy is there to tell the reader about it, standing hidden on a toilet seat while Dutch is desperately wounded with .45 slugs while still trying to button his fly. The novel is a daydream, and Billy's invisibility is a daydream state.

Lulu and Irving are dead, and Berman the mathematician has only breath to whisper in Billy's ear a few last numbers-the combination to Dutch's portable safe, the contents of which prove to be $362,112, surely enough for Billy and his mother to purchase new lives. But Doctorow is still not done with his prose daydream. "Murders are exciting and lift people into a heart-beating awe as religion is supposed to do," Billy observes. And Dutch is still tenuously alive. There are still fabulous secrets.

Billy not only attends to Dutch's last hours in the Newark hospital, he even eats the crime czar's last meal for him (consommé, roast pork, lime Jell-O). Then, now invisible behind a folding partition of cotton cloth (but really behind an author's indifference to even the sketchiest sort of likelihood), Billy takes down the man's last soliloquy with a pencil stub he keeps sharpening with his thumbnail. "He died dispensing himself in utterance . . . as if all we are made of is words and when we die the soul of speech decants itself into the universe."

Dutch's words contain cryptic information that only Billy can decode, for the police reporters on the other side of the partition hoping to capture some clue to the whereabouts of Dutch's hidden loot are confounded by his hallucinatory monologue. But Billy grasps the hidden meaning of one of the dying gangster's sentences: "Money is paper too and you stash it in the shithouse," and he and his orphan pal Arnold Garbage recover an immense fortune in an unbunged beer barrel from the "shit and refuse" on the floor of one of Dutch's old beer barns. Doctorow's cornucopia of miracles is still not exhausted: "From that midnight we became partners in a corporate enterprise that goes on to this very day," Billy tells us enigmatically. And magically, Billy's mother regains most of her mental balance, and soon Billy goes back to high school, and then on to "an Ivy League college I would be wise not to name," then to a lieutenant's commission in the army and certain hush-hush work in World War II, returning magically unharmed, and he magically unearths somewhere yet *more* of Dutch's "pirate swag," millions and millions of dollars of it "stuffed in a safe, packed in mail sacks." And just as in *Loon Lake*, Doctorow *still* has a final magic twist of plot up his sleeve.

Even though the murder of Dutch and Berman have made Billy "feel fatherless again, a whole new wave of fatherlessness," the novel ends with a restoration of the circle of family even more stunningly unforeseen than Bennett's adoption of Joe at the conclusion of *Loon Lake*. Billy does not find another father, he becomes one. A liveried chauffeur delivers to the new apartment he shares with his mother nothing less than the son he has sired with Drew Preston, and, like Mother in *Ragtime*, Billy's mother receives the child serenely, as if she realizes intuitively she has been selected, blessed. "My life as a boy was over," Billy declares, and the three of them will live, the reader can be sure, happily ever after, Billy's apprenticeship with evil now redeemed.

Stephen Schiff is correct in his assessment of Doctorow's use of popular culture and disreputable genre materials as the point of departure for his stories and novels:

> When you trace the fantasy materials that recur throughout his fiction, they look almost touchingly boyish and antiquated:

> gangsters and cowpokes; broken-spirited poets; tough but frail-looking blondes whisked out of reach by sleekly dangerous hooligans. If Doctorow is indeed the artist as conduit, then what he's channeling is the great American dreamwork: his materials are the stuff of our legends—and our schlock.

Perhaps especially in *Billy Bathgate* the reader is constantly aware of Doctorow's use of junk from the pulp and celluloid bins of 1930s mass art. But just as he was able in *Ragtime* to fill in the outlines of historical personages with a vivid life of his own invention and to reclaim overfamiliar situations from the attic of American popular culture, so here in his big crime novel the force of his intèlligence transforms the preposterous characters and plots from the comic-strip kingdom of schlock into a creation that rewards our mature attention. Doctorow spoke in an interview of purposely choosing to go back to the mind of a young boy in order to lend once more a sense of wonder and what he called "empowerment" to the voice of his narration, "a kind of rhapsodic appreciation of what adults have stopped thinking about." Boys' adventures, he has noted, were the genesis for memorable tales from such masters of boys' fiction as Twain, Dickens, and Robert Louis Stevenson.

"At his best," says Schiff, "Doctorow is able to reimagine [these humble materials] from the ground up, and to reignite the moral and political issues buried in their ashes. Doctorow is like a medium for our dead fictions; as they flow through him, they come out alive and sizzling."

One of Doctorow's sharpest departures from popular narrative convention is the manner in which he rewards self-serving opportunism and even outright villainy instead of punishing it, as the novelist, screenwriter, and director in the commercial arts almost always feel constrained to do. In *Ragtime*, for example, Tateh abandons his wife, his social conscience, and his religion, and yet ends up happily ever after in Hollywood. In *Loon Lake*, Joe abandons his past, his parents, his social conscience, and his child fiancée with her babe in arms and yet ends up as the millionaire Master of Loon Lake. This is perhaps one aspect of those "moral and political issues" Schiff said were buried and disregarded in the genre material from which Doctorow derives his narrative energy. Reviewing *Billy Bathgate* for *Time*, Paul Gray noted that both the adventures and the boy who tells of them "are as far as they could be from innocent visions of Tom Sawyer or Horatio Alger." This lack of innocence and willingness to be exploitative marks all of Doctorow's fiction and sets it apart from mere genre stuff. His central figures come in out of the cold to "families" of one sort of another—homey and loving in some cases, criminal and outcast in other situations, aristocratic and arrogant in still other instances. Thus, Blue in *Hard Times* is a middle-aged drifter who discovers in himself a talent for the fathering of orphans, the husbanding of fire-scarred whores, and the creation of villages in the wasteland of the American high plains; in *Big as Life*, Red Bloom lives by his uncompromised jazzman's code and kids Sugarbush that "your trouble is you're not an outlaw"; Daniel Isaacson is the outlaw son of martyred parents who suicidally aspired to a higher morality than the bourgeois public life of their country could ever achieve, and he comes to see in the hippie activist Artie Sternlicht the very incarnation of late-1960s radical cool.

Ragtime, *Loon Lake*, and *Billy Bathgate* are all novels which in various ways investigate with contagious fascination that unique American archetype, the criminal genius. Marginal man is Doctorow's favorite subject, just as the city and the family are his laboratory. "My life is bad for my image," Doctorow told *Time*, referring to his financial success and respectability, his academic chair at NYU, his children and his tennis, the fact that he wrote so much about crime but never in fact hung out in what he calls "lowlife saloons." "Dedicated criminals live on the extreme edge of civilization, where manners and morals unravel and the underlying impetus of our tribal, primordial origins breaks through," Doctorow has said about his fascination with criminality. "My background, which was safe and conventional, may have made me attentive to life beyond the pale." The quality of events being "beyond the pale" is certainly intrinsic to *Billy Bathgate*, just as it is to so much of his fiction. But this very criminality and extremism is subject to a powerful countervailing centripetal force: the desire to belong to a family.

Billy Bathgate is not quite a successful novel, but a less ambitious writer would never have tried to bring off this bizarre tale of what Doctorow characterized as a solitary boy's "search for patrimony and justice." From the crisp deadpan ironies of *Ragtime* through purple thunderclouds of *Billy Bathgate* there is no doubt that Doctorow is a writer always pushing at the far edges of his talent in an attempt to achieve work of significance and authority. *The Book of Daniel*, *Ragtime*, and *World's Fair* are perhaps Doctorow's greatest successes, but everything he has published demonstrates not only his talent but his restless search for a new means of expressing what Joseph Conrad considered the treasures that only fiction can bestow: "encouragement, consolatuion, fear, charm—all you demand—and, perhaps, also that glimpse of truth for which you had forgotten to ask."

MARSHALL BRUCE GENTRY

Ventriloquists' Conversations: The Struggle for Gender Dialogue in E. L. Doctorow and Philip Roth

Gender politics is a crucial issue in contemporary American Jewish literature. One of the things that separates writers like E. L. Doctorow and Philip Roth from earlier American Jewish writers is the growing pressure to renegotiate relations between the sexes. A historical opposition between feminism and Judaism presents Doctorow and Roth with problems insofar as they want to be both Jews and contemporary Americans. To become feminists may appear an exercise in assimilation; to resist feminism may appear to leave them in a patriarchal rut. For a long time, of course, there have been American Jewish women feminists, but the opposition between feminism and Judaism remains. As Elinor Lerner states, "Until the revival of the feminist movement in the late 1960s the feminism of American Jewish women had been expressed in secular, rather than religious, terms." A new vision of what it means to be Jewish in America could result from the growing efforts—by women and men, theologians and secular writers—to reconcile feminism and Judaism, but the vision does not come easily.

Emily Ellison and Jane B. Hill, in the introduction to their anthology *Our Mutual Room: Modern Literary Portraits of the Opposite Sex*, suggest that a sign of "vitality" in contemporary American writing is the wealth of "cross-gender writing," in which the author enters the perspective of a character of the opposite sex. A similar route is proposed by Wendy Lesser in *His Other*

From *Contemporary Literature* 34, no. 3 (Fall 1993): 512-535.

Half: Men Looking at Women through Art. Talking about male artists whose work "evokes the human figure and its surrounding world," Lesser claims that

> the highest criterion on which such art can be judged is the extent to which the artist succeeds in freeing his creations, his human figures, rather than retaining possession of them as puppets of his own ideas and desires. . . . Fairness—not in the sense of total objectivity. . . , and not in the sense of rigidly observed evenhandedness . . . , but in the sense of true openminded ness, true willingness to tolerate difference and disagreement and disobedience—that kind of fairness is essential.

Such sentiments may call to mind the theories of M. M. Bakhtin, for whom the novel as dialogue, as a field of play in which characters may rival their authors for authority, is the height of literary art. Because Bakhtin himself has a "hearing loss" with regard to women's voices, it is especially interesting to consider how successfully the crossing of gender lines on the part of authors like Doctorow and Roth produces the freedom for females that would constitute a successful Bakhtinian dialogue of genders. For John G. Parks, apparently, Doctorow's works are dialogically open to women's voices, for Parks uses Bakhtin's definition of the polyphonic novel to describe Doctorow's strategies and concludes that his works achieve the goal of being "both disruptive or even subversive of regimes of power, and restorative of neglected or forgotten or unheard voices."

At times both Doctorow and Roth seem interested in conveying feminist ideas. It is not hard to find female characters in Doctorow's fiction who seem, at least on the level of theme, to be symbolic of the wisdom, the insight, the valuable mystery that the male characters should approach: Mother and Emma Goldman in *Ragtime*, Clara in *Loon Lake*, Billy's mother and Drew Preston in *Billy Bathgate*, perhaps even Sugarbush and the female giant in *Big as Life*. Mildred Culp has argued that the women in *The Book of Daniel* collectively "prove integral to the novel" in the guidance they provide to Daniel and to the reader. And in *Ragtime*, Doctorow's combination of the perspectives of a boy and a man in a narrative voice achieves for a male the privileged qualities of freedom and flexibility that Doctorow considers more characteristically female. Doctorow's tendency to idealize feminine traits may even go too far; in *The Book of Daniel*, where much of the focus is on women characters, we are asked to admire women for what Daniel is able to make of them rather than for what they are. Several of Doctorow's major female characters nearly disappear by the end of their novels, as if they must be hidden from view so that their flaws, too, may be hidden, so that what is positive in their portrayals may be preserved, as with Emma Goldman in *Ragtime*, Clara in *Loon Lake*, and *Billy Bathgate*'s Drew Preston (whose crucial power has been demonstrated by Janice Stewart Heber).

His statements about fiction show that Doctorow considers his treatment of sexuality and gender important to his work. He has claimed that although he favors feminism, he is not conscious of having "written from an explicitly feminist point of view." But Doctorow clearly admires openness to the point of view of the opposite sex: he praises Hemingway's *The Garden of Eden*, in an otherwise negative review, for developing "the rudiments of feminist perspective" and elsewhere approvingly restates Henry James's idea that an inexperienced woman, if she is essentially a novelist, can write a novel about the military on the basis of a walk by a barracks during which she keeps her eyes and ears open. Asked in another interview about his "preoccupation" with sexuality in his fiction, Doctorow suggests that gender issues are important to him as a form of politics: "I think more likely it is a preoccupation having to do with sex as power, either perhaps using sex as a metaphor for political relations, or helplessly annotating what passes for sex in a society that suffers paternalistic distortions." Doctorow implies here that one of the goals of his writing is to release society from "paternalistic distortions," a claim also found in his famous distinction, in the essay "False Documents," between "the power of the regime" and "the power of freedom." The power of the regime, the realist sensibility of facts that makes art into a trivial pastime for leisure moments, is also the sensibility, Doctorow says, that once "proposed as a biological fact that women were emotionally less stable and intellectually less capable than men."

As for Roth, whose bad boy reputation with feminists is legendary, it is worth pointing out that he has said he wishes feminist critics would discover that he dramatizes men's frailties rather than arguing for their superiority. He intends to show that men are "clay with aspirations." Gender is clearly one of the issues about which both Doctorow and Roth claim to care, so it is fair to ask whether they have found the best literary techniques to put themselves on the side of liberation.

When one looks at the entire careers of Doctorow and Roth, one discovers what looks like an increasing intention on the part of both writers to open up their, works to the voices of women; they are trying to use not just themes but also forms compatible with feminism. Doctorow lets women speak in several recent works, most notably in his novel about a Jewish childhood, *World's Fair*, in which females narrate several interchapters. The story collection *Lives of the Poets* and the play *Drinks before Dinner* also provide examples of Doctorow's continuing struggle to loosen up, to relax male control over the text. While one popular image of Roth is that he uses antifeminism to launch an attack on Judaism, it is also true that recent works like *The Counterlife* and *Deception* (and even the autobiographical *The Facts*) use sophisticated techniques to introduce female voices into novels that happen to discuss what it means to be Jewish. To demonstrate how difficult genuine dialogue with women is for both Doctorow and Roth, one must first analyze the problems these writers encounter when they create forms to allow speech to women. They more successfully make women's voices believable in early works that happen to be "non-Jewish"—*Welcome to Hard Times* and *When She Was Good*—where there is no clear intent to be fair to women, where the intent may even be hostile. Perhaps these two writers have recently become too intent on fairness to women.

The 1984 story collection *Lives of the Poets* provides interesting evidence of Doctorow's struggle with gender dialogue in his fiction. We may decide, for example, that we empathize with a female teacher in the story "The Hunter" as she is harassed by the men in her rural community, despite the fact that (or, perhaps, because) her supposed creator, Jonathan of the title novella, makes several misogynistic remarks. Carol C. Harter and James R. Thompson have even discussed "The Hunter" as "a rare example" for Doctorow "of experience rendered from a woman's point of view." There is a significant moment at the end of the story when the school teacher insists on controlling a male photographer's picture of herself and her group of students, but it seems to me that "The Hunter" still leaves one with severe doubts about the schoolteacher's opinions and motives. The sympathy we do feel clearly does not ultimately derive from any of the narrative innovation found in *Lives of the Poets*. The narrator of this story is what we typically call omniscient, adopting the schoolteacher's angle of vision occasionally but without producing intimacy; and the schoolteacher can boss around a photographer to exercise some control over his taking a photograph without having any effect on the narrator's control over her. While Harter and Thompson suggest that Jonathan probably writes "The Hunter" to express his contradictory feelings toward the mistress who is abandoning him, and while it would be possible to argue that Jonathan is somewhat fairer to women in his art than in his life, the only freedom the schoolteacher manages is the freedom to be ambiguous. It is actually easier to notice the gap than the connection between Jonathan and "The Hunter." If I accept Jonathan as the writer of a story in the Lives collection, it is the story "The Writer in the Family," where the male narrator's goal is to retain control of his writing, which female relatives—especially Aunt Frances, who will reappear in the novel *World's Fair*—are trying to take over.

It may seem that Doctorow is particularly open to gender dialogue in

World's Fair, a reminiscence about a Jewish childhood, for two reasons. First of all, the most nearly ideal character in *World's Fair*, Norma, is female. The protagonist's playmate's mother, Norma works at the World's Fair, swimming nude and wrestling with the mechanical Oscar the Amorous Octopus. The male protagonist, Edgar, realizes near the novel's end that "Norma's freedom made life more thrilling and more dangerous" and that Norma's daughter Meg, his playmate, "had been born to the thrilling freedom that I only now suspected was possible." But Norma's ideal status has less to do with gender than with her ability to move comfortably between age and youth. She is admirable to the protagonist because of her sexuality, but also because of her willingness to play games on the floor with the children and to have her daughter Meg call her by her first name. It is also significant that the ideal Norma never takes part in the narration. While *World's Fair* manages to avoid the problem of keeping all its women totally idealized and silent, it still equates ideality with silence. Perhaps Doctorow keeps Norma quiet so that she will remain ideal.

This ideal character's silence is even more noticeable in light of the presence of female narrators in the novel. The second reason one might consider *World's Fair* to be more open to a woman's perspective is that women narrate parts of it—including the first three pages, in which Rose, Edgar's mother, reminisces. The interchapters of the novel—four narrated by Rose, two by the protagonist's brother, Donald, and one by the protagonist's Aunt Frances—might seem likely to distribute the narrative authority and give women recurring, separate voices. But most of the time the female narrators use their words to demonstrate how constricted their minds are, how much they are authority figures against whom the male protagonist will rebel. Listening to Rose, we are reminded by her use of "you" that she is telling her story to instruct the protagonist, to give rules from a position of dominance we want Edgar to reject: "Things were different then, you didn't meet someone and go out and go to bed with them one two three." And as Christopher D. Morris suggests, her speech responds to prompts provided by the male narrator; her remarks seem to answer questions that Edgar asks so that he will have the material he wants for the book he controls. Doctorow himself has suggested that his intention was to strengthen the male narrator's control, saying he wanted "to lend [the male narrator's] voice verisimilitude by dropping in some oral-historic statements by other members of the family." On the last page of *World's Fair*, one of the things Edgar considers putting into his time capsule is a book called *Ventriloquism Self-Taught*. He explains that he thinks the book represents his life "not because I had succeeded but because I had tried." Here, I think, we have an unintentional symbol for the novel's problem with narration—

indeed, for Doctorow's problem in many works, where one voice controls all others. *World's Fair* is an attempt to break away from such narration using a technique that will not do the whole job.

Drinks before Dinner, Doctorow's 1979 drama with female characters and no controlling male narrator in the background directing their voices, would also seem likely to facilitate gender dialogue. Doctorow recalls in his introduction to the play that he started writing it with ideas that I consider Bakhtinian, specifically that character is a function of the community and that the characters of the play "can only have their being from their positions in the dialogue." The protagonist, Edgar, makes sense, therefore, when he philosophizes, "we could all be each other." But the play as a whole finds as much horror as joy in that possibility. While longing for new community, the play also desires gender difference, even as it assumes that it is nearly impossible for men and women to differ. Doctorow produces female characters who, for all their disagreement with the protagonist, never produce more than minor variations on his voice. Everyone has a difficult time expressing personal freedom, of course, after Edgar pulls a gun at a dinner party and suggests he will use it to end the world. Two characters, one female and one male, Andrea and Michael, do threaten to go beyond the limits of Edgar's obsession; however, at the moment of crisis, as Edgar is about to pull the trigger, Andrea retreats from Edgar's radicalism and Michael calls for delay. While the hope that remains at the play's end is more likely in the male character's call for delay than in Andrea's stance, it is interesting that Andrea and Michael themselves seem so very similar to each other, even though both have suggested that they are troubled by the various threats to clear differences between genders.

Doctorow describes the end of the play as the formation of "a community of perception." But is that not where the play started? The perspective of a free female barely challenges the control of the male voice. The play's dilemma of community and its goal of community become fused and confused. Doctorow allows the last line— "And now we'll go in to dinner" —to be spoken either by Edgar or by the hostess Claudette, but even this possible suggestion of gender equality as the result of dialogue can be interpreted as ventriloquism, if not vampirism, in which the male takes on and uses a female voice he controls. As Doctorow himself points out, if Edgar speaks the last line, he is implying sarcastically that the evening has been useless and that the hostess will continue in banality. It is interesting that Doctorow cites as the sources for the method of dialogue in *Drinks before Dinner* two authors, one female and one male, who could reasonably be called a pair of the twentieth century's great monologists: Gertrude Stein and Mao Tse-tung. *Drinks before Dinner* never becomes more than Edgar's show using puppets of barely differentiated gender. It is not clear that either Edgar or Doctorow wants the ventriloquist's dummy to speak for itself or declare itself female.

Perhaps Doctorow's notion that character is a function of community is the source of a narrowness in his works. At the end of several of them, if not earlier, we discover that all the voices we have heard are from a single source—a male narrator. The clearest examples are *Ragtime*, *Loon Lake*, and *Lives of the Poets*, and one could make the same case about *Drinks before Dinner* if one considers the introduction the part written last. As the contributions of female perspectives are reduced to the conclusive goal of creating a man, we are left feeling that Doctorow's women are typically silenced, controlled, nearly dead—only slightly removed from what is called the "starfish" state of Susan Isaacson in *The Book of Daniel*. I wish Doctorow could go back to *World's Fair* and tell his protagonist that the ventriloquism need not be perfected, that the book on ventriloquism need not be plucked from that time capsule.

Voices in conflict with each other are also at the center of Philip Roth's Zuckerman novel *The Counterlife*. This novel is made more interesting by technical experiments seemingly intended to undercut the author's and narrator's authority so that female characters will have their say, but the experiments are not completely successful. Despite my considerable admiration for this novel, I read *The Counterlife* as a demonstration of the inherent difficulty in constructing a dialogic novel without having it function primarily to reconfirm the authority of the narrator and author through the credit they earn by engaging in something close to dialogue. To Roth, *The Counterlife* achieves considerable freedom and openness. He describes the book as "five mutually entangled, somewhat contradictory narratives that sometimes appear to be joined and then are not, and then there's outright contradiction." To some extent, *The Counterlife* achieves Roth's apparent intention to reveal men's frailties and open up his fiction to women's voices. Much of the novel concerns the parallels between the lives of the narrator, Nathan Zuckerman, and his brother Henry, who is described in one section as having an operation for the sake of overcoming his impotence and in another as becoming a religious zealot suddenly devoted to living in Israel as a follower of a radical Israeli political leader. It eventually becomes apparent that Nathan has used Henry to discuss some of his own problems, for in undergoing the surgery that is to improve his love life, Nathan dies. Henry takes revenge on his dead brother by discovering the manuscript of the novel we are reading and then attempting to destroy parts of it, but Henry still comes off as ridiculous: as he throws Nathan's papers into a garbage can, he is overcome by his own behavior and begins to vomit.

Apparently, the primary beneficiary of Roth's playfulness, of his willingness to open up *The Counterlife* to others' views, is the narrator's wife (or mistress, depending on which part of the novel one is reading), called Maria (although that is not her name), who in the fourth of the novel's five sections finds Zuckerman's novel just after Henry does and expresses a variety of opinions about Nathan's violence and irrationality and about where the novel describes her and her side of the family incorrectly. Consequently, as we read the final section, entitled "Christendom," which focuses on Zuckerman's attempts to understand Judaism, English Christianity, and his marriage, we question what Zuckerman tells us, especially the amazing final page in which he decides that he has discovered the crucial significance for modern civilization of his circumcised erection. Maria ultimately decides not to destroy the manuscript, despite the fact that she dislikes much of what Zuckerman says, because she considers it "my way out," a book that will give her freedom from a marriage in which she is unhappy.

Her "way out," however, may not be as clear as Maria thinks. The end of the fourth section is the key to a reading that makes the novel fit together more coherently than Roth has suggested. Maria's doubts about the book appear in an interview conducted by the ghost of the deceased Zuckerman. His dialogue with Maria, along with his understanding of the reactions of others to his death, persuades him to alter somewhat (basically by addition) the manuscript Maria has read. The format of the fourth section's final pages suggests that they may have been the last part of the novel to be written. One is led to discover order in the book based on the fact that Nathan's ghost has graciously taken into account all of Maria's complaints.

In his 1988 autobiographical work *The Facts*, Roth goes so far as to claim (in a prefatory letter addressed to Zuckerman) that Zuckerman in *The Counterlife* "miraculously manage[s] to be revived from death" *because* of Maria. If Roth's assertion is correct, if Maria brings about the dialogue, then her power is greater than I think it is. Even Roth's most fascinating and daring devices for opening up the novel reinforce his male authority. Maria says she went to Nathan's apartment and "had a kind of conversation with him," but one that turned out to be "one-sided," apparently because Nathan was not ready to cooperate. And although she tells Nathan at the end of the fourth section, "It's my turn now to invent you," one never has the sense that she manages to initiate genuine dialogue. The ghost writer Zuckerman seems to be the one responsible for starting the most nearly genuine dialogue with Maria—the one at the end of the fourth section—for she seems not to realize with whom she is speaking through much of it. Late in the conversation, asked who he is and why she thinks he is speaking to her, she answers that he wants to know "What it's like now. What I did. You have the rest of the story to tell. You need the hard evidence, the details, the clues. You want an ending. Yes, I know who you are—the same restless soul." Maria perceptively notes that he is looking for more control over the story, not less, and the final pages of *The Counterlife* do little to call her conclusions into question. At the end of the book, Nathan, in doubt about whether Maria will stay with him or return to her husband, composes a letter to himself that he imagines Maria could write, in which he expresses for her many of the doubts about him that she might have. That Maria is not responsible for this letter is clearest when Zuckerman has her say "that all the way back on page 731 saw where you were preparing to take us." Zuckerman has managed to anticipate that Maria might read *The Counterlife*; she had not read it when he wrote the letter. Thus the status of the fourth section as Maria's chance to speak completely freely is undercut. Her imagined letter is followed by Zuckerman's imagined reply, in which he cleverly answers her complaints. The problem with these pages is that the false dialogue in the fifth section makes us suspect the dialogue in the fourth section. Rather than being humbled by his engagement in dialogue, Zuckerman becomes at once the ideal Jew and a self-sacrificing and resurrected Christ, and it is precisely his most interesting device for engaging in dialogue with the female that makes Zuckerman superhuman. It is a leap into fantasy for Roth to make Zuckerman godlike as he engages in dialogue with a female who is only supposedly successful. Roth gives her a hollow voice rather than a genuine chance to speak for herself without being pre-empted.

Even as Maria makes one of her most effective attacks on Zuckerman's manuscript—that he has projected his own self-loathing onto Maria's sister Sarah, whom Zuckerman portrays as a rabid anti-Semite—we are encouraged to feel that he is learning his lesson, that the final draft of the novel is revised by a perfected author. As we read Maria's complaint that the material "he had taken from my sister was so far from what she was that I thought there was something deeply twisted in him that he couldn't help," as we read her conclusion "that *he* was my sister," we are so conscious of the fact that Nathan has come back from the dead to include these complaints that the complaints may be turned to praise. That Nathan can will himself into a woman becomes an indication of his virtue, at least at this point in the ongoing story of Zuckerman.

Even at the end (which is not a conclusion) of the work, what may make us most confident about Roth's genuine openness to dialogue with women are traditional characteristics of *The Counterlife*: his willingness to state—through dialogue and narratorial ruminations about others' views—why other characters may be closer to the truth than Zuckerman is, and his inclination to keep open the story of Zuckerman, to resist monologic closure.

Certainly we find these characteristics in *The Facts*, which ends with a letter to Roth from Nathan Zuckerman in which Nathan and Maria disagree about whether *The Facts* should be published. As in *The Counterlife*, Maria decides at first that it is acceptable for *The Facts* to be published, while Nathan is more inclined to complain that he and Maria will never achieve their freedom while Roth is their author. But then, as Nathan puts it, Maria worries "that never will it be our good fortune, or our child's, to live like those whose authors naively maintain that at a certain point the characters 'take over' and do the storytelling themselves on their own initiative." This at least seems to be an insight that Maria is not allowed in *The Counterlife*—or, if it does come up, only through a speech Zuckerman rather domineeringly writes for her.

In *Deception*, a male writer, a version of Roth, writes passage after passage of dialogue without Roth's customary amount of narrative connection. In some ways this book extends the discussion of gender issues in previous ones, but *Deception* also finds new angles. Many of the dialogues seem to relate to the man's own sexual affairs. In one dialogue, interestingly, the man is put on trial on the charge of hating women: "Why did you portray Mrs. Portnoy as a hysteric? Why did you portray Lucy Nelson as a psychopath? Why did you portray Maureen Tarnopol as a liar and a cheat?" But the cross-examination turns out to be foreplay between Roth and his lover; such dialogue poses no genuine threat to Roth. The stakes are raised considerably when the man's wife finds and reads the notebook and makes what seems a reasonable charge against the man—that he loves another. In defending himself, the man turns everything into a compliment for himself, while the wife sinks toward despair, as this exchange demonstrates:

> "You know, I ought really to interpret your jealousy as a terrific tribute to my persuasiveness."
>
> "And I suppose I ought to interpret what I've read here as a measure of my terrific failure. Whether I believe she exists or whether I believe she doesn't exist, certainly the love for her exists, the desire for her to exist exists. And that is even more wounding. The whole notebook is nothing more than an attempt to escape the marriage and me."

Nevertheless, as the wife is eventually placated, it is hard for the reader not to be. And yet, late in *Deception*, the man goes back to his notebook, to engage in another dialogue with a woman, in which he says that he has managed to trick his wife into believing the notebook is almost purely imaginative, that his affair with the woman he addresses remains safely covered up. The woman playfully threatens to tell the truth about the man in her own book, to be called *Kiss and Tell.* Such a threat might be read as implying that in the outermost frame of this novel, the female speaker can play the man's game and is thus his equal. But the man's joke about using this very conversation in his own book has already come true, obviously, and it is much easier to believe that all of Roth's novel is imaginative (and, presumably, fully under his control) than to believe that it is all a deceptive transcription of reality. There is no *Kiss and Tell.* We admire Roth's cleverness, but it is the cleverness of imagining a rival that does not exist. Even the wife seems less real once we finish the novel, one more in a series of ventriloquist's dummies.

Ellison's and Hill's praise for writers' use of cross-gender narration as found in the works discussed to this point is based on the assumption that such writing opens the minds of writer and reader. Lesser also confidently assumes the value of men's writing from the perspective of women and in fact defends several male artists who have been attacked for their representations of women. In summarizing her standards for evaluating such art. Lesser suggests that good writing depends on conscious choices by male authors, who decide to seek out and then appreciate differences between their perspectives and those of women. When, however, an author's intent seems to contradict rather than reinforce such appreciation, as is the case in Doctorow's first novel and in Roth's second, female voices come through more forcefully because the author seems not to be on their side. Molly Riordan of Doctorow's *Welcome to Hard Times* and Lucy Nelson of Roth's *When She Was Good* achieve powerful voices; their sorry predicaments only partially hide their toughness and perspicacity. Thus Doctorow and Roth can be said to have written novels that make feminist statements, if in an oblique manner.

While he is hardly hostile toward the women in *Welcome to Hard Times*, Doctorow has done little to counteract the readings he sees critics and interviewers attaching to that novel. Critics have generally accepted the narrator-protagonist, Blue, as the book's most sympathetic figure as he tries to write a history of the western town Hard Times, its destruction, rebuilding, and redestruction. Blue sees himself as potentially the savior of Molly Riordan, a prostitute and the novel's primary female character, as they drag themselves from the first wreckage and worry that the Bad Man from Bodie may return to demolish the town that they work to put back together. When Blue writes the book, after the second destruction, which includes the deaths of Molly, the Bad Man, and (soon) Blue himself, he blames the town's second failure on Molly, who has repeatedly predicted the Bad Man's return. Critics have basically followed Blue's lead in their estimations of Molly, even implying that she is to blame for her own death. Harter and Thompson go so far as to associate Molly with a "language of sexuality" they equate with what Doctorow calls "regime language," while they see Blue the artist attempting to use a "language of freedom."

In opposition to the dominant readings, Christopher D. Morris has provided a sophisticated analysis of Blue's motives, in which Blue is as "selfish" as "selfless" and his attempts at writing history are riddled with self-deception. Morris comes closer than anyone else does to taking Molly's side in the novel, but then he retreats from an endorsement of her: "The point is not that Molly's view . . . is true and Blue's hopes . . . false; instead, both coexist simultaneously, but to comprehend one is possible only through blindness to the other." Morris is not particularly receptive to John G. Parks's inclination to find Bakhtinian dialogue in Doctorow, and Parks himself is no fan of Molly, but I want to take Morris's argument where he almost takes it—to a dialogical reading in which the nearly silenced Molly's perspective is more accurate than Blue's controlling male perspective.

The opening of *Welcome to Hard Times* both suggests and strongly undercuts the idea that the narrator Blue generally empathizes with women. When the Bad Man from Bodie "[sticks] his hand in the collar of [Florence's] dress and [rips] it down to her waist so that her breasts [bound] out bare under the yellow light," one assumes Blue is horrified. But Blue's description of his reaction makes it clear that he, along with the other men in town, is quickly putting together the rationale that Florence need not be defended because she is, after all, a prostitute: "We all scraped our chairs and stood up—none of us had looked at Florence that way before, for all she was." While on the one hand Blue wants to convey the message that the men liked Florence too much to consider her a mere prostitute, one also sees that they consider their past blindness toward Florence an overly courteous illusion. From the book's very beginning, then, Blue labels himself the Bad Man's accomplice. When Florence screams from upstairs, where the Bad Man has taken her, Blue and the others enviously label her screams the result of orgasm, wondering "what kind of man it was who could make her scream." After the Bad Man kills Fee, Florence's lover, Blue returns to the saloon and discovers the Bad Man snoring upstairs while Florence is downstairs drinking. Blue says "I tapped on the window, but she knew Fee was dead and she wouldn't come out." Why will she not come out? Blue changes the subject instead of investigating her motives, perhaps to suggest that Florence has some sort of irrational desire to stay with the Bad Man. The rest of the novel would seem to support a reading Blue does not consider, that Florence, justifiably in despair, considers Fee her only defense. Despite Blue's suggested disapproval of Florence's failure to escape the Bad Man's control,

Blue duplicates her behavior. When the Bad Man gestures for Blue to drink, Blue recalls, "Right then my hand began to move and I meant for it to go for my gun. But it went instead for the glass on the bar; I felt at that moment that I wanted to please him, I was almost glad to drink."

And Blue is also glad to follow the Bad Man's lead in his relations with women. Blue introduces Molly Riordan as the saloonkeeper Avery's "other girl" and treats her unfairly throughout the book. His initial description of the relationship between himself and Molly puts Blue in a superior position from which he can condescendingly admire her spunk while anatomizing her faults: "Molly was never to my taste, pale and pocked, with a thin mouth and a sharp chin, but I liked the way she stood up to Avery." For her part, Molly initially considers Blue an honorable man—in contrast to Avery, at least. Later, when Molly is discovered burned in the remains of the town. Blue carries her away, making her his possession in a manner resembling the Bad Man's handling of Florence. A clue to the parallel is that as Blue and two other men transport Molly from the cinders, Blue does nothing about the fact that "The front of her dress hung down like a flag." Clearly Blue has little respect for this woman from whom he says he wants respect. He compares her to "a big cat," blames her lack of forgiveness for his supposed inability to hope, and calls her an "unrelenting whore." Even Molly's posture strikes Blue as a "rebuke," but that is surely a matter of his imagination. Her stiff posture, "her chin . . . always in the air," is a result of the way "the healed burns pulled her up tight." Writing after the novel's major events, Blue assumes that Molly would trade sex for the death of the Bad Man. Blue fantasizes that anyone able to shoot the Bad Man would have had "Avery standing him a drink and maybe redheaded Flo and Molly smiling his way." This fantasy is probably a reaction to Molly's curses against Blue for his cowardice.

Blue's deep insecurities are what lead him into distorted perceptions. When Molly reminisces about her years in New York City in order to contort the orphaned Jimmy Fee, Blue senses a "terrible pride" in her that he calls "blinding." But to react as if the story were for his benefit is another of Blue's distortions. Molly insists that Blue not look at her and later that evening whispers to him, "I swear I can't bear the sight of you!" Does she allow Blue to listen? Does she expect that he "will never forget her words," will take possession of them? Probably not. She concentrates on Jimmy, speaking with her eyes closed. Rather than being obsessed with tormenting Blue, she seems oblivious to Blue's feeding upon her. When Molly has to hold him that night for warmth, Blue tells himself that he has some fond feeling for her, but he achieves this self-congratulatory stance by eliminating himself from the situation; he tells himself that "At the worst her hate is something between herself and herself." This insightful line applies less accurately to Molly than to Blue, who clearly projects his self-loathing on her. Probably Blue's most self-incriminating statement is "I felt anyone new helped bury the past," which he says just after admitting that "Molly was right, I would welcome an outlaw if he rode in." While Blue thinks that he welcomes settlement and renewal, his words suggest that he also welcomes the destruction performed by the Bad Man. Blue believes there were a few "last free moments after the [Bad Man] came" and is puzzled when he is unable to persuade anyone to leave town. He fails to see his part in limiting the freedom of the men of Hard Times just as he has limited Molly's freedom. As he tries to persuade the businessmen to flee, Molly giggles wildly over the irony of Blue's advice.

Although Molly may seem to reject automatically everything Blue says, she is generally correct in her estimation of the situation in which she finds herself. One indication that Molly has her own voice, even if it is difficult to hear at times, is the fact that she prays. When Blue speculates lamely, "Maybe a cup of coffee is what she's praying for," the reader is cued to wonder what she does want—probably the defeat of overlapping evils, Blue with his fraud and the Bad Man with his destructiveness. When Blue presents Molly with a dress donated by another prostitute, he has to admit his ignorance of Molly: "It was to plague me for a long time, like this, that I couldn't tell what she would answer or if I might find a moment's favor in her eyes." Molly opposes Blue's plan to rebuild Hard Times, perhaps because she knows that towns draw Bad Men. She even demonstrates a bit of precognition, almost figuring out before Blue himself does that Blue wants to persuade the newcomer Isaac Maple to settle in Hard Times. Later, as Blue heads out to investigate the appearance near the town of the Swede and his wife, Helga, Molly yells to Blue, "I know what you're doing! Go get 'em Mayor, more fools for your town!" Such wisdom links Molly with characters like the always reliable Emma Goldman of *Ragtime*, who sees civilization as inherently corrupt. Molly is understandably shocked when Helga later spits at her, but Helga's picking out of Molly is appropriate. Helga does not blame Molly for going along with the town or for compromising with Blue. What Helga wants, at least as her husband tells it, is a settlement, probably a more established one, made up of Swedes. Helga's curse labels Molly as the major opponent of towns. When Helga and Molly later have a fistfight, it signals Molly's desperate plan to take advantage of the few strategies allowed by the town. The women fight over the protection Jimmy Fee may provide, and their desire makes sense. Molly teaches the reader how to read Blue when, speaking about him to a government official, she proclaims, "this is more than an honest man standing before you, you can trust his records for they show against him!" Blue is most believable when he provides data that does not fit his interpretations.

While Molly is sometimes regarded as passively accepting of disaster she consistently tries to act when action might matter. Molly's opinion of Blue plummets near the beginning of the novel—as the reader's may—when she realizes that she is going to be the only one who will try to kill the Bad Man. She fails because of her human reaction to seeing Florence dead in the saloon—Molly drops her stiletto—but this failure is surely preferable to the reaction of Blue and the other men who ignore Florence's body and play along with the Bad Man's script for a celebration. Molly saves Blue in a situation similar to that in which Blue failed to save Florence. In the gunfight that breaks out in the saloon, Blue says, "Molly was struggling and pulling [within the Bad Man's grip] or I'm sure he would have killed me." Blue admits, at the beginning of the novel's final section, "Third Ledger," that Molly takes control of the entire course of events. Although Blue is the recordkeeper, Molly steps into the role of the precognitive cause of events, a role that we most easily associate with the Little Boy in *Ragtime*. Molly is sometimes considered to be stuck in a cycle of repeated disaster, but surely Blue is more committed to a myth of return and repetition than is Molly. Blue relates that Molly pleads almost daily that Blue, she, and Jimmy flee the town, even though she doubts that flight will help matters. Blue is left with the odd argument that a town is safe if it does not welcome Bad Men, and, of course, as Blue fatally wounds the Bad Man, he gives Molly the blame once again.

Christopher D. Morris has challenged Doctorow in an interview with the possibility that Doctorow's women are White Goddesses leading men toward catastrophe. Doctorow defends himself by referring to several of his female characters as "subject to the male world's rules." Doctorow does not mention Molly in this exchange, but it seems to me that his explanation applies to her as accurately as it does to his other female characters.

The closest thing in Roth's fiction to genuine gender dialogue, and the book that most rewards a feminist reading, is a novel that, like *Welcome to Hard Times*, contains a female voice to which we should listen more carefully. *When She Was Good* is often dismissed as Roth's gentile experiment, his pale imitation of Flaubert, and Roth himself has encouraged the mass of commentators who take the novel to be a portrait of the Great American Bitch. Traditional as it is in terms of technique, *When She Was Good* may be made more powerful if the reader assumes that Roth's intent is to crucify the protagonist, Lucy Nelson. Unlike the manipulative resurrection in *The Counterlife* (or the resurrection of Anne Frank in *The Ghost Writer*), Lucy Nelson's refusal to remain dead makes *When She Was Good* a powerful novel because our admiration for Lucy is the result of more than an authorial stacking of the deck. Her crucial choices—of marriage to a man she does not love, of childbirth rather than the abortion others push her toward, of insistence that her unpleasant family live up to what they say are their values—can earn the reader's respect even as these choices lead to her death.

In Reading Myself and Others, Roth gives conflicting evidence about his intentions when he wrote this novel. On the one hand, Roth says that he "identified with strongly" and "imagined myself into" both Lucy Nelson and her mother, Myra, that it is "stupid" to say his presentation of Lucy is hostile, that instead he made her express "feminist rage." On the other hand, Roth suggests that Lucy is essentially responsible for her destruction, that she "rejects every emancipating option," and even, amazingly, that Lucy's "rhetoric," used "to disguise from herself her vengeful destructiveness," is like "language our government used when they spoke of 'saving' the Vietnamese by means of systematic annihilation." Roth's discussion in *The Facts* of how *When She Was Good* had its roots in his marriage to Margaret Martinson Williams ("Josie" in *The Facts*) also suggests the complexity of his motives. More than *My Life as a Man*, a novel even more thoroughly based on that marriage, *When She Was Good* is close to what Zuckerman advises Roth to write: "thirty thousand words from [Roth's ex-wife's] point of view."

Critics have always reacted to Lucy with impressive negativity. Mary Allen calls her "one of the most monstrous bitches" American writing has produced. Sanford Pinsker implies that Lucy wants to be "rich" and "famous," says she is what "overwhelms" her father, and implies that it is Lucy who deceives Roy in his car's back seat as she is seduced. Raymond Rosenthal calls her "a kind of poisonous distillate of something soft and rotten in the American sexual psyche." Josh Greenfield, following Roth's lead, calls her an "example of that prevailing self-righteous, unreasoning, insatiably grasping, man-hating, female bitch spirit now spreading like a cancer throughout our country . . . , impelling us to do battle and heap destruction in foreign lands, threatening to drive us yet as a nation to a frigid and icy doom."

Lucy is diminished even by the critics who are most sympathetic to her. In an otherwise perceptive reading, Murray Baumgarten and Barbara Gottfried overemphasize Lucy's weakness when they say Lucy "can discover no way to change either herself, her own circumstances, or anybody else." Even Sam B. Girgus, who generally treats Lucy as a "role model" for feminists, says that concerning abortion, "Lucy proves incapable of being reasonable, of compromising with her moral standards"; like many critics more outspokenly negative toward Lucy, Girgus asks, "What force in Lucy's personality causes her to destroy her own happiness?" Some critics even complain when they feel some sympathy for Lucy. For Robert Garis, although Lucy is hard to like. Roth attacks her so much that, reluctantly, "we are moved to protect her." Glenn Meeter also questions Roth's handling of Lucy: "When Roy asks Lucy, 'Have a Hydrox?' he . . . offers a kind of sacramental sharing; but the reader, without any symbolic tips, and seeing the offering through Lucy's eyes, is too apt to feel only her irritation at her husband's infantile cookie-and-milk."

Lucy deserves a defense. Critics often accuse her of inflexibly seeing herself as right and others as wrong, but in several instances she displays admirable self-awareness, flexibility, and open-mindedness. She can be critical of her faults, as when she tells herself it is against her principles to leave the high school band, doubts herself as she interrogates Roy about his failure to buy condoms, admits she has a "habit" of jumping on others' words, suspects she may have at times "been stone," and even near the end of the novel feels she may have been unfair to her father. Lucy is open to the possibility of reconciliation with her father —until she finds out he pushed his wife into an abortion—and even, momentarily, with her husband's most unpleasant relatives, the Sowerbys. Rather than always seeing others as simple, Lucy muses over her failure to realize how complex are the personalities and lives of her mother and of Mrs. Sowerby. Rather than considering herself always right, Lucy occasionally desires opposition; the major instances of this feeling concern the proposed marriage and her disgust for Roy's always saying what he thinks she wants to hear.

Critics regularly complain that Lucy hates all men without any sort of discriminating eye because she hates the men in her family, but Lucy is capable of labeling her friend Kitty's family "worse even than her own," and when Lucy first has a conversation with Roy's father she concludes that she likes him and Roy's uncle. In her marriage, Lucy gives Roy every chance to make the relationship work. On the day he first seduces her, she works hard to believe his apology for a previous argument, and then she wants altogether too much to believe him when he pleads, in the back seat, "Just trust me." She tries to be trustful of and even obedient to Roy after they marry, consenting, for example, to weekly visits with both sets of parents. Even when things are very troubled, Lucy believes Roy when he starts to talk about his dream of a second child, a daughter, as the key to a happy marriage; it seems significant that Roy makes Lucy most happy when she hears him talking about desires she has not had to encourage. When Lucy thinks that she has forced Roy to be a good husband, she does not enjoy the feeling of power over him so much as she longs for a better marriage.

Much is made of Lucy's occasional confusion and lack of understanding, but when one looks at these qualities from a Bakhtinian viewpoint, they may turn into advantages. According to Bakhtin, "Stupidity (incomprehension) in the novel . . . interacts dialogically with an intelligence (a lofty pseudo intelligence) with which it polemicizes and whose mask it tears away." The best example of Lucy's wise ignorance is in her conversation with the doctor in the college infirmary, concerning Roy. Lucy senses immediately that it is a mistake to reveal that Roy would "marry [her] tomorrow," but she is mystified as the doctor suggests marriage. Lucy's incomprehension calls into question not only the opinions of the men within the novel but also the male author/narrator of *When She Was Good*. The narrating voice fails to produce solutions to problems Lucy uncovers, and the fact that Lucy does not foresee all of the effects of her actions should make even clearer that she acts in search of truth rather than devilishly to manipulate others.

One of Lucy's best qualities is her refusal to practice denial. When a classmate giggles at Lucy's childhood lies aimed at denying her father's drunkenness, Lucy "refuse[s] ever to tell a lie again" for such purposes. Ellie Sowerby, on the other hand, reveals to Lucy that her father, Julian Sowerby, Roy's uncle, is having affairs, and then Ellie lies for him. Ellie's family's collective denial of his affairs until Lucy forces the issue at the novel's end — and not the affairs themselves—is probably the crime that sends Lucy to her death. The inclination of critics to accuse Lucy of insanity at the end of the novel is also a kind of denial because it blames Lucy, not others, for her predicament. Lucy herself, halfway through the book, asserts, "Maybe . . . you *make* me insane, Roy Bassart." And she implies—perhaps without intending to—that the label of "insanity" is a way to deny and dismiss the injustices to which she directs attention.

Roy is the one consistently at fault in their relationship. At first he does seem innocuous, and we should not blame Lucy for being attracted to a man who says that his life is changing and that he refuses to tell lies. Soon he starts photographing her in such a way as to make her look like an "Angel" of "stone," precisely the image he will later condemn. He seduces her after delivering near-threats: he will not tear her clothes if she will stop fighting him. After their marriage, he consistently runs away from her, and when he does apologize, he also accuses: "everybody" should have, he says, "a chance to make his accusations—and also to admit where he might have been in the wrong (because it's never so simple as one being all in the right, of course . . .)." Roy's claim that Lucy torments their child, Edward, is clearly false. His departures are what disturb the child: in one scene Roy starts "to grumble again" about his job, whereupon, "Before [Lucy] even had a chance to reply, Edward had . . . rushed away." Even as Roy finishes a strongly accusatory outburst over the phone against Lucy's childrearing, we may be impressed by

Roy's childishness when Lucy realizes that "Either Roy had hung up, or someone had taken the phone away and hung up for him."

Lucy is regularly accused of cruelty to her father, of making outlandish choices simply because she wants to displease him. But when she rejects his offer of an abortion, we should recall that he forced her mother to have one and also forced her to agree that Lucy was the reason for the abortion. One should not blame Lucy but admire her strength in rejecting his recommended abortion. She has much to fear in Whitey: echoing Roy's seduction speech, Whitey says, "Why don't you just trust me! I'm not going to kill you!" When Lucy repeatedly has a vision of her father toward the novel's end in which the word "INNOCENT" is written on his teeth in lipstick, we do not have a sign, as some suggest, that Lucy is forced to admit she has been unfair; she sees the absurd extremes to which her family will go to deny his guilt and project it onto her.

Another interesting defense of Lucy is to be found in the first of the novel's three sections. Here her grandfather Willard's thoughts after Lucy's death demonstrate, without his realizing it, the folly of following the major alternative to the path Lucy chooses. Willard once believed his own father was more cruel than nature, but unfortunately, unlike Lucy, he has learned to accept his father. One possible implication here is that Lucy incorrectly chose to believe that her father was more cruel than nature, and several critics accept such a reading. But Willard's attitudes lead to his receiving Whitey back into the house for yet another repetition of the family's disasters, and Willard excuses even Whitey's blackening his wife's eye with a belt, rationalizing that "no real physical harm" resulted. Lucy at least tries to break the cycle of family violence.

The reading in which Lucy blames everything on her father is also contradicted by a passage later in the first section, in which she remembers her college paper on "Ozymandias." Although some critics take her reading of the poem as a sign of her own commitment to a "sneer of cold command," Lucy's writing suggests that such a stance is useless, even if a sneer "is all many mere mortals have at their command, unfortunately"; most critics ignore the fact that Lucy does not blame parental authority for what she refers to as "the inevitability of the 'colossal wreck' of everything," but rather a larger-than-human force she calls "Fate." The novel's final pages may prove that her father is more cruel than the "nature" in which Lucy freezes to death. Lucy's clutching of one of her father's letters to Myra as Lucy dies has been taken by some as an indication that she finally changes her mind about her father. There is no need to accept such a reading. Whitey's letter denies the pain in his family's life, asks Myra for assistance shortly after promising not to trouble her, self-justifyingly claims that his punishment in jail will diminish his ability to change, and ends with a poem about his desire to repeat the past. Roth's presentation of Lucy's story may at first seem to promise comforting, reasonable encouragements to ignore her voice, but Lucy can affect her audience deeply despite the odds. Her fate and her forceful action speak louder than any sort of overt feminist statement she voices.

While it may be disturbing that Doctorow and Roth seem to have to release some anger toward a woman to be able to let her tell her story, this pattern in their works does not give us a reason to condemn either writer. It may be that works in which murderously threatening forces in society are dramatized are precisely those in which it is most important for the authors to let others' stories be told. It may be tempting (and troubling) to suggest that somehow the success of Molly and Lucy in telling their stories is connected to the fact that both are Gentiles, but one should remember that silenced gentile women also appear later in works by both Doctorow and Roth. Both of these writers have been engaged for years in a struggle toward openness to the perspectives of women, a struggle that is significant for these writers' sense of themselves as Jews in contemporary America even when they may seem to neglect obviously Jewish subject matter. I am inclined to admire Doctorow and Roth for their stubborn refusal to accept anything but tentative solutions as they work with their commitment to the difficult dictum that Nathan Zuckerman prepares in *The Counterlife* for his brother: "We are all each other's authors."

STEPHEN MATTERSON

Why Not Say What Happened? E. L. Doctorow's Lives of the Poets

Lives of the Poets, E. L. Doctorow's seventh work, first published in 1984, occupies a unique space in his writings. Its most obvious difference from the other work is announced in its subtitle, *A Novella and Six Stories*, because, apart from the 1979 play, *Drinks Before Dinner*, Doctorow's previous work had been in the novel form. A case could be made for considering *Lives of the Poets* almost an aberration within the Doctorow canon. Among its diverse themes and settings the collection becomes an exploration of the nature of writing itself and of the relation of writing to the life of its author. Doctorow had never before treated this issue so explicitly, though a debate about the reliability of fiction had often been implicitly present in his work. The style of the book is also markedly different from the other work. Doctorow appears willing to allow his self and voice to emerge more fully than they ever had before. *Lives of the Poets* could also be said to lack something of the ambitious breadth of Doctorow's novels. The multiple plotting and discontinuities that might be considered typical of Doctorow's writing are here apparently disregarded in favor of a series of self-contained stories. Doctorow's typically sustained focus on a particular time period is also absent. Whether writing of the 1870s, the turn of the century, the 1960s or the 1930s, Doctorow had maintained the focus on that time even while diffusing the action. In contrast, the short stories here range broadly in time

From *Critique* XXXIV, no. 2 (Winter 1993): 113-125. Published by Heldref Publications.

and setting. However, in spite of the elements that would make *Lives of the Poets* an oddity among Doctorow's works, the book illuminates and adds much to our understanding of the novels. It may remain an aberration, but one that it was essential for Doctorow to write and that is in itself a major achievement.

For the reader to appreciate fully the unfolding of its meanings, *Lives of the Poets* must be read in sequence. It would be possible to detach particular stories and consider them complete in themselves, but Doctorow's achievement in the book is an overall one in which the stories are interdependent and contribute to a developing meaning. *Lives of the Poets* works in part through a series of correspondences that are established in the first story and are developed by the others. These correspondences achieve two effects. First, they establish a series of connections, which, when taken together, make up the theme of the whole book. Second, the correspondences between this book and Doctorow's other writing indicate the seriousness and urgency of the themes and issues it raises. It addresses fundamental questions about the nature and function of the writer, questions that Doctorow is applying to himself and to his already published work. In some respects, chiefly through what it reveals about the writer and the need to write. *Lives of the Poets* could be said to alter our understanding of Doctorow's preceding novels. After reading this work we reconsider some aspects of *Welcome to Hard Times*, *The Book of Daniel*, *Ragtime*, and *Loon Lake*. *Lives of the Poets* is an outstanding example of the supposition that T. S. Eliot made in 1917: "The existing order is complete before the new work arrives; for order to persist after the supervention of novelty, the whole existing order must be, if ever so slightly, altered." Indeed, it can be argued that one of the urges driving *Lives of the Poets* is Doctorow's need to re-examine some of the ideas that Eliot originated in that essay.

I

The situation established in the book's first story, "The Writer in the Family," is important for appreciating this dual series of connections. The narrator, Jonathan, is in his early teens when his father dies, leaving a widow and two sons, Jonathan and his older brother Harold. The father's elderly mother, however, is still living, in a nursing home. Fearing that the shock of her son's death will be too much for the old lady, the narrator's wealthy Aunt Frances persuades Jonathan to write a letter purporting to come from his father, pretending that the family has moved to Arizona. Aunt Frances is delighted with the letter and prevails upon Jonathan to write more.

Eventually the deceit disturbs the boy and to end the letters, he writes one that he knows Aunt Frances cannot show her mother.

Because of the dual system of correspondences in *Lives of the Poets*, "The Writer in the Family" is not a self-contained, straightforward story. It establishes within the book, a set of fundamental questions and observations about writing and the role of the writer. It is suggested that Jonathan has to give up the letters because they are dishonest. In anticipation of the novella "*Lives of the Poets*," young Jonathan is already haunted by Robert Lowell's question from the poem "Epilogue," quoted in the novella: "Yet why not say what happened?" On one level, "The Writer in the Family" is about the boy's almost heroic stand, his refusal to use writing for deceit. Yet the story introduces other, potentially more important, areas. First, in spite of the deceit involved, Jonathan actually comes to a truthful image of his father by writing the letters through the fiction that he makes up. Thus, in the final letter, he invents the father's longing for the sea, and, in so doing, he uncovers two kinds of truth about his father, the factual and the psychological. His father actually was, as Jonathan later discovers, in the navy for a year. Psychologically, the father was restless and unsatisfied, a man for whom living in Arizona would have been a kind of death.

The second significant point about the fictive letters is that they come to have a function far beyond their ostensible one of deceiving the grandmother. Their immediate effect is somehow to keep the father's memory alive, to keep him real and living to the boy (he has a vivid dream that his father is still alive), and to Aunt Frances. The first brief letter has a profound effect on Aunt Frances:

> My aunt called some days later and told me it was when she read this letter aloud to the old lady that the full effect of Jack's death came over her. She had to excuse herself and went out in the parking lot to cry. "I wept so," she said. "I felt such terrible longing for him. You're so right, he loved to go places, he loved life, he loved everything."

The talent of the young writer has given the father a truth, a reality, that keeps him alive for others. Jonathan never really grasps this fact, and Aunt Frances' motives are misunderstood. His brother, Harold, points out that the letters are unnecessary: "Grandma is almost totally blind, she's half deaf and crippled. Does the situation call for a literary composition? Does it need verisimilitude? Would the old lady know the difference if she was read the phone books?" Both the brothers misunderstand Aunt Frances because they fail to realize how much the letters help in dealing with the loss of her brother.

For all of its darkly comic situation, "The Writer in the Family" concludes subtly with a complex and dual message: although fiction is deceit, made-up stories, it can reveal truths that facts alone cannot. Jonathan is as yet too young to grasp this fully; to him the letters are deceptions that he cannot continue. It is significant here to suggest the ways in which this dual approach to fictions pervades Doctorow's other works. "The Writer in the Family" forces the reader to recognize how much of Jonathan's situation has been repeated in the novels. This happens most obviously in *World's Fair*, which followed *Lives of the Poets*; there, Aunt Frances and the family all reappear at much greater length. There are particular changes; for instance, the brother Harold is renamed Donald, and the family situation is amplified from "The Writer in the Family." Edgar in *World's Fair*, who wins a prize in an essay contest, resembles Jonathan in the earlier story. Though absent in "The Writer in the Family," the father is a prominent figure in *World's Fair*, and his longing for the sea is further outlined, appropriately enough, by Aunt Frances herself.

There are also correspondences with the earlier novels. The reader recognizes much of the family situation from *The Book of Daniel*. Although the figure of Paul Isaacson is never explored as fully as the father in *World's Fair*, there are striking similarities between them. Like the father in *World's Fair*, Paul Isaacson has a shop; in *World's Fair* it is a record and radio shop, in *The Book of Daniel* a radio repair shop. The fathers also share a reciprocated devotion to their mothers and similar politics. The mother in *The Book of Daniel*, *World's Fair* and "The Writer in the Family" remains a constant and recognizable figure.

The similarities shared by these three works are especially striking because they suggest how far Doctorow has inserted himself and his own experience into *The Book of Daniel*, which often has been considered an exploration of an historical moment and an examination of the postwar period and of how the temper of the times could bring about the execution of the Rosenbergs. But, like "The Writer in the Family," it also is concerned with the nature of writing and truth. On one level, this is obvious because Daniel self-consciously writes the novel in front of us as he sits in the library at Columbia. But, more covertly, Doctorow is considering the same questions that are raised explicitly in "The Writer in the Family." In repeating something of the childhood situation that existed in *The Book of Daniel*, he is already asking Lowell's question that will haunt him in *Lives of the Poets*.

In his first novel, *Welcome to Hard Times*, Doctorow had apparently avoided a reliance upon personal truth and fact. In part, the setting of *Welcome to Hard Times* in the 1870s, and in the West, which Doctorow had never visited, safeguarded him from the dangers of the overly autobiographical first novel. As he has said, "Somehow I was the kind of writer who had to put myself through prisms to find the right light—I had to filter myself from my imagination in order to write." However, in reconsidering even *Welcome to Hard Times* from the perspective made available by *Lives of the Poets*, the reader is likely to place more emphasis on the questions the central character, Blue, asks himself about writing and its effect. In the novel, Blue receives identity by his role as a historian; the role is analogous to his role as rebuilder of the town Hard Times. Yet he too doubts the validity of his writing as a means of interpreting and changing the world: "as if notations in a ledger can fix a life, as if some marks in a book can control things."

When Doctorow said that he needed a prism through which to write, he was suggesting a strategy that is crucial to an understanding of *Lives of the Poets*. "The Writer in the Family" introduces a dilemma about the honesty of writing compared to the kind of truth that fiction offers. Taking Jonathan as the writer of the stories that follow, one sees how the dilemma is either avoided or further developed. The connections between "The Writer in the Family" and the subsequent stories are apparent even though they are not made explicit for the reader. In "The Water Works" a boy who is apparently shadowing an undertaker follows him one day as he collects a drowned corpse from the water works. The corpse, that of a child, is taken away, and the story ends with the boy observing the water workers drinking whisky; it represents one of their rituals for dealing with death: "There is such a cherishing of ritual too among firemen and gravediggers." The boy and his family are curiously absent from this story. We do not learn his name or anything of his family situation. Strategically, the story represents one way of writing—distancing oneself from the theme. The self is extinguished, erased, in exactly the way that T. S. Eliot had described in "Tradition and the Individual Talent": "Poetry is not a turning loose of emotion, but an escape from emotion; it is not the expression of personality, but an escape from personality" and "The progress of an artist is a continual self-sacrifice, a continual extinction of personality." It is obvious that this erasing or distancing strategy is only apparently successful. Given the context of "The Writer in the Family," "The Water Works" develops in different ways. It can be read as a deepening of the boy's fascination with death deriving from the death of the father in the other story. It also develops from one brief statement in "The Writer in the Family"; faced with his grief at the father's death, Jonathan is comforted by Harold who tells him:

> Look at this old black stone here. . . . The way it's carved. You can see the changing fashion in monuments—just like everything else.

"The Water Works" is much more than an isolated epiphany, a Joycean moment of recognition and truth. It has a context that is provided by the previous story and by the overall questions about writing that *Lives of the Poets* considers. The story suggests the boy's unstated recognition that there are ritualistic ways of dealing with death. In seeing the water workers drinking the whisky, he immediately recognizes the ritual that is followed also by "gravediggers and firemen." The unspoken realization or implication is that the act of writing about the dead is in itself a ritualistic means of coping with grief and loss. But at that moment the boy gives no sign of recognizing this fact; and in effect, "The Water Works" is evidence of a split between the persona adopted for the telling of the story and the author of the tale. Mention of the rituals of firemen, is a glance toward *Ragtime*; one of its chief plots depends on how a ritualistic practical joke that the fireman play on their victim Coalhouse Walker turns into a shocking and extreme situation.

The division between author and narrator widens in the next story, "Willi." Essentially, "Willi" is a boy's reminiscence of his mother's infidelity and what happens when he tells his father of the adultery. Like "The Water Works," this story involves a moment of recognition and realization, not about death but about sexuality, jealousy, and, more personally, about the boy's learning that he is not exempt from feelings of sexual longing and arousal. "The Water Works" is in effect a fictionalization of Jonathan, using fiction to explore his feelings; this strategy is even more extreme in the case of "Willi." Jonathan is erased from "The Water Works," necessarily absent from it, and a further displacement takes place through the suggested displacement in time; the undertaker has a horsedrawn hearse. In "Willi," there is displacement of time, place, and persona. The story is set in Galicia in 1910 and has a certain familiarity, even a predictability, with its props of aristocratic husband, younger wife, and adultery with the boy's tutor. On a more significant level, "Willi" is about displacement and comes to echo the displacement that made feeling into fiction. Galicia in 1910 is firmly invoked by the narrator (untypical of *Lives of the Poets* where most of the stories are not specific about time and place), as is the fact that the father is not at home there:

> He was a Jew who spoke no Yiddish and a farmer raised in the city. . . . We lived alone, isolated on our estate, neither Jew nor Christian, neither friend or petitioner of the Austro-Hungarians.

Galicia itself occupied a precarious position in 1910, divided between Austria and Russia and agitating for autonomy. "Willi" has various effects. A satisfying and stimulating story in itself, but like a chameleon it takes on a variety of colors from the stories and contexts in which Doctorow has placed it. The narrator has created the persona of the boy and used the historical position of Galicia to find concrete analogies for his own puzzlement and alienation. The father, of course, reflects Jonathan's father; the Jew in a land of Gentiles, the would-be sailor living in the city. The implications of "Willi" are deepened further when, in "Lives of the Poets," Doctorow uses the same phrases to describe the fighting of Jonathan's own parents. Whatever its theme, of adolescent longing, awareness, alienation, "Willi" is also concerned with how fiction starts in feeling and seeks concrete situations and symbols—objective correlatives—to explore and express that feeling. The feelings themselves may be explored more deeply through the very act of displacement, of locating them in a fresh context.

With this last recognition one starts to reach to the center of *Lives of the Poets*. Although the individual stories succeed on their own, the book as a whole takes for its theme the origin and purpose of fiction. The stories not only exist separately as units but also join together to form a much greater whole. Indeed, *Lives of the Poets* can be considered as a book that helps to unify Doctorow's own work up to that point. Like Jonathan in the book, Doctorow had transposed the self, seeking historical analogies and circumstances, recreating over and over the father, the mother, the family situation, the Jewishness. Even a brief tale such as "Willi" has implications for re-viewing Doctorow's other fiction because it makes explicit what had been implied in the recurring situation of father and mother seen from the child's perspective, the one offered in *The Book of Daniel*, *Ragtime*, and *Loon Lake*. Further, it suggests how the remote settings of *Welcome to Hard Times* and *Big as Life* can be considered self-consciously manipulative on Doctorow's part.

II

The first stories establish this questioning of the origins of fiction, in the second half of the book the stories go further and ask another, related question. In part, this is Lowell's question, "Yet why not say what happened?" It is another question too, which is not about the origins of fiction but about its usefulness and its responsibilities. That "The Hunter," which follows "Willi," raises these issues is not fully apparent until reading "Lives of the Poets." The novella reveals that Jonathan had (and possibly is having) an affair with a woman who had taught in a grade school to pay for her university tuition. "The Hunter" represents Jonathan's imagining her situation; perhaps, though we cannot know this, deriving it from a story she had told him. Once this fact is revealed, "The Hunter" takes on various meanings. At first the story seems more remote from Jonathan than even "Willi" because the central consciousness is the young woman. But the story may also be read as Jonathan's self-examination because, being the story's maker, he has also entered into the life of another character, a young bus driver. Again, "The Hunter" explores aspects of alienation: the landscape is cold and bleak; the young woman is out of place in the town and is also deeply unhappy. In the story she apparently invites the bus driver's sexual attentions, but, then, in a moment of disgust, she spurns him. The act is one of both hope and despair; hope for love, yet despair at the predictability of the young man and at the restrictions in her life. She recognizes that an affair with the bus driver, rather than being a liberating force, will confirm her imprisonment in the small town and her self-restriction. In effect, she is the "hunter" of the title because, unlike the other characters, she seeks a life that is not predictable but imaginative and spontaneous.

Ostensibly "The Hunter" has a fairly standard theme, but "Lives of the Poets" suggests that it has other ones. On one level it is concerned with the writer's empathetic ability to enter and understand other lives, and perhaps it is also about the writer's need so to do. If we accept that the story is written by Jonathan, then it is also a story of self-examination because he has created the persona of the bus driver. Even the setting of "The Hunter" is glossed in "Lives of the Poets" as the town to which Jonathan and the woman go to be discreet in their love making. In this regard, the story could be read as a kind of disguise: guilt will not allow Jonathan to write frankly and honestly about the woman, but he needs to write about her, and thus the fictive displacement represented by "The Hunter" is born of guilt and the need to camouflage feelings. If this is the case, then the adult Jonathan is confronting the question of fiction in a much more complex way than could the child Jonathan. In "The Writer in the Family," the dishonesty of the fictive letters forces him to stop writing them. But here Jonathan is, as it were, using Eliot's "objective correlative" and the notion of the distanced, disguised self as a shield, a self-protective device, as if the insertion of one's self into a fictive self were one of the "deliberate disguises" that Eliot's "Hollow Men" sought. Jonathan has not yet reached the crisis brought on by the devastating simplicity of Lowell's question that is evident in the novella.

In the next two stories, "The Foreign Legation" and "The Leather Man," Doctorow uses these by-now-established questions about fiction as a basis for exploring other themes, particularly variations on the theme of the writer's responsibility. Morgan, the chief (and, really, sole) character in "The Foreign Legation," is not a creative writer but is used to represent aspects of the writer's apparent isolation and supposed self-reliance. Morgan's wife and children have left him (his story could have been suggested by those told in the novella about broken and failing marriages); alone in the house, he tends to brood. One day his habitual morning run takes him by the house of an unspecified foreign legation. At the end of the story Morgan is again jogging by the legation one winter morning when a bomb goes off, and he is injured.

Like the other stories, "The Foreign Legation" establishes its meanings from different contexts. In part this story is about the impossibility of withdrawing from the world, either as an individual or as a nation. For instance, Morgan recognizes an analogy between his job as "assistant curator of pre-Columbian art at the Museum of the Under Americas in New York City" and the international aspect of a diner he visits.

> The counterman handed him a large laminated menu and smiled a gold-toothed smile. Hey, compadre, he said.
> Morgan looked at the menu. He could have the chili, or the chicken soup, he could have pigs' feet or Irish lamb stew or lasagna or souvlaki.

This recognition precedes the bombing, where the implication is that because we are all involved, no one can be entirely innocent or claim to have no interest in "foreign affairs." Doctorow makes the lack of insulation between the private and the political shockingly clear. Morgan's erotic fantasies about the girls in the convent school are brutally echoed when, after the bombing, he finds himself holding the severed leg of one of the girls. This theme alone makes the story a powerful one, but, once again, its placement in *Lives of the Poets* makes it resonate with other possibilities and analogies. It corresponds to "The Leather Man" and "Lives of the Poets" in that it is about the writer's responsibility in the world and his inability to withdraw from it. In several ways, Doctorow signals Morgan as surrogate writer. Like Jonathan in "Lives of the Poets" Morgan has, as it were, withdrawn temporarily into the self. If we read "The Foreign Legation" as a story explicitly written by Jonathan, we see again how he is exploring the self through displacement and how essential displacement is for such an exploration. Jonathan's voluntary withdrawal from his wife and family in "Lives of the Poets" is something he does not especially want to examine. In "The Foreign Legation" he avoids scrutinizing the act simply by making it an involuntary one. Morgan's wife and children have left him, allowing Jonathan to concentrate on the story's other themes. Further, Morgan's insight in the local diner is also Jonathan's, inserted into fiction:

> When I walk into the Bluebird Diner on lower Broadway the counterman gives me the gold-toothed grin. Hey, compadre, he says. He tosses me the laminated menu. . . . The plates slap through the slot, oh chili, soup of chicken, oh pigs' feet, oh lamb stew, lasagna (homemade), fried steak and souvlaki.

Jonathan uses Morgan to exemplify the inability to be separate from the world, and this inability is part of his own self-examination as a writer, an examination that had started in "The Writer in the Family" and will reach a climax in "Lives of the Poets." However, the realization that the writer cannot be immune from politics and choice is also made by the authorities, as is evident in "The Leather Man." At first reading, this story, which directly precedes "Lives of the Poets," makes little sense. Only on subsequent and careful readings does its point emerge.

"The Leather Man" has the not altogether convincing setting of a semi-formal meeting by a group, apparently the CIA. The meeting is concerned with whether vagrants and drop-outs can be considered politically or socially subversive and, if so, what subsequent course of action should be adopted toward them. Slater, who dominates the meeting, sees drop-outs and vagrants, characterized by a centenarian, the Leather Man, as necessarily subversive because they possess, and potentially provide, an alternative perspective on society.

> What is the essential act of the Leather Man? He makes the world foreign. He distances it. He is estranged. Our perceptions are sharpest when we're estranged. We can see the shape of things.

Because Slater accepts this as fact, his position is that the group should infiltrate and make contact with these individuals. One of the clues that this group is a CIA meeting is in Slater's reminiscence of having been part of the group that infiltrated the Woodstock festival. Once more, it is the writer, not just the drop-out who is the focus here. When Slater argues that the vagrant forces us to re-see the world, he is also detailing one of the effects that the writer achieves. Furthermore, Slater's final point concerning infiltration seems to be aimed deliberately at the writer rather than at the vagrant. The writer provides a perspective on society similar to that of the outsider, the Leather Man, and at first it appears that Slater wants to utilize the writer's perspective as a resource: "We've got thousands of people in this country whose vocation it is to let us know what our experience is. Are you telling me this is not a resource?" The twist, however, is that rather than learning from the writer's perspective, Slater visualizes controlling the writer through infiltration. His group will seek to curb the writer's power by limiting the range or effectiveness of fiction as resource. The exact means of achieving control is not stated, but Doctorow is likely to have had in mind government patronage of the arts as a covert means of control. The *New York Times* of 11 January 1986 reported that Doctorow objected to then Secretary of State George Shultz's addressing the PEN conference.

III

From the very opening of "Lives of the Poets," it is obvious that the postures and stances that Jonathan has assumed in the other stories are now dropped and that the novella itself is exploratory, self-conscious. "My left thumb is stiff, not particularly swollen although the veins at the base are prominent and I can't move it backward or pick up something without pain." As the novella develops, it is clear that the fictive *personae* Jonathan has used are not merely dropped but are being explained. He provides hints that lead to our detecting the sources of the preceding stories. In one regard, the novella is about a mid-life crisis, about turning fifty. Jonathan chronicles the anxieties and problems of his class and his age group. "Lives of the Poets" works successfully on this level alone, but it becomes immeasurably richer and finer because Doctorow is also examining the nature of writing and living. The questions that Jonathan faces—ones that he cannot even fully articulate—are about the nature of being a writer, about what the writer can hope to achieve, and about the responsibilities of fiction. In considering these issues, "Lives of the Poets" corresponds to the doubts that other writers have expressed in their work. These would include Shakespeare's "How with this rage shall beauty hold a plea,/ Whose action is no stronger than a flower?" Auden's statement that "poetry makes nothing happen," ("In Memory of W. B. Yeats") and, as Jonathan himself indicates, Lowell's question, "Yet why not say what happened?"

One way of considering "Lives of the Poets" is to see that Jonathan is asking such questions within a framework that provides their answers. The preceding six stories become variations of the possible answers about why one writes. Jonathan invents stories to make something real to him, to give comfort to himself and others, to deceive, to disguise the self, to explore his emotions and conflicts. Another answer to Lowell's question is that a kind of truth can emerge through fiction, though that truth is not necessarily factual. For example, Jonathan may learn something of himself through displacing his own situation, setting it in Galicia or making a fresh character for himself.

Displacement represents another aspect of the Leather Man's significance: in making the world foreign for the reader, writers may also provide themselves with a fresh point of view. These are all sound reasons for writing. In "*Lives of the Poets*" Jonathan is at the end of his fictional resources, his Eliotean deliberate disguises. He drops his *personae* and in so doing, deftly (or, perhaps, to him, accidentally), reveals to us the sources of the preceding stories.

Doctorow's title for the novella and the book, *Lives of the Poets*, now reveals more of its significance. Perhaps more than any other art form, twentieth-century poetry has faced a crisis in the perceived relation between author and persona. For Eliot, at the start of modernism, the poet's progress, as outlined in "Tradition and the Individual Talent," was a "continual extinction of personality." When this process is made apparent in his poetry, however, it often appears as disguise, as in the "deliberate disguises," but it is there also in "Portrait of a Lady":

> And I must borrow every changing shape
> To find expression . . . dance, dance
> Like a dancing bear,
> Cry like a parrot, chatter like an ape.

The oblique revelation of the self through the dramatic monologue is a variation of this strategy of the impersonal. But Lowell's question strikes to the heart of this strategy, exposing it as somehow dishonest. Indeed, Lowell's question, "Yet why not say what happened?" comes from one of his last poems, published in his last book, *Day by Day* (1977). To reach the simplicity of the question in "Epilogue" Lowell himself had undergone the same process that Doctorow explores in *Lives of the Poets*. Starting off, as he often acknowledged, as a poet under the influence of Eliot and the New Critics, Lowell had espoused the impersonal in poetry. But his break with this aspect of modernism came with *Life Studies* in 1959. Strikingly, *Life Studies* itself follows something of the same pattern as *Lives of the Poets*. Lowell's book starts with monologues, as he invests his personality and feelings in figures such as Marie de'Medici and a mad negro soldier. He continues through a prose reminiscence, which, like Doctorow's "Lives of the Poets," provides essential clues to the other works in the book. After a section on four writers—Lowell's own "Lives of the Poets"—he comes to a series of poems that are, apparently, more nakedly about the self and the personal, undisguised by persona. Rather than being a continual extinction of personality, both *Life Studies* and *Lives of the Poets* represent a gradual emergence of the personality behind the fictions. An astute reader of "Lives of the Poets" makes a connection between Jonathan and Lowell because Jonathan attended Kenyon College, where Lowell and Randall Jarrell had followed their teacher John Crowe Ransom. Indeed, the ostensible gloss on the title *Lives of the Poets* derives in part from Jonathan's interest in poetry; it seems to have been the title of a projected reminiscence about the poets he knew.

After he finished *Life Studies*, Lowell said that he was unsure whether the book was a "life-line" or a "death-rope." Something of the same question is tackled in "Lives of the Poets" because Jonathan's new style of writing could represent either a dead end or a way out of his crisis. However, Doctorow complicates the question in several ways. The story ends with Jonathan's starting to become engaged in a political action, shielding Salvadorean refugees. This act can be seen as the logical consequence of one of the debates that has emerged in the second half of the book, about the impossibility of being self-reliant and disengaged from political realities. In theory, it could also mean the end of writing; hypothetically, Jonathan could find in political action an outlet for his temporarily suppressed creative energies. The choice between silence and action would be by no means new; it derives from Auden's "poetry makes nothing happen" and reflects, for example, the silence at the end of Saul Bellow's *Herzog* when Herzog is liberated from the compulsion to write his letters. The actual ending of *Lives of the Poets* is not so straightforward, however; it closes with the child refugee now assisting Jonathan at the typewriter:

> hey who's writing this? every good boy needs a toy boat, maybe we'll go to the bottom of the page get my daily quota done come on, kid, you can do three more lousy lines.

The positive suggestion at the end is that political engagement, or, at least, a reawakening of the quality of compassion, can reinvest writing with the energy and power that are otherwise in danger of being lost. There is a neatness to this ending because man and boy now compose together, thus echoing and developing the situation in "The Writer in the Family." But rather than looking back to the first story, the novella ends by looking outward to a future that in other parts of the book seemed hopeless. Jonathan's action resolves nothing. It solves none of the dilemmas he had outlined, but it reveals a source of energy from outside the self. It is as though to be re-engaged as a writer Jonathan finds the advice of Yeats insufficient. Rather than returning to the "foul rag-and-bone shop of the heart" as Yeats advised in "The Circus Animals' Desertion," he must do the opposite and look outside the self.

In "Epilogue" Lowell's complaint about his "threadbare art" involved a doubt over whether he was a true artist. The artist, he suggests, transforms reality rather than reproduces it. Lowell's sense of failure derives primarily from a romantic view of the role of the poet, a view that stretched from Coleridge and Wordsworth to, in Lowell's time, Wallace Stevens. Rather than a romantic, Lowell designates himself a recorder, a photographer rather than an expressionist painter. Nevertheless, "Epilogue" ends with a note of triumph at this fact; art itself should be accurate, should exist in order to preserve because it involves the recognition that we are mortal and human:

> Yet why not say what happened?
> Pray for the grace of accuracy
> Vermeer gave to the sun's illumination
> stealing like a tide across a map
> to his girl solid with yearning.
> We are poor passing facts,
> warned by that to give
> each figure in the photograph
> his living name.

In some regards, *Lives of the Poets* closes with the same recognition, and, as for Lowell, "why not say what happened?" becomes not so much a question as a half-aggressive statement of post-romantic sensibility. For Jonathan, dropping fiction and saying "what happened" can be a refreshing, if temporary, triumph. Indeed, it is possible to see that "The Hunter" touches on this time. After her frustrated night with the bus driver, the teacher calls in the school photographer. To do so is most unusual because there is no special occasion, and the children are not dressed up for so unexpected a visit. They become uneasy and upset over the event and the teacher's vehement insistence. On one level, the teacher's gesture could be considered symptomatic of her overall frustrations. But the event becomes almost a trope for *Lives of the Poets*. Like the teacher, Jonathan finds authenticity in the snapshot rather than in the composed, formal portrait, in saying "what happened" as well as in the ways of disguising it.

JOHN WILLIAMS

Canonizing Welcome to Hard Times *and* The Book of Daniel *1980–85*

The popularity of *Ragtime* and subsequent discussion of its use of history ensured a reexamination of *Welcome to Hard Times* and *The Book of Daniel*, both of which had received favorable reviews but little attention from academic critics. In the case of the former novel, critics in the 1980s tended to explore generic and philosophical issues raised by this metaphorical Western, and in the case of the latter, politics became the dominant issue, related but not always connected to the view of history implicit in the book. Including these and other approaches, this half-decade proved to be one of the most fertile for Doctorow's studies; more than fifty critical works appeared in all, two of them book-length. Almost half of these were devoted in whole or part to *The Book of Daniel*, another half-dozen to *Welcome to Hard Times*. In discussions of both works, a postmodern eclecticism becomes more obvious and the subject of writing takes on more importance. The articles lead toward the first books devoted to Doctorow's work as well as perhaps the most distinctive essay yet written about it, Geoffrey Galt Harpham's 1985 article that announces a definitive poststructuralist approach to Doctorow.

From *Fiction as False Document: The Reception of E. L. Doctorow in the Postmodern Age*.

Politics, Psychoanalysis, and Postmodernism: *The Book of Daniel*

The suspicion of Doctorow's politics evident in some reviews of *Ragtime* found voice in the renewed attention to *The Book of Daniel*. Although several essays dealing with the novel appeared in the 1970s, the most vocal critics analyzed the text less than they condemned or praised the political nature of the work. Conservative critics shouted louder, it seems, and Joseph Epstein's 1977 attack on what he called the adversary culture, using Lionel Trilling's phrase, includes *The Book of Daniel* as an example of fiction spoiled by the political views of authors, views which can be summed up as a distrust, even hatred of America. No doubt the immediate occasion of Epstein's attack was the appearance of Robert Coover's *The Public Burning* (1977), a dark satirical look at the infamous Rosenberg trial and execution (1951–53) that, Epstein says, makes *The Book of Daniel* seem "disinterested" by comparison. Conceding Doctorow's book to be skillful, Epstein charges him with "rigging" its point of view for "what can only be political purposes." As evidence he cites changes in the facts to make the accused couple more sympathetic and their accuser more repugnant. What seems to upset Epstein the most, however, is the anti-American stance taken by the narrator. As Carole Harter and James Thompson point out in their Twayne study of Doctorow, Epstein's determination to see only the book's politics causes him to overlook that it is *Daniel's* point of view the reader gets, not necessarily Doctorow's, and while that perspective is largely anti-American, it includes criticism of communism and is itself undermined by the book's context. In other words, Epstein fails to see Daniel as an unreliable narrator whose beliefs are shown to be flawed.

The mantle of Epstein's hostility was assumed in the early 1980s by Robert Alter, who again uses Trilling's word to describe *The Book of Daniel* as "an adversarial political novel" that grossly oversimplifies issues. According to Alter, a work such as Robert Penn Warren's *All the King's Men* is a truer political novel because it "tells us not so much what politics as such is like as how politics might fit into some larger vision of the human condition." Here Alter invokes a traditional criterion by asking fiction to make universal statements about reality, but in the emerging postmodern age of the 1980s his effort could be characterized as a rear guard action, the moral wing of New Criticism fighting a losing battle against the avant-garde. Alter's 1980 article appeared in the *New York Times Book Review* but Harper's, which had published Epstein's reasoned critique, followed in August of 1981 with another reactionary essay by Bryan Griffin called "Panic Among the Philistines," a scathing attack on postmodern writers in general. Earlier that same year, Griffin had used the pages of *The American Spectator* to attack Doctorow for, among other things, a lack of "intelligence and moral purpose." He is, says Griffin, a writer who prospers only because his works "serve the political, cultural, and professional ambitions of . . . empty critics." Both Griffin's hatchet jobs and Alter's attack echo Epstein's hostility toward a privileged university class of professor/writers who persist in the modernist distortion and rejection of mainstream American life. Of course, Alter admires Warren's *All the King's Men*, but can accept its modernist critique of American politics because it lifts us out of politics to a "larger human vision." Perhaps he and other readers of *The Book of Daniel* were too close in time to the politics reflected in it to appreciate its view of the human condition. By no means as widespread as reaction to *Ragtime*, conservative attacks on *The Book of Daniel* were less likely to consider the broad issue of history than to read the book as a direct statement by its obviously liberal author. At any rate, by taking on a political subject, Doctorow had galvanized a segment of the conservative establishment.

In this time period (1980–85), several essays can be grouped into two related categories: those that deal with the relationship of politics and art, and those that discuss politics in terms of psychology. Interestingly, they sometimes mingle elements of all three disciplines in their discussions. Actually, two 1975 essays, the earliest work in the scholarly journals, anticipate the early eighties focus on the political dimensions of *The Book of Daniel* and illustrate something of how critics saw in the book a nexus of politics, psychology, and art. John Stark's "Alienation and Analysis" in *Critique* classifies types of alienation and argues that Daniel must overcome alienation not by means of rational (primarily Marxist) analysis, but by means of "analysis by image," or imaginative analysis. In contrast to Stark's view that Daniel resolves his problems, Barbara Estrin, writing in the *Massachusetts Review*, sees the novel as a failed confession of the narrator's deep psychic wounds; he is a "lost child" deprived of home and self by the state's cruelty. The McCarthy era, with its threat of persecution and atomic doom, has in fact produced a cruel Daniel who repeats in his new family what the state did to his old one. This corruption of identity extends to the act that Daniel hopes will restore his lost legacy; that is, writing becomes another form of cruelty as it exacts its own torture by presenting endless "sequence," or rehearsal of the past. Eventually the narrator must "bury" his Isaacson self in the act of finishing the book in order to achieve a "minimal subsistence" as the assimilated Daniel Lewin. Despite their obviously different readings of the novel's ending, both Stark and Estrin see a dynamic interplay of political, artistic, and psychological forces.

While retaining an interest in psychology, Peggy Knapp (1980) and Susan Lorsch (1982) approach *The Book of Daniel* as heir to traditional literary themes and works. Lorsch reads the novel as a political *Künstlerroman* (or artist novel) which varies the traditional format by *beginning* with the alienation of artist from state and showing his successful use of art to cope with that alienation. The book's disjunctive voice is Daniel's attempt to break through traditional style, itself an ideological construct that reinforces alienation. By learning the power of images, Daniel avoids the extremes of suicide (to which his sister Susan succumbs) and acquiescence to social forces represented by a character known as the Inertia Kid. Lorsch responds directly to Epstein and Alter, rejecting their characterization of Doctorow as "adversarial"; he is rather "pro-art." In so doing she also sides with Stark's more general assessment and refutes Estrin's pessimistic interpretation of the act of writing.

If Lorsch pays Doctorow the compliment of placing *The Book of Daniel* within the tradition of the *Künstlerroman*, Peggy Knapp dares to compare the novel's theme with that of one of Shakespeare's greatest tragedies. Her essay "Hamlet and Daniel" explores the "political consequences" of the bereavement of the two sons in question as each negotiates a relationship with a state perceived to be hostile to him. For Knapp, the death of their fathers creates a political and Oedipal crisis for the sons. The two works fuse "a sense of cultural tumult . . . with the firm and detailed psychology of persons." Knapp's case for the display of psychic defenses erected by the sons against female and state provides a more sophisticated analysis of the novel. Invoking Eliot (and as her subtitle playfully suggests, Marx and Freud), she says that, like *Hamlet*, the novel depicts the effect of the past on the present. The essay also argues that personal relationships cannot escape social and political entanglements. Thus Daniel's cruelty to his wife and son reenacts the cruelty of the father/state, his family constituting a "tiny kingdom" of helpless dependents. Knapp sees his wife Phyllis as a weaker substitute for the strong mother Daniel had lost to the state. He can deal with neither his mother's nor the government's power, so he politicizes the family structure. Although both characters come to terms with their political and familial identities, they exemplify a radical skepticism about the nature of ideology, including even language itself, that makes them exemplars of modern writers.

Since Knapp describes her essay as a "wholesome haunting" of Doctorow by Shakespeare, it might be regarded as a simplified version of Harold Bloom's theory of influence (1973). Certainly Bloom's curious mix of literary and Freudian terminology echoes in Knapp's mingling of political and psychic defenses. Although there is no scheme of "revisionary ratios" here, Knapp does suggest the modern writer's struggle to assert his version of a strong precursor. Doctorow's Daniel is the postmodern Hamlet, achieving a "comic victory" shadowed by the tragedy of a diminished vision of knowledge and power.

One of Knapp's interesting points is that contemporary readers do not necessarily understand but nevertheless accept the presence of an irrational "sex-disgust" as a response to social upheaval. Doctorow once responded in this way to an assertion about the preoccupation with sexuality in his fiction: "I think more likely it is a preoccupation having to do with sex as power, either perhaps using sex as a metaphor for political relations, or helplessly annotating what passes for sex in a society that suffers from paternalistic distortions." Doctorow's recognition of a link between public and private, between politics and sex, and the writer's inevitable reflection of the union, suggests the widespread acceptance of psychoanalytic principles among the literati. Despite rampant revisionism of Freud—indeed, his marginalization in the profession of psychiatry—artists and critics continue to be fascinated with theories of the unconscious and especially of the Oedipal conflict.

Among the most notorious of Freud's revisionists is Jacques Lacan, the maverick French psychiatrist whose work now informs so much of radical feminist as well as psychoanalytic criticism. So far no Doctorow critic has adopted a full-blown Lacanian approach, but in a 1982 article, Robert Forrey makes use of Lacan to reconfigure Knapp's view of *The Book of Daniel*. Where Knapp and others see the effect of political power on sexuality, Forrey sees "sexual politics," namely the struggle over Daniel's incestual longings, as the real site of conflict. For Daniel, "parental copulation" is the "cruel paradigm" of all relationships, one which he extends to his view of government. Forrey bolsters his interpretation of the Oedipal triangle by alluding to a pair of Lacanian principles. First, Lacan describes a pre-Oedipal identification with the mother, the mirror stage, in which a harmonious narcissism prevails with no need of an unconscious because there is no unfulfilled desire. The second major principle mentioned by Forrey is the role of the father as representative of the Law, or the symbolic order entered into after the inevitable loss of the mirror stage. Adapting a Saussurean view of language as a system of differences without positive terms, Lacan sees the symbolic stage as a continual demonstration of "lack," or unfulfilled desire. The father forever stands as the primal negation of the union with the mother. For Lacan, the "ego" is a false construct; in its place exists only the "subject," a "fluid site" in which the "signification of desire" takes place. Essentially, then, the unconscious is more a matter of language than drama.

Forrey explains Daniel's pursuit of truth (the Father's law, or justice) as a sublimation of his real sexual desire for his mother. Significantly, Forrey cites not a text of Lacan's, but a book on Lacan for the theoretical principles used. This use of secondary material is understandable because in 1982 only a few of Lacan's texts had been translated into English, but more importantly perhaps, because Lacan's prose is difficult in any language. Most students of literature must rely at least in part on explanatory material from "experts." Granting this need to the reader untrained in psychoanalysis, however, it must be said that Forrey does not seem to integrate Lacanian theory into his reading of Doctorow. He relies on the concept of an ego and, despite the Lacanian terminology, depicts Daniel as a Freudian "mother-lover" who rebels against America to sublimate his own guilt. Forrey claims his reading of the novel makes sense of Daniel's otherwise cryptic description of Edgar Allan Poe as the master subversive of American history. The naming of an "apolitical poet" instead of more likely candidates reinforces Forrey's argument that the book is more about the Oedipal theme than politics. To sanction his observation, Forrey cites Marie Bonaparte's Freudian analysis of Poe. Of course, Lacan's most famous literary analysis—of "The Purloined Letter"—is a rebuttal of Bonaparte's interpretation and amounts to a proclamation of the primacy of language in structuring Oedipal positions. Lacan would have it that anyone caught in the Oedipal struggle does not possess a disintegrating ego, as in traditional Freudian analysis, but merely acts out the position assigned him or her in the linguistic structure, or as he puts it, the signifying chain. Thus Forrey illustrates the attractiveness of innovative nonliterary theory as a tool for literary analysis as well as the difficulty of adequately absorbing it into more traditional readings.

Writing for *Studies in Jewish American Literature*, Forrey takes another step away from Lacanian analysis by interpreting Daniel's incestuous fantasies as a denial of his Jewish heritage, which is built on the very law that his Oedipal desire flaunts. Forrey ingeniously cites several passages ripe with sexual imagery to make his case, but he also interprets the climactic execution scene as sexual: "the ultimate screwing" not only of his mother (as narrator Daniel does in words what the state had done in reality) but of their common Jewish heritage. Although it does not convincingly support his main thesis, Forrey's introduction of Daniel's Jewishness does bring up an important consideration—the relative scarcity of readings of Doctorow as part of the Jewish tradition.

From the start, critical reception of Doctorow has focused mainly on his historical/political themes and his experimentation. None of the major Jewish critics of the older generation has paid much attention to his work at all, much less as part of the canon that includes Bellow, Malamud, and Roth. Undoubtedly Doctorow's own rejection of religion has influenced this relative critical silence. Although many of his characters are Jewish and much of his fiction is based on his own family, the dominant influence there was not religion but, as Doctorow himself notes, "humanist, radical, Jewish. . . . All the solutions were to be found right here on earth." The content of his work certainly suggests that influence; the Jewish religion plays less a role than a Jewish sensibility compounded of suffering and secular tradition. Also, Doctorow often works within genres—the Western, science fiction, and more recently the gangster novel/film—that steer him away from standard Jewish themes.

Nevertheless, some critics made the case in the early 1980s that Doctorow could be placed within the canon of American Jewish writers. In an essay written for Richard Trenner's anthology on Doctorow, John Clayton argues that despite his modernist tendencies, Doctorow comes out of the radical Jewish humanist tradition, which Clayton describes as a universal response to suffering and a critique of society's injustice that amounts to "a kind of faith." In Clayton's view, the committed Jewish Doctorow with a redemptive view of history struggles against a disengaged modernist Doctorow. In a highly debatable assertion, Clayton claims that all of Doctorow's protagonists act on behalf of a community—even Blue, the frontier mayor in *Welcome to Hard Times*, exhibits a Jewish compassion, guilt, and devotion to law. As for *The Book of Daniel*, it contains both Jewish culture and sensibility. In his search to relieve guilt and suffering, Daniel must employ "the forms of Jewish culture . . . to express his pain."

Clayton's brief essay may strain to define as Jewish what is a more universal phenomenon (Is Jewish humanism so described any different from other humanism?), but his conclusion that Doctorow's protagonist must reclaim his Jewishness to exorcise historical demons agrees with a more detailed argument by Sam B. Girgus concerning Doctorow's place in the ongoing debate over assimilation. Girgus's 1984 book, *The New Covenant: Jewish Writers and the American Idea*, devotes a chapter to Doctorow, approaching him as one of the "new Jeremiahs," whose sermon-like diatribes issue "a call for both introspection and cultural renewal in the light of an ideology that sees America as a new way of life." The writers surveyed by Girgus either espouse the myth of America as the "new covenant," attack the culture for failure to live up to the myth, or "disavow" it both ideologically and psychologically. Using primarily *The Book of Daniel*, Girgus argues that Doctorow's view combines conservative (assimilationist) and radical perspectives to make the myth of America relevant. Daniel must overcome two kinds of alienation: the psychic estrangement of the artistic sensibility, symbolized in his mind by Poe, and the moral alienation of a stranger in a strange land. His search for the truth about his parents takes him on an inward journey for the moral authority of his namesake—a visionary in corrupt times who can offer a "moral metaphor" to cope with the source of his suffering. Echoing Clayton, Girgus argues that to find any meaning in his parents' death, Daniel "must go beyond its political context" to the structure of Jewish ritual.

In Girgus's view, however, *The Book of Daniel* locates Daniel's Jewishness squarely in his American experience, so that his history is incomplete until a "marriage" between his two heritages takes place. The wedding happens, according to Girgus, in Doctorow's unflinching portrait of a variety of American Jews, including two positive examples of assimilation: Aescher, the Isaacson's lawyer, and Lewin, Daniel's adoptive father. Lewin in particular epitomizes a faith in American institutions combined with the patience and status that Paul Isaacson never had. The book's three endings offer proof of Daniel's successful assimilation. The first, a visit to his old Bronx home, marks an ability to leave his past, but the second, an account of his sister's funeral, makes clear his reliance on Jewish heritage. By invoking the practice of hiring official mourners, Daniel accepts the need for ritual. Significantly, despite his typically ironic depletion of the old men saying prayers, Daniel also admits that at last his grief has been tapped. According to Girgus, Daniel's ability to cry represents a renewed humanity obtained through the moral authority of Judaism. The act of writing, a major motif in the novel, culminates in Daniel's liberation depicted in the book's third ending. His finished book completes the awakening of his "moral and historical consciousness."

Although references to ethnic themes pepper subsequent criticism on Doctorow, Clayton and Girgus remain among the few readers to emphasize the "Jewish" in Doctorow's formulation about his influences: "humanist, radical, Jewish." In so doing, they identify Jewishness with broad philosophical or moral values. As for *The Book of Daniel* specifically, critics during this period respond to the swirl of politics, psychology, and aesthetics in the book, but show only hints of radically new critical perspectives. We have already mentioned Gross's Marxist reading of all of Doctorow's work. Beyond Gross and the conservative reviewers, few seem interested in discussing Doctorow as a political novelist. Rather they see politics as a theme to be explored alongside others by analysis of dominant imagery, essentially echoing Alter's criterion for a good political novel that it take us beyond politics.

Neither is there anything yet terribly poststructural in these analyses, merely glimmerings of things to come. By the end of 1985, recognition of Doctorow as a postmodern writer was widespread, but lapidary journal essayists still depended on traditional vocabulary and approach. The consensus of those who discuss *The Book of Daniel*, for example, is that it represents at least a partial triumph for an artist-figure over psychological and political problems. Commentary on style is limited mostly to its portrayal of the narrator's state of mind, and the majority of the critics mentioned above conduct essentially New Critical analyses of imagery patterns such as Doctorow's use of electricity.

Resurrecting the "Disreputable Genre Materials" of *Welcome to Hard Times* 1980–85

As with *Ragtime*, critical discussion of *The Book of Daniel* often centers on its view of history, but generally readers who deal specifically with the earlier novel do not venture into the same theoretical waters that we saw in chapter two. During this same time period, the critical revival of *Welcome to Hard Times* remained even more traditional, as befits the popular genre of Western fiction, and is relegated to relatively minor or narrowly focused journals. Barely reviewed on its first publication in 1960, the novel drew comment in the 1970s from only David Emblidge in his study of Doctorow's view of progress as illusion (1977), and from Daniel Zins, in his praise of the historical imagination of Doctorow's three major books at that time. Tracing the sequence of articles from 1980 to 1985 reveals, however, that *Welcome to Hard Times* raises issues for devotees of popular literature similar to those expressed by critics of *Ragtime* during the same period. In fact, it can be argued that *Welcome's* critics do not really get beyond Emblidge's conclusion that all of Doctorow's early work is about the illusion of progress in America.

Emblidge and other critics treat *Welcome to Hard Times* as a historical novel. As Frank Shelton asserts, by the time of *Loon Lake* (1980), Doctorow had produced "a panoramic view of American history from the 1880s through the 1960s." Many later critics would elaborate on Emblidge's view of *Welcome to Hard Times* as the first of Doctorow's works to debunk American history. This view is certainly evident among the revivalist critics of *Welcome to Hard Times* in the early 1980s, but the subject of history is seen through the prism of genre. Doctorow himself had announced that his choice of a Western for his first novel originated in a desire to take "disreputable genre materials and [do] something serious with them." Such a remark, by the author who once hinted that he may have inserted an allusion to Conrad to "confound the Ph.D.s," probably intends irony at the expense of elitist genre distinctions, and it does suggest the ongoing attitude of many serious literary critics toward so-called popular culture.

Indeed, a certain anxious need for significance invades the style of those critics who write about the Western. They see Doctorow as a welcome addition—a serious novelist using their popular form, or more precisely, subverting its conventions for the purposes of his serious art. Frank Shelton, for example, argues that *Welcome to Hard Times* modifies the hopeful picture of the American dream offered by the traditional Western. Doctorow's novel also questions that most venerable of theses, Frederick Jackson Turner's claim that the frontier experience helped produce the rugged self-made individualism in the American character. J. Bakker makes explicit Shelton's implicit critique of popular forms. He asks, "Can the Western be great?", and his answer shows a bias for "serious" literature. The popular Western cannot be great because it depends on commercial success or insists on being escapist fare. Only a small groups of revisionist Westerns are willing to ask the "great questions." After using Owen Wister's *The Virginian* to illustrate the tendency of popular Westerns to lead up to but then retreat from difficult moral or social issues, Bakker examines three works that do engage them: *The Oxbow Incident*, *Little Big Man*, and *Welcome to Hard Times*.

Bakker calls Turner's influential thesis a poetic one that confirms the power of myth rather than historical truth as shaper of attitudes about history. Turner, James Fenimore Cooper and other purveyors of the frontier myth lock history into the mythic genre of the Western where it reinforces some of our most enduring cultural stereotypes: the righteous individual hero, the female as repository of civilization, the foreboding timeless or edenic landscape, or what Bakker calls the "prevailing ideologies." For Shelton and Bakker, the genre as thus conceived has ignored history, especially the pernicious effects of capitalism, a system for them synonymous with greed. Bakker sees *Welcome to Hard Times* as a truly subversive work precisely because it filters the various conventions, which represent a nineteenth-century mythic view of America, through a twentieth-century perspective informed by the Korean War, Viet Nam, and racial unrest. In the book, Doctorow is willing to ask difficult questions about both personal and collective responsibility for tragic events. On this basis, Bakker calls the novel great. Similarly, Shelton compares *Welcome* to *The Great Gatsby* in its exploration of the corrupt American dream. Both critics agree that despite its debunking of easy optimism, the novel retains hope based on the humanity of its central character—Blue.

Representing critics of a popular genre, Shelton and Bakker invoke what are essentially modernist criteria to praise *Welcome to Hard Times*. It stands apart from boosterism, reflects the ambiguities of experience, and challenges old literary forms. They also appear to reinforce the separation of popular and serious literature that has been around since the industrial revolution. On the one hand is the formula fiction that supports the dominant culture's view of itself, and on the other is the subversion of formula in order to challenge dominant ideology. As a novice effort,

Doctorow's book could not command much attention, but after *Ragtime* made him a novelist discussed in the *New York Times Book Review*, his foray into a "disreputable" genre would validate the worth of that genre for its critics and champions. Ironically, that validation consists of repudiating or challenging the characteristics that made it popular in the first place: an affirmation of cherished American principles and character. Bakker goes so far as to say that for the first time in Westerns, Doctorow creates a tragic figure destroyed by "historical conditions." For Bakker, the book represents a new myth of the West to replace Cooper's original one. In a modest way, Bakker wants to make Doctorow the James Joyce of Westerns, employing a mythic structure but undermining it with irony in definitive modernist style.

During this period of rediscovery and praise, at least one dissenting voice could be heard. Stephen Tanner finds the style in which Doctorow goes about his debunking to be bookish. Doctorow announced with some pride to one interviewer that his whole sense of the novel's barren landscape had originated in a description from *The Great Plains*. According to Tanner, however, the stereotype of a treeless West is not only false, but it also leads to a pathetic fallacy that demands barren lives to match the barren landscape. Doctorow's lack of genuine experience, he says, generates factual errors in his depletion of the frontier, and more importantly it produces an inaccurate, academic conception of the frontier spirit. Thus in place of felt-life, the book offers Freudian stereotypes and artificial conflicts that violate the fundamental genre convention of Westerns, what Tanner calls righteous rage on the part of a hero to restore communal order. Tanner is here thinking of Blue's agonized questioning of his own and others' motives in destroying the Bad Man from Bodie. The novel insists on introducing repression and neurosis into a clearly justified attempt to ward off evil. What in a traditional Western would have produced a purgative effect—the destruction of a despicable outlaw by the sheriff—becomes a muddled moral dilemma without logic. Doctorow's tinkering with the formula weakens the mythic pattern that gives the genre its power.

Tanner's complaints notwithstanding, *Welcome to Hard Times* became a legitimating artifact for some critics in the Western genre because it demythologized traditional and therefore superficial ideas connected with American history and myth. The notion of literature as oppositional to main street is not new, but the term "ideology," used by Bakker, suggests the post-structuralist project of examining texts for ways in which they either reveal or undermine dominant views. One result of such a trend has been to efface the difference between popular and serious literature, since any text will do for such analysis. Of course, these critics of *Welcome* are caught in the middle, unwilling to lose the distinction entirely but wanting to endorse popular forms as capable of modernist complexity. This desired union is explicit in Doctorow's stated project—to use "disreputable genre materials" in serious ways. Bakker points out that unlike many debunkers, Doctorow eschews farce and satire, but with or without humor, one of the hallmarks of postmodern fiction is the blurring of lines between genres so that questions of appropriateness get trickier. In the postmodern world, a writer or critic need not apologize for "using" a genre in an unorthodox way.

Paul Bové represents many poststructuralists when he argues that the term "genre" may be outmoded, to be replaced by "discourse" as used by Foucault and his followers. For them, discourse means not a distinct way of speaking or writing, but the organization of a field of knowledge, a system that authorizes certain ways of knowing and "disciplines" members of a discursive community in their responses. Given that discourse functions to control how reality is seen in particular times and places—since it in certain ways is a society—the real task of the literary critic turns out to be "genealogy," the tracing of the kinds and effects of discourse, rather than interpretation.

Certainly variations on genealogy have emerged in New Historicism and post-colonial studies, but many critics cannot or will not follow Foucault too far. In the case of Doctorow criticism of *Welcome* during the revival, there is a reluctance to move from thematic study to analysis of discursive fields. Obviously Shelton and Bakker do not engage in genealogy. Nonetheless, Bakker's talk of breaking the bounds of genre is a fetal version of genealogy: suggesting how the forms of literature condition our knowledge of history. In their approval of Doctorow's exposure of capitalism's seamy side, for example, Shelton, Bakker and others agree implicitly with Foucault that knowledge cannot be separated from power because what and how we know determines the limits of control that may be exerted over us. These Doctorow critics simply stop at a general assent that it is healthier to realize America's imperfections; they do not trace the implications of either popular or debunking views within the culture. They obviously show no interest in examining how the academy itself may be subject to genealogical study (In what ways, if any, do genre studies impact departments of English?) or outside of it (What political uses, if any, have been made of the popular Western?). Other Doctorow critics have pursued such implications more eagerly, but relatively few scholars have regarded the concept of discourse in Doctorow's work or its political ramifications.

Advocacy and Explanation: The First Books on Doctorow

Clearly, by 1985, with his work discussed in the *Massachusetts Review*, *Critique*, *Genre*, and other such periodicals, Doctorow had arrived at least on the lower rungs of the contemporary canon. And although as yet no major critic had welcomed him as a great writer, lesser members of the academy were lining up to carve out a place for him. Two such champions published the first books on Dortorow's fiction during this period. Richard Trenner edited a collection of interviews of Doctorow and essays about his work that appeared in 1983 as *Essays and Conversations*. Then in 1985 Paul Levine, perhaps the most prolific of Doctorow's admirers, combined versions of several previous essays into an introductory volume for Malcolm Bradbury's Contemporary Writers series. Both books succeed as advocacy for the importance of his work through *Loon Lake*.

Trenner's volume has become the standard reference material for work on Doctorow. It came after the author's first major phase—a series of novels on American history—and brought an end not only to the decade of seventies criticism with its emphasis on *Ragtime* and *The Book of Daniel*, but signaled the demise of Doctorow's period of relative anonymity among scholars as well. What Trenner foresees in his introduction has come to pass: "the coming years" have extended the variety and amount of attention given to Doctorow, who is now recognized among scholars as well as journalistic reviewers. The timing of *Essays and Conversations* also marks the acknowledgment of poststructuralism's influence on Doctorow criticism. Trenner hints at being a poststructuralist-pluralist with a tinge of humanist remaining. He values the "composing and recomposing" of diverse critical theory and asserts for this collection the status of lively debate between different voices. To achieve this debate, Trenner gathered three interviews, two essays by Doctorow ("False Documents" and "For the Artist's Sake"), and several previously published articles. He also commissioned three new pieces for the book. The result is, as he promises, a variety of approaches: Doctorow as Jewish humanist (Clayton), as Freudian-Marxist (Gross), as postmodernist (Saltzman and Foley), and Doctorow as closet allegorist (Arnold). Trenner includes one article on the influence of Kleist (Ditsky) and even inserts Ellen Chances's brief study of Doctorow's reception in Russia. As already noted, in lieu of a biography, the interviews have been relied on by most of Doctorow's critics as sources for a variety of interests. *Essays and Conversations* still may be the single most valuable volume in the secondary literature on Doctorow.

Despite obvious diversity, the book reflects what had been up to the mid-1980s the dominant concerns of Doctorow critics: his use of American history and his moral-political vision. The interviews especially set this tone. Despite employing different titles, Larry McCaffery, Trenner, and Paul Levine return to similar questions about the novelist's politics, views of the American idea, and of course, his method and philosophy of composing. Interestingly, Doctorow sidesteps direct questions about his politics to make general pronouncements about the role of artist as outsider and about the inevitable political nature of any work. In fact, portions of the interviews are like little dramas in which the critics try to draw the protagonist into declarations that he is uncomfortable making. For example. Trenner states his own thesis about Doctorow's canon: "I see in your work an explicit political rhetoric and an insistent concern with how political and social forces help shape the lives of your characters." Having been challenged to affirm the assertion, Doctorow admits the radical influences from his childhood, but refuses to acknowledge any political philosophy, instead setting fiction apart as an "illuminated way of thinking" beyond politics.

In the same interview, however, Doctorow does reveal a political background out of which his postmodern aesthetic takes shape:

> The assumption that makes fiction possible, even modernist fiction—the moral immensity of the single soul—is under question because of the bomb. To write fiction now as it has been written may be to misperceive or avoid the overriding condition of things, which is that we're in the countdown stages of a post-humanist society.

Without using the exact word, Doctorow describes a variation on the post-modern condition. Speaking before the fall of communism, he assigns the cause of jeopardy to "the bomb," which to his generation had become a convenient and powerful symbol of the threat posed to human nature and values by an almost bewildering complex of factors. His remark is actually a self-revealing speculation about his craft in such an era. He seems to wonder if this new "post-humanist" age requires some new mode of fiction; his most recent work at the time of this interview was *Loon Lake*, a novel questioning the nature of the human "subject." On the other hand, one can presume that Doctorow does not want to relinquish the assumption—the integrity of the "subject"—that makes fiction possible. This musing explains much critical debate over his work. Do his innovations correspond to the spirit of a post-humanist society or do they preserve the "moral immensity" of the soul? Or can they do both? The critics in Trenner's volume, all sharing to some extent the humanist bias, believe he achieves both a rendering of post-modern skepticism and saves the soul. The most detailed argument to that end is by Arthur Saltzman, in one of the pieces commissioned by Trenner.

Saltzman's essay is the most comprehensive of the collection, dealing with all of Doctorow's novels through *Loon Lake*, and it announces a pattern that will become almost standard: Doctorow is a postmodernist who still cares about "sociopolitical realities." Saltzman attempts to show how each novel follows this pattern of "demythologiz[ing] America" and "demystify[ing]" fiction itself. The first aim more or less echoes the interviews in substance. America's nostalgic or official view of itself is false. Thus the country's history becomes a series of power-seeking institutions victimizing its citizens while constructing pleasing illusions for public consumption. Doctorow's second purpose, according to Saltzman—the demystifying of literature—derives from an awareness that language is incapable of representing reality. Anticipating Christopher Morris's later arguments, Saltzman offers several images from the novels to illustrate this deconstructive dimension of Doctorow's work.

The Doctorow novel that emerges from Saltzman's analysis is both self-reflexive and socially conscious. On the one hand the artist-figures who populate each book try unsuccessfully to represent reality; on the other they manage to critique American social institutions with powerful irony. Saltzman never fully reconciles the radically different pictures of fiction inherent in his thesis. The paradox of a writer who manages to say something important with the unreliable tool of language is one that few poststructuralist critics have dealt with successfully. Nevertheless, Saltzman's embrace of the post-modern element in Doctorow anticipates the wave of the future. On the other hand, his unwillingness to let go of the novel's project of cultural critique allies him with the thesis of the first book on Doctorow, Paul Levine's.

Actually, Levine's *E. L. Doctorow: An Introduction* is monograph length, one of a common species in post-World-War-II literary culture. Academic presses have inundated the market with introductions to modern writers. Not so long ago Lionel Trilling had to wage his campaign on behalf of modernist fiction outside the academy; now students can read a Twayne volume on John Irving, for example, after only a handful of books by the author. The obvious disadvantage in this instant analysis is lack of perspective. For better or worse, the publishing industry shares in the fast pace of contemporary consumerism. Levine's book, however, even in the rapidly shifting critical scene of the decade since its publication, holds up rather well. Because he had been a student of Doctorow's work for several years and had talked to as well as written about him, Levine avoids the trap of superficiality. And, as a reviewer in *American Literature* notes, the book benefits from an intelligence that he sardonically ascribes to the project's origin in Great Britain, "where the general reader is still envisioned as serious and bright."

The Contemporary Writers series is edited by Malcolm Bradbury and Christopher Bigsby. Bradbury, a British novelist and critic whose credentials include editorship of the excellent *Modernism: A Guide to European Literature 1890–1930*, has made a career of bringing modern literature to the general reader. In the preface to E. L. Doctorow, he characterizes contemporary writers as among the most "sensitive interpreters" of contemporary culture. In Levine, the editors found someone who believes in Doctorow as just such an interpreter of America's past and present. He offers a sympathetic portrait of Doctorow as a serious artist who combines experimental style with cultural critique.

Levine's approach, then, returns us to the heritage of American studies discussed in chapter two. Tied at first to historical studies, then to what Giles Gunn calls the myth and symbol school, American studies found a series of oppositions in the culture that showed a lost ideal, for example the garden, which is destroyed by the "machine" of modern technology. They suggested an idea of America tarnished by time and corrupt social development. Later cultural critics found more and more canker in the rose, at times dismissing the first wave of Americanists as apologists for the system, but behind even their harsh revisionism lay the hope for something better. This critical, socialist-influenced longing informs Levine's view of Doctorow.

Levine's interview with Doctorow in *Essays and Conversations* centers on the relationship between America and radicalism. In that context he asks at one point: "Do you have a sense that there was a golden moment in American history where it could have all been different?" Arising in a discussion of *The Book of Daniel*, that question says much about Levine's emphasis on politics and history. In his study of the political novel, Irving Howe (1957) comments that political novels are born when "the idea of society, as distinct from the mere unquestioned workings of society," occupies the characters and conflict of the book. Howe's remark seems to describe Levine's sense of Doctorow's canon, which elsewhere in the interview he characterizes as "a conscious attempt to revise history in such a way that we can understand American society politically." For Levine, the first four novels all deal with the idea of America gone wrong, off of some original or ideal course. Put most simply, Levine returns again and again to the theme of America's failure to live up to her idea of justice.

His reading of *Ragtime* offers an example of this emphasis and serves as a summation of the arguments on behalf of Doctorow's use of history. First, Levine accepts the prevailing notion that history is constructed—the premise of Doctorow's own "False Documents." Doctorow's mixture of fact and fiction stands traditional history—as written by the dominant culture—on its head, or, as Levine puts it, *Ragtime* "rewrites [history] 'from the bottom up.'"

Doctorow's inclusion of immigrants and blacks as major, even triumphant figures, indicates his vision of their contributions to American culture. Repeated and widespread references to emerging popular entertainments such as baseball, motion pictures, and, most centrally, ragtime music, offer further evidence of the project to rewrite history from the vantage point of the excluded. At the same time as he celebrates popular culture, Doctorow satirizes and critiques "mass culture" after the manner of Herbert Marcuse, who sees in it an artificial version of popular culture that is dehumanized, exclusionary and a historical.

Not mere leftist dogma, Levine's analysis shows awareness of the complexity of factors in America's past, the conflicted fate of its classes and dreams—and Levine credits Doctorow with a corresponding subtlety of vision. In fact, he ends the chapter on *Ragtime* by appealing, as Doctorow himself does on many occasions, to the artist's imagination as the aesthetic tool by which facts can be "reclaimed" from history. Put another way, Levine believes in fiction's ability to transcend the realm of facts to get at "psychological truth." With Levine's assertion that Doctorow has participated in the invention of a new kind of historical novel, we are in some sense back to Aristotle and fiction's rivalry with other explanations of life. The imagination provides a better way of knowing because it can distill from the realm of facts some "universal" or essential truth. Levine is quite aware of the poststructural revolution that by 1985 had declared truth an elusive or irrelevant goal, but his own liberal moral vision cannot accept the judgment that fiction is irrelevant. As a result, Levine refuses to call Doctorow a postmodern writer as the term is often used—he is postmodern perhaps in his refusal of master narratives, but humanist in his insistence on the relevance of literature to life. He especially avoids grouping him with the "self-reflexive school," although it is hard to read *The Book of Daniel* or *Loon Lake* without seeing that quality. Instead he opts for older terms which he then qualifies to locate Doctorow in the mainstream of American fiction. In a later version of the chapter on *The Book of Daniel*, Levine chooses the term "new realism" to label the style arising from the "imaginative crisis" of the 1960s and producing what John Earth calls the "literature of exhaustion." Instead of yielding to the "arid formalism" of some experimentation, the new realists, among whom he names Joan Didion and Robert Stone, find new ways to approach the social and political content of American experience. When in his book he does deal with Doctorow's formal innovations, Levine prefers the term "modernist" to describe the novelist's concern with revealing relationships between the inner and outer reality of his characters.

On style, however, Levine has little to say. Each chapter mentions innovative formal features, but the major concern is Doctorow's revisioned myth of America. In his discussion of *Loon Lake*, for example, a novel that by 1985 had not yet produced much commentary, Levine devotes only one paragraph to the most difficult of Doctorow's experiments in narrative voice. What occupies him in the chapter is the "idea of the thirties," namely the myth of success, a cheapened, Gatsby-like American dream that masks a betrayal of working-class solidarity. The protagonist, Joe, is caught in a web of corrupt capitalism that in the 1930s made the world safe for consumerism.

Levine's introduction to Doctorow makes good use of secondary material to suggest a variety of themes and images in the works. It includes the first treatment of *Lives of the Poets* and one of the first discussions of *Loon Lake*. Its defining trait remains, however, a celebration of Doctorow as a critic of American history and culture. Conservative reviewers who lambasted Doctorow for leftist sympathies no doubt see an apologist in Levine, and he champions the sometimes "insoluble pellets" of ideology that, as Howe points out, exist in any political novel. Leftist sympathy notwithstanding, Levine makes a reasonable attempt within the scope of his assignment to do what the Americanists of an earlier generation had hoped to see come out of a wedding between literary and historical study: a way to make "larger statements about American culture."

With his acknowledgment of postmodern theories but preference for cultural critique, Levine takes the road increasingly less traveled by literary studies in this period. Although he prefers the terminology and sensibility of pre-structuralist English studies, other Doctorow critics show the influence of decidedly different vocabularies and sensibilities. At the outset of 1985, an essay appeared that confirmed this new direction for literary studies of Doctorow.

The Poststructuralist Turn: Geoffrey Galt Harpham's "Technology of Narrative" 1985

Geoffrey Galt Harpham's "E. L. Doctorow and the Technology of Narrative" is cited approvingly by three of the four full-length critical studies of Doctorow's work that came after its publication in 1985. Harter and Thompson call the essay "perhaps the single most perceptive short study of Doctorow's narrative vision," and both Parks and Morns rely on its insights more than any other essay. Additionally, if the pecking order of English academic journals means anything, "The Technology of Narrative" is noteworthy as the first essay on Doctorow published in *PMLA* (January 1985).

Such distinctions aside, Harpham's essay deserves a special place in the reception of Doctorow because it moves the discussion of his work into a set of clearly poststructuralist concerns. First, he shifts the debate over history and politics in *Ragtime* and *The Book of Daniel* to an emphasis on narrative technique itself, which Harpham claims is the "central continuing concern" of those two novels as well as *Loon Lake*. Such an assertion is not new, of course; several previous critics had mentioned Doctorow's innovative and challenging style. In addition to Arthur Saltzman's emphasis on self-reflexivity, Barbara Cooper had argued for Doctorow's attempts to find the proper narrative perspective, raising the issue of the connection of self to narrative technique. By performing a close reading of imagery as related to narrative theory, however, Harpham makes fiction itself the subject of fiction, akin to the preoccupation with language in deconstruction.

As Harpham announces at the outset, "issues of narrative technique interpenetrate and constitute the political, social, or historical subjects of narrative." Here shows the influence of Hayden White, one acknowledged by Harpham, who borrows White's concept of "narrativity" to discuss how the issue of authority in narrative becomes an issue of political authority. At stake is control over the past. Despite its sanction by the ruling powers, history can only pretend to deliver the past authoritatively; what we have instead are versions of the past. Harpham cites Doctorow's own gloss on this idea from "False Documents": "There is only narrative." Then in his discussion of *The Book of Daniel*, Harpham offers his own expression of this relativistic view: "narrativity takes precedence over referentiality." Adopting the jargon of poststructuralism as well as one of its chief insights, Harpham begins with the premise that reality is knowable only through texts. Thus the shift in which he takes part is actually not just from history to narrative, but, again drawing upon White, from political and cultural issues to epistemological ones. Narrative is, quite simply, how we know, or think we know.

Even more marked is Harpham's invocation of poststructuralism's most threatening claim, which he phrases thus: "there is no such thing as a uniquely human character . . . . The self is both the cause and effect of processes generally thought to be external to the self." The death of the subject had been heralded by Foucault and Lacan, of course, but the entire project of poststructuralism—to show that "there is nothing outside the text"—played with the stability and integrity of the human self. In a universe constructed by language, a "psychologized ego" seems irrelevant. Harpham does not acknowledge any one source outside Doctorow's work for his interpretation, but it obviously does not derive from traditional humanist scholarship.

To arrive at his conclusions, Harpham discusses each of three novels that "tell the same story": that of a boy seeking an alternative to a narrative imposed from without. In *The Book of Daniel* the master principle of narrative is electricity, in *Ragtime* it is the "process" of transformation, and in *Loon Lake* it is the computer. Each of these technologies, Harpham argues, represents external forces that "compose" the individual as well as provide analogues to the narrative process.

The first of these, electricity, is the most significant for Harpham. Daniel's fractured story builds to a recreation of his parents' electrocution, the event that changed his life forever. Along the way Doctorow's unstable narrator obsessively incorporates imagery related to electricity into his descriptions and analyses. In one respect, of course, Daniel associates the electric chair with the oppressive injustice perpetrated against Jewish socialists by a Babylon-like America. For Harpham, electricity moves beyond an image of authority to symbolize at one level the unifying elements of narrative—images that provide coherence—and at a deeper level the very desire that gives rise to narrative in the first place. Narrative derives from our need to find meaning, to make connections within the numbing particulars of sequence. Closure, however, although it masters flux, "deadens" reality in the same way as the current flowing through the bodies of the Isaacsons deadens them even as it proves their case against America. A completed circuit—a finished novel—reveals the forces flowing through humans, not any traditional idea of meaning as a full explanation of the human condition or personality.

When it comes to *Ragtime*, Harpham continues to explore the principle of narrativity's precedence over referentiality—this time as revealed in the anonymous "pedantic" voice that has elicited passionate praise or condemnation from the first reviews of the novel. Harpham's interpretation of the style offers a post-humanist retort to reviewer Richard Todd's fundamental criticism of the book. Because its themes and style suggest that a "human life" cannot "become a coherent narrative," *Ragtime* earns his disdain. On the contrary, for Harpham such a notion is near the center of Doctorow's achievement The book demonstrates the absence of meaning by showing endless process, which, like electricity in *The Book of Daniel*, permeates all supposedly fixed, safe places on the social and moral maps. Human life and history form a process of recomposition; thus the selves that are remade—Mother, Tateh—are successful, while those like Father, who hold to some ideal essence of self, are doomed to failure. Harpham calls the Boy a successful personage in the novel because he has gotten to be an older narrator who mixes facts and fantasy to both represent and "falsify" the ragtime era. Such falsification is legitimate, Harpham says, because the era was "never fully present to itself." There is no essence to the era, only parts left behind to be gathered up by our entrepreneurial Boy/author in his version of it. Harpham suggests that satisfaction depends on accepting the inevitable "serial construction" of self out of the technologies of a given epoch.

The central image of this process of composing and recomposing is the assembly line, suggesting as it does the ability to use interchangeable parts to build a product. In *Loon Lake*, Doctorow continues to explore anonymous style in the form of computerese, a technology akin to mythic presentation in its "bricolage," or reassembly of preexistent parts. Here Harpham relies on Lévi-Strauss's characterization of myth. Consistent with his structuralist project, Lévi-Strauss analyzes myth as a language of constituent parts, or mythemes, which produce meaning in their ever-changing "bundles" or recombinations through the ages. Upon this foundation, Lévi-Strauss could exclude individual creativity from his analysis; meaning is relational, a product of a system and not of the artist. The sum total of bricolage creates whatever coherence any myth may have within a culture.

In *The Savage Mind*, from which Harpham quotes, Lévi-Strauss identifies this "bricolage" as improvised analogies between culture and nature that are a property of all human response: "mental structures which facilitate an understanding of the world in as much as they resemble it." A savage might represent himself in terms of a bear because that correspondence—between a human being existing in culture and an animal dwelling in nature—gives meaning to his place in the environment. Harpham tries to extend Lévi-Strauss's theory to more formal narration by showing how major images drawn from the fictional world constitute the very structure of Doctorow's narrative. The computer in *Loon Lake* serves to "detach" the narrative from any single narrator and place it in the realm of bricolage. Further, the computer becomes a symbol of structural forces in the modern environment that "dissolve" human character itself, in a unique fulfillment of Lévi-Strauss's call for structuralist anthropology to exchange focus on the individual for a study of the systems which produce our sense of individuality.

By raising the specter of a socially or linguistically produced self, Harpham opens himself to the charge of determinism. As Vincent Leitch points out, Lacan, Foucault and other poststructuralists who argue for the "death of the subject" have much in common with Marxism and psychoanalysis, the two major deterministic systems of thought in the century. But Harpham sees this emphasis in Doctorow as a liberation of the self "from the restrictions of the ego." *Loon Lake* especially demonstrates for Harpham that although identity may be corrupted by unwanted presences—

social forces producing recurrent types—it also may be redeemable by self-invention or production. Under the threat of imprisonment, Joe reinvents himself as the son of wealthy industrialist F. W. Bennett. On the other hand, evidence suggests that he is from the first a clone or fractioning off of Bennett, a product not of his own refashioning but of capitalism's "central myth," the self-made man. Again, the computer symbolizes the gray area between the two possible explanations of self—as production or reproduction. Whatever personal element contained in the novel is a product of impersonal force, but the "possibilities for self-invention" alive in *Loon Lake* reveal an enthusiasm for the process by which the self is made and the extent to which manipulation of social systems is possible. Despite this note of adventure, Harpham cannot quite escape the determinism sounded by Stephen Greenblatt, who finds that self-creation inevitably inter-twines with cultural impositions on the self, so that no such things as "pure, unfettered subjectivity" can exist. Greenblatt concludes his landmark Rennaissance Self-Fashionings by wondering if the self is not "the ideological product of the relations of power in a particular society;" Harpham's fine essay seems to confirm that suspicion.

As a result of the importance attached to the self as a site of power and knowledge, Harpham sees a progression in Doctorow's work away from political themes to what he calls "epistemological intrigues." Whether he is right or not, his essay demonstrates the movement of literary theory and criticism in the direction of such intrigues. In his thesis, language, and sources, Harpham represents the dominance that was achieved by post-structuralism approaches by mid-decade.

The early 1980s proved to be a fruitful period for Doctorow's studies. A variety of critical approaches were used to examine not only *Ragtime* but the earliest and latest novels in his growing body of work. Half a decade can hardly reveal any major or permanent pattern in the criticism, but these five years do show the continuing rise of poststructuralists theory. Using 1985 as an artificial but convenient dividing line for a clear change in the terms of the debate, we can now return to the reception of Doctorow's as historical novelist.

MATTHEW A. HENRY

Problematized Narratives: History as Fiction in E. L. Doctorow's Billy Bathgate

E. L. Doctorow has made a career out of historical fiction, and he is renowned for both examining and rewriting the American past, most notably in the novel *Ragtime*. Such rewritings of history are possible because for Doctorow there is no fact or fiction, only narrative. That "textualist" stance, however, does not imply that Doctorow's approach to historical writing is necessarily anarchic. He is neither a radical experimentalist nor a traditional social realist, though his works contain features of both. As a historical novelist, Doctorow is concerned foremost with the cultural myths of the immediate past and their role in contemporary American culture. Where Doctorow differs from traditional historical novelists—and takes a postmodern approach to history—is in the intentional confusion he sets up between documented historical events ("facts") and invented ones ("fictions"), thereby problematizing the process of historical writing. For Doctorow, the value of documentary forms of history comes under serious scrutiny, and "truth" becomes a relative term. In each of his novels, Doctorow admirably exploits the "dark areas" of history, offering interpretations of the past which, although not denied by the historical record, jar our assumptions and undercut our trust in the "official" record. Doctorow is thus able to investigate history through fiction and arrive at a version of the past that, at least for him, rivals the one available from largely

From *Critique* 39, no. 1 (Fall 1997): 32-40. Published by Heldref Publications.

unreliable documentation, i.e., the media. Doctorow employs that technique in virtually all his works, but it is perhaps best represented in *Billy Bathgate*.

In the essay "False Documents," Doctorow succinctly states the philosophy that underlies his work as a novelist and gives foundation to *Billy Bathgate*: "I am thus led to the proposition that there is no fiction or non-fiction as we commonly understand the distinction: there is only narrative." For Doctorow, history and fiction are nearly inseparable narrative forms—no neat dividing line may be designated between the texts of history and literature, so the author is free to draw upon both. The writer is, therefore, privileged in his view because "alone among the arts, literature confuses fact and fiction."

The acceptance of such confusion in historical writing is, however, a relatively recent development. In the traditional historical narrative, history has a privileged place because it is believed to be fundamentally linear, coherent, and verifiable. For Doctorow, the relationship between fiction and history is a complex one of interaction and mutual implication. In his view, postmodern historical fiction works to situate itself within historical discourse without surrendering its autonomy as fiction. Thus, the intertexts of history and fiction take on parallel—though not equal—status in the parodic reworking of the textual past. The past is textual because history, like fiction, is a product of culture, a belief Doctorow highlights in "False Documents":

> History is a kind of fiction in which we live and hope to survive, and fiction is a kind of speculative history, perhaps a superhistory, by which the available data for the composition is seen to be greater and more various in its sources than the historian supposes.

Doctorow understands history as a construct of the willful or unconscious imagination. Therefore, he subordinates historical accuracy to accommodate the demands of his fiction. Thus, in postmodern historical narrative, the writer need not adhere as strictly to the realm of plausibility. An event so audaciously invented as the trip of Freud and Jung through the Tunnel of Love in Doctorow's most celebrated novel, *Ragtime*, is clearly a violation of the canon of historical decorum, a blatant fiction that poses as history. But Doctorow utilizes the reader's knowledge that those historical figures existed to challenge the reader's preconceived notions about the validity of what has been too readily named historical "truth."

Billy Bathgate is, nevertheless, an example of a relatively restrained approach toward history in postmodern historical fiction. In the novel,

Doctorow only fictionalizes history to a limited degree, elaborating upon those areas where the historical record is vague or lacking. But he also intentionally blurs the boundary between factual and fictional events. The essential difference, then, between *Billy Bathgate* and the more traditional historical novel, which respected historical "truth," lies in Doctorow's rejection of an accepted, documented history and his self-conscious manipulation of the historical record.

As a postmodern historical novelist, Doctorow thus avoids the paradox that places the traditional historical novelist in the precarious position of favoring either historical consensus or imaginative reinterpretation. Doctorow succeeds in favoring both; his novels are filled with historical circumstances and personages fleshed out to meet the standards of his fiction and facilitate his interrogation, and subsequent rewriting, of the past. It is clear that, at least in Doctorow's hands, no historical narrative can escape reshaping the past in the light of present issues, and this interpretive process is precisely what postmodern historical fiction is calling to our attention.

Those concerns with the subjective bases of both historical and fictional "truths" are the foundation of *Billy Bathgate*. The novel recounts a fifteen-year-old boy's rather meteoric rise from poverty, through the portentous underworld of organized crime during the 1930s, to a status, we infer, of wealth and prestige in conventional business. As in previous works, Doctorow has blurred the admittedly elusive distinctions between history and fiction, blending the story of his fictional character Billy with that of a historically verifiable one, Arthur Flegenheimer, alias Dutch Schultz. What we receive in *Billy Bathgate* is a fictionalized reshaping of the past, one that makes central what has been historically marginalized—the role of Billy in the Dutch Schultz saga.

It is evident that Doctorow did a great deal of research for this novel, for many of the events are historically verifiable. Following the traditional techniques of historical fiction, Doctorow establishes early in the novel both the time period (the 1930s) and the locale (New York City). The historical aspect of *Billy Bathgate* is dense, comprised of "real" characters like Dutch Schultz and of the phenomenon of organized crime during Prohibition. But Doctorow self-consciously manipulates many of the circumstances, violating the historical accuracy he has been so careful to establish. In "False Documents," Doctorow defends that post-modern prerogative by averring that the themes of a real character's life are worked out publicly; they are media figures who have "invented themselves." People like Dutch Schultz have "made themselves into fictions" already; therefore, Doctorow claims, the writer may write fiction about them. That is evident in *Billy Bathgate* in the contrast Doctorow establishes between the myth surrounding mob figures such as Dutch Schultz, especially as created in the newspapers, and the realities as Doctorow himself sees them: the reader is privileged to see Schultz fictionalized by the media into someone Doctorow repeatedly shows us he is not.

In *Billy Bathgate*, Doctorow manipulates historical events for his own fictional purposes, causing us to question what we know to be, what we assume to be, and what might possibly be. For example, the novel opens with Billy's recounting of the circumstances surrounding the mysterious disappearance of Schultz's real-life crony Bo Weinberg. It was widely rumored at the time that Weinberg found his way to the bottom of the sea, via cement shoes, at the hands of Schultz himself, a proposition that fits in well with the myth of organized crime. However, the event is trivial in the historical record. Doctorow foregrounds what has been historically marginalized by vividly displaying the rumor as truth in a rather cinematic and fast-paced opening scene. Doctorow gives details that are unavailable in the historical record and capitalizes on the uncertainties surrounding Bo Weinberg's death, thus offering answers that history has not and cannot provide. The uncertainty about truth is then paralleled and complemented by Billy's uncertain emotional reaction to the murder.

Although Billy's assistance in the death of Bo Weinberg is his first serious initiation into the rackets, we soon learn in a protracted flashback that juggling originally helped him to ingratiate himself into the Schultz gang and win the approval of Dutch Schultz. Billy is a loner, a self-made orphan who lives a separate and individual life. What separates him further is his uncanny ability as a juggler, a talent that may be viewed as a metaphor for the construction of the self. One momentous day, Billy is performing for his friends, believing he was "not only the juggler but the only one to appreciate what the juggler was doing." Schultz also sees and appreciates Billy's performance, and with the pronouncement that Billy is "a capable boy" hands him a crisp ten-dollar bill. That small act of generosity convinces Billy that whatever happens in his life from that point forward will involve Dutch Schultz, a belief that sets in motion the chain of events that form this narrative.

Juggling is used, however, as more than just a mere device for bringing together the fictional and historical elements in *Billy Bathgate*: Doctorow transforms the act into a significant motif throughout the novel. We see Billy in the overt act of juggling only in the scene just described, which functions to explain Schultz's initial attraction to Billy. As the novel progresses, we see Billy in the covert and continual act of juggling his own fate, for his status in the Schultz gang is uncertain throughout. Billy is forever questioning his role and each of his actions, realizing, as in juggling itself, that the slightest of errors would irrevocably alter everything: "All I had to remember was how small a mistake was sufficient to change my fortune, maybe even without my knowing it."

In creating *Billy Bathgate*, Doctorow himself may also be seen as a juggler, an artist juggling the past and the present, the fictive and the real. And in doing so, Doctorow makes Billy central to the narrative. The events of Billy's life are what come to concern us the most; Dutch Schultz and his activities are in large part peripheral, and what we do see of Schultz is always filtered through Billy as narrator. Doctorow is concerned, we must remember, with exposing Dutch Schultz from the "inside" through a partially innocent perspective. Creating Billy is his method of accomplishing that goal. Doctorow's own characteristically postmodern act of juggling thus allows the fictional to displace the historical in *Billy Bathgate*.

That displacement is evident from the start. Billy quickly inserts himself into the Schultz gang through a combination of skill and luck, and in the process we see many of the historical elements emphasized. Doctorow is able to further his incorporation of the past by including such "real-life" characters as Schultz's right-hand man, Irving, and his burly bodyguard, Lulu Rosenkrantz. However, the subsequent tutelage of the fictional character Billy makes up the larger portion of the novel. From Irving and Lulu, Billy learns the fundamentals of being a gangster, including the use of a gun. For the reader, Irving and Lulu represent the common denominator and the violent aspects of organized crime.

Even more influential in Billy's life, perhaps more so than Schultz himself, is Schultz's financial wizard Otto "Abadabba" Berman, a man who "lived and dreamed numbers." Otto stands as a complement to Schultz, Irving, and Lulu, representing the intellectual rather than the physical aspects of organized crime. Otto is, above all, a business man, one who desires, in true capitalist fashion, to continually make money. However, it is not avarice that drives Otto but control, the manipulation of numbers; money itself becomes for him merely a series of numbers to be calculated. Thus, it is from Otto that Billy learns the value and necessity of business savvy.

In essence, though, Doctorow has shaped Otto and Schultz as two halves of a whole: together they make for Billy the complete criminal. Initially, Billy believes that the unpredictably violent nature of Schultz is what gives organized crime its power; without it, the system would fail. However, before long Billy questions his beliefs, and by the novel's end he realizes that Schultz's methods are outdated and must be combined with Otto's business sense and social acumen, particularly as America moves past the prohibition era. Thus, from Otto, Billy also receives the most significant lessons, in not only gang decorum but life itself.

Doctorow intensifies his study of Billy's coming-of-age with a powerful lesson in love from the novel's femme fatal, Drew Preston, one-time girl friend of Bo Weinberg and present moll of Dutch Schultz. Forced together under the pretense of governess and ward. Drew and Billy spend much time together. When they are sent to Saratoga, so as not to complicate Schultz's upcoming trial, their love finally reaches fruition. In a wonderfully hedonistic scene that speaks to both the animality of man and the sexual act, Doctorow has Billy and Drew make love in the foul-smelling mud and scum of a country pond, a merger of the "real" and "imaginary" in its fullest sense.

With this illicit love affair, Doctorow places a further tension in the dance between history and fiction. Billy knows that his feelings complicate matters and that his relationship with Drew is a betrayal of his mentor; and he knows the possible consequences. Even so, Billy is insightful enough to see that the change of situation has a parallel in Schultz's underworld, where things rapidly are changing for the worse. Billy is also intuitive enough to understand the true cause of such disloyalties:

> Dutch Schultz . . . brought betrayers forth from his nature, each in our own manner shape and size but having the common face of betrayal, and then he went murdering after us. Not that I didn't know, not that I didn't know. I took the elevator each night to the Schultz family dinner table and sat there aching in love or terror, it was hard to tell which.

The terror sinks in for Billy when he is callously used to help cover up Schultz's impulsive and malicious murder of a visiting New York restauranteur, Julian Martin. Brought into the room after Martin has been shot, Billy is confronted with the gasping and bleeding body slumped over the coffee table. After first finding the spent shell, Billy is given a nose-breaking punch from Lulu and then positioned so that his blood mixes with Martin's on the stained carpet. That moment may be Billy's true initiation into the lifestyle of these men, but it is also a moment of revelation: that sort of gratuitous violence shocks Billy; it is something he cannot seem to come to terms with or rationalize. Billy, therefore, remains separate from Schultz's gang even though he is an integral part of it.

In detailing the exploits of the Schultz gang in *Billy Bathgate*, Doctorow uses the information available in newspapers and other forms of documented history with remarkable creativity. In the summer and fall of 1935, *The New York Times* made prolific use of news about Dutch Schultz: the paper reported on his racketeering, his court appearances for tax evasion, his purported criminal connections, and of course his death. That material gives

Doctorow a historical foundation from which to build his fiction. One of Doctorow's more creative uses of the "factual" past in the novel is his elaboration on Schultz's trial upstate in Onondaga. Doctorow allows us to see much that recorded history does not reflect, including the possible reasons behind Schultz's eventual acquittal.

Schultz wanted his trial in a place where he was unknown and would be assured of success. Aside from the events of the trial itself, however, the documented history provides very little information about his activities in Onondaga. Schultz's acquittal, then, came as a surprise to many at the time, including the presiding judge, who apparently expressed dismay over the jury's having "reached a verdict based not on the evidence but on some other reason." Doctorow acknowledges the significance of that remark and intensifies it in his narrative. His judge was somewhat more rancorous:

> "Ladies and gentlemen, in all my years on the bench I have never witnessed such disdain of truth and evidence as you have manifested this day. That you could on hearing the meticulous case presented by the United States Government find the defendant not guilty on all charges so staggers the faith in the judicial process that I can only wonder about the future of this Republic. You are dismissed with no thanks from the court for your service. You are a disgrace."

For the reader of *Billy Bathgate* the verdict is less inexplicable, not a surprise at all; infact, it seems, quite expected. In Doctorow's account, we have been privileged to observe previous circumstances and to see Schultz's ongoing and willful subversion of each juror's impartiality. From the moment he arrives in Onondaga, Schultz plays upon the emotions of the town's members and establishes himself as a good Samaritan. He deposits a large sum of money in the bank, enrolls Billy in bible school, visits local hospitals, recovers foreclosed mortgages, and, most effectively, returns people's farms for free. It is likely Schultz's magnanimous gestures are fictionalized, but they fit into the historical framework as precisely as the pieces of a jigsaw puzzle. Thus, Doctorow provides answers to the "why" and "how" questions that were likely prevalent at that historical juncture, giving us the underside of newspaper-documented "truth" and, in large part, explaining the historical record.

In connection with Schultz's trial, Doctorow also self-consciously creates a situation that underscores the centrality of history in *Billy Bathgate* and reflects upon the underlying structure of the novel. Having no responsibility, and being unnecessary in Onondaga during Schultz's trial,

Billy is sent back to New York City. While there, he keeps himself abreast of the events of the trial by reading the local newspapers. His actions are interesting in that they mirror our own method of both knowing and understanding not only the past but also the present. We rely upon documents for our knowledge of history. However, as Doctorow here shows, only the surface is reported; the "reality" behind the events, as supplied by Billy, is missing. Through Billy, Doctorow has been able to offer the reader truths unavailable elsewhere, thus reaffirming his position that history is a brand of fiction. But Doctorow now places Billy in the position of having to perceive history as everyone else does, not by personal association with Dutch Schultz. The choice is both self-conscious and bold, for in doing so Doctorow removes from the historical context the fictional voice that has elucidated that history from the onset. The choice is also significant because it highlights the inability of documentation to fully relate history, past or present.

Doctorow has created Billy as a character who is more attuned to the notion that history is manipulated, and that characteristic is emphasized repeatedly in the novel. For example, just prior to leaving for Onondaga, Schultz impulsively murders one of his rivals in a New York barber shop. When Billy mentions the newspaper headline about it, "GRISLY GANGLAND MURDER," Schultz responds: "There wasn't nothing grisly about it. That was newspaper bullshit . . . it was as beautiful and professional as could be." Somewhat later, Billy philosophizes that news reporters are opinion-shapers, "composing for you the sights you would see and the opinions you would have . . . like magicians whose tricks were words." And when Billy returns to his neighborhood in the Bronx, he sees that people's perception of him is altered, shaped in large part by what has been reported in the local newspapers: ". . . I realized that wherever I had been, whatever I had done, the people knew about it not in its detail but in its fulfillment of their myth-knowledge of the rackets."

Central to *Billy Bathgate* is the myth-knowledge that the general populace has of organized crime, especially its accompanying violence. To convey that sense, Doctorow uses very detailed descriptions to create vivid and striking images, as evident in the climactic scene relating the slaughter of Dutch Schultz and his men. The scene is filled with the sort of incidental detail that may be found in media accounts of the event. One article on the shooting related not only the facts—that Arthur Flegenheimer and three companions were "felled" by gangland bullets at the Palace Chop House and Tavern on October 23, 1935—but also minutely detailed descriptions of the place itself. Those particulars all find their way into Doctorow's narrative.

More significantly, however, Doctorow undercuts the inevitable violence by embracing it and having it filtered through the lens of his protagonist, Billy, who is immersed in—and at the same time repulsed by—the violence he must narrate. Doctorow shapes this final scene to be both antimythic and anticlimactic: his fictionalization of historical particulars shatters the media's "factual," yet exaggeratedly heroic and violent, portrait of gangland activities in the 1930s and places the focus upon the fictional, upon Billy. Moreover, the scene is antimelodramatic. Instead of being an ending, it is a hook that leads us along with Billy into the future, where organized crime has been transformed into big business. Once again, we see fiction giving us truths that history cannot.

Billy Bathgate ends in a similar fashion. We see Billy escape the fate of his mentors; he lives to recover both the monies on hand and—after analyzing Dutch Schultz's death-bed ramblings—those hidden in numerous city stashes. According to history, the Schultz "fortune" was never found; according to Doctorow, Billy got it all. In short, Billy becomes the fictional answer to the historical mystery, and Doctorow's fictionalization of history once again allows him to successfully rewrite the past.

Doctorow's use of history in *Billy Bathgate* is impressive in both its accuracy of detail and its faithfulness to original sources. By this I do not mean an adherence to documented "fact" but rather an unassuming fictionalized re-creation and transformation of history itself. What we receive in this novel is a fictional reshaping, dependent largely on verisimilitude, of the historical "media story" of Dutch Schultz. *Billy Bathgate*, therefore, reveals our understanding of the past to be nothing more than a media fiction. Doctorow undercuts that misrepresentation by fictionalizing history and emphasizing that Billy's education is also one in which he learns how to make his own life a fiction. We are left to believe that Billy has used the lessons of his experience with Dutch Schultz to questionable ends and has transformed not only himself but the era in which he came of age into the present. Business, like crime, is for Billy simply a new arena in which to juggle and reap financial reward.

Although Doctorow's work is marked by a realism not found in the writings of many postmodern novelists, that does not negate his place as a significant writer of postmodern historical fiction. Although he is less jocular and ironic than others, and certainly less radical and shocking, his successful combination of fact and fiction accentuates our preconceptions about both literature and history, forcing us to examine each and question old verities. That questioning is central, for it differentiates the traditional historical narrative from the postmodern: the former uses accepted history fleshed out with imagination, whereas the latter is interrogating and rewriting the accepted past through a dialectic of history and fiction. It is precisely that blurring of fact and fiction that gives postmodern historical novels their vitality.

It is fairly easy to dismiss the complexities involved in fictionalizing history by claiming that it is the process of an artist "inventing" reality, and then asserting that documented history is not at issue; it is, however, naive to do so. The documented past is precisely what is at issue in the work of postmodern historical novelists. Doctorow's statement that "there is only narrative" attests to that. The issue of historical "truth" becomes central, and the postmodern historical novel forces us to consider the nature of that truth and the means for arriving at it.

MICHELLE M. TOKARCZYK

Postmodernism Reconsidered on an Urban Landscape: The Waterworks

Even more than *Billy Bathgate*, *The Waterworks* has been called an allegory of the Reagan era. Both works deal with the nature of greed and depict societies in which there is little community; rather, a Darwinian ethos of survival of the fittest prevails. Yet *The Waterworks* might as easily be seen as an extension of, or even an answer to, themes in *Welcome to Hard Times*. If *Welcome to Hard Times* is at heart a city novel championing the values of civilization against the savage energies of the countryside, *The Waterworks* is a quintessential city novel exploring the sensibility of an urban environment specifically during the beginning of the Gilded Age. Roy Lubove has argued that the urban slum problems had their origins in the same values that guided western land development, the values of greed, self-centeredness, and rabid individualism depicted in *Welcome to Hard Times* and railed against in "A Gangsterdom of the Spirit." While *Welcome to Hard Times* is set against the harsh, empty plains, *The Waterworks* is filled with descriptions of the dense urban architecture and population. New York City and the Gilded Age (the latter part of which is depicted in *Ragtime*) represent intensified, exaggerated versions of the United States. The metaphor operating in *Billy Bathgate* is a gangsterdom of the spirit attributable especially to the Wall Street barons and speculators of the 1980s; the metaphor of *The Waterworks* is a collusion among science, government, and wealth.

From *E. L. Doctorow's Skeptical Commitment*. ©2000 by Peter Lang Publishing.

The echoes of Hawthorne (the treatment of science, nuptial ending, fantastic elements) particularly bring to mind the American romance novel and its political orientation. Again, as we see in *Ragtime*, "The confrontation of the hopes of romance with the actualities of realism runs throughout political fiction. It is a pattern that arises from the nature of political engagement. The formal polarities arise from the situation, the politics, the character choices." In *The Waterworks* the harsh urban scenes and historical veracity of Boss Tweed's corrupt power constitute realistic actualities; the nuptial ending and demise of Sartorius, the hopes of romance. Doctorow is thus able to use the romance genre, as he did in *Ragtime*, to suggest the depth of social problems and, in *The Waterworks*, the possibility of change. Harter and Thompson argue that both *Welcome to Hard Times* and *Ragtime* enact fables of the repeated undoing of hope; depending on how the ending is read, we might see *The Book of Daniel* as enacting the same fable. *The Waterworks*, in contrast, can be interpreted as enacting a fable of hope, a story of battle against evil in which, unlike in *Welcome to Hard Times*, the "good guys" win. Considering Edmund Donne and McIlvaine's relentless search for Martin Pemberton and the truth about his father, Augustus Pemberton, the novel could be read as a detective novel in which, as is typical of the genre, law and order prevail. Ultimately, *The Waterworks* fulfills the promise of Doctorow's midfiction brand of postmodernism.

According to Alan Wilde in "Strange Displacements": "Midfiction seeks to affirm in the face of the void, although its assent is 'local, limited, and temporary.' In other words it seeks positive knowledge . . . without ever losing sight of the fact that knowledge in any absolute sense . . . is completely out of reach." In *The Waterworks* positive knowledge is discovered and utilized to end evil deeds, thus suggesting the possibility of praxis. The novel might be read as enacting an agency advocated by some cultural critics. New historical critics have argued that poststructuralism is of limited use to those who need not only to deconstruct discredited histories, but also to construct new histories in which they are represented. *The Waterworks* is an imaginative reconstruction of history that restores forgotten voices and suggests positive change is possible. Unlike any other Doctorow novel, in *The Waterworks* an evil collusion is dissected and broken; unlike any other Doctorow novel, a way beyond the impasse of postmodern indeterminacy is suggested.

Indeed, the sense of *The Waterworks* is close to Appleby et al.'s consideration of postmodernism, which finally insists, "upon the human capacity to discriminate between false and faithful representations of past reality and beyond that to articulate standards which help both practitioners and readers to make such discriminations." While the novel does not articulate standards for determining truth, it certainly delineates the characteristics of "villainy." Sartorius represents a radical disruption of the categories of life and death, although these categories are continually reinscribed by the policeman Edmund Donne, who is described as bringing order to chaos, and by the narrator's own discoveries. As McIlvaine explains it, "There are moments in our lives that are something like breaks or tears in moral consciousness, as caesuras break the chanted line, and the eye sees through the breach to a companion life, a life in all its aspects the same, running along parallel in time, but within a universe even more confounding than our own. It is this disordered existence . . . that our ministers warn against . . . that our dreams perceive." Such a state has been described by Hannah Arendt as the banality of evil: the sense that evil people often, like Sartorius, appear to be respectable, but violate society's norms of human decency and respect for life.

As does most of Doctorow's fiction, *The Waterworks* insists upon the importance of community through numerous suggestions that human lives and actions are interrelated. One of the central symbols of the novel is the newspaper as it was laid out during this period. Each of the major news stories occupied one of the seven columns and each story ran beside the others. Symbolically, these stories juxtaposed with one another suggest that ". . . the sense is not in the linear column but in all of them joined together." McIlvaine sees a symbolic importance in this layout, ". . . as if our stories were projections of the multiple souls of a man . . . and no meaning was possible from any one column without the sense of all of them in . . . simultaneous descent . . . ." In promising that the columns will ultimately be joined together, McIlvaine is first promising to put relevant stories in context and secondly suggesting that individual lives and occurrences are in fact more related than many of us imagine, a suggestion reinforced by the name of the investigating officer Donne, evoking John Donne's poem "For Whom the Bell Tolls," "ask not for whom the bell tolls/It tolls for thee." The double weddings of Sarah Pemberton and Edmund Donne, Emily Tisdale and Martin Pemberton, underscore how interconnected these lives have been. The fates of the exploited urchins represent those of all helpless residents for whom citizens should care. As one critic argues, the horror of Sartorius's experiments is in the extent to which they break ". . . the moral consciousness itself, revealing the darkness and chaos of a universe that negates the understanding and faith of the human bond."

While *The Waterworks*' themes and plot signal a move toward determinacy, its experimental prose is characteristically postmodern. Stylistically, one of the novel's most striking features is the number of ellipses. Grimshaw's lines relating his conversation with Martin are typical:

"Yes. You know I have learned over the years . . . about souls in need of pastoring . . . how they often bristle, or present a superior attitude." The use of ellipses and sometimes dashes has the effect of reproducing the sense of oral speech. Perhaps more important, it, like the novel's relatively long, often complex sentences, slows down the pace of an urban detective novel in much the same way as the thick descriptions of jungle landscape slow down *Heart of Darkness*, ensuring that readers take the necessary time to ponder the tale's meaning. And finally, they moderate the certainty of the tale's moral by underscoring the incompleteness of memory, leaving readers to ponder an alternate tale left out in the elliptical spaces.

As in much of Doctorow's work, the story is conveyed by a narrator who struggles to render a horrible truth he has experienced. In this struggle, Doctorow suggested in conversation, McIlvaine is similar to Marlow in *Heart of Darkness*. Again, as did Blue and Daniel, McIlvaine represents the historical process itself. In this respect, McIlvaine's account may be interpreted as "recomposing" (in Doctorow's vocabulary) a part of the American political consciousness: the collusion of powerful figures and institutions.

The novel's efforts to involve the reader in constructing and understanding the city are suggested in McIlvaine's recollections: "I'm reporting what are now the visions of an old man. All together they compose a city, a great port and industrial city of the nineteenth century. I descend to this city and find the people I have come to know and for whose lives I fear. I tell you what I see and hear. The people of this city think of it as New York, but you may think otherwise. You may think it stands to your New York today as some panoramic negative print, inverted in its lights and shadows . . . a companion city of the other side." As did Blue in *Welcome to Hard Times*, McIlvaine writes with a consciousness of future readers' ability to shape the past with their image of the present, and with a hope that they will learn from his lessons. The image of the inverted panoramic negative recalls the mirror image in *Billy Bathgate* and thus suggests the artist's role. McIlvaine's decision not to publish his story implies that by the time he has seen Sartorius defeated, McIlvaine is no longer interested in personal glory, but in community welfare, the kind of community welfare Blue consistently tried but failed to promote, the community welfare for which Jonathan yearns.

Reviewers have noted that *The Waterworks* is a prototypical city novel, that in fact the city is a major character. Set in New York in the decade after the Civil War, the novel depicts a period in American history that is important to understanding the development of urban areas and their relationship to the American dream. At one point the narrator of *The Waterworks* states that he ignored the great story of the westward push to write about New York. Yet no less startling than the frontier's settlement was the rapid push toward urbanization in the late nineteenth century. The 1870s were associated with accelerated industrialization as well as with westward expansion. In 1860 only nine U.S. cities had populations of 100,000 or more; by 1880 twenty cities did. Urban centers were important not only for their size but, as *Ragtime* suggests, for their relationship to America's promises. In his book on New York, O'Connell argues that though much of America's mythology revolves around rural landscapes, "the real test of American democracy would occur in the cities, in particular in New York City." He also asserts that New York City is both an intensification of the nation and its antithesis. With its large immigrant population dreaming of a better future, New York reflects the country's commitment to the ideal of individual potential to excel, "that the free expression of many individual wills can compose a great and unified nation." (The word "composed" is, of course, charged in Doctorow criticism, and *The Waterworks* itself is in many ways a study of the composition of individual enterprise in the city.)

If cities in general and New York in particular are where American ideals are tested, they are also where these ideals break down. Cities expose the myth of a classless society through divisions, one scholar argues. In essence, *The Waterworks* represents an urban equivalent of the western frontier evoked in *Welcome to Hard Times*—what Annette Kolodny refers to as a borderland of liminal landscapes on which distinct human cultures first encounter one another's otherness. While *Welcome to Hard Times* faintly suggests the clash of cultures between the Native American John Bear, immigrants such as Zar, and migrants from other sections of the United States, *Ragtime* evokes a city's multicultural landscape, and *The Waterworks* suggests the class conflicts between the Augustus Pembertons and the street urchins.

In addition to class differences, *The Waterworks* represents other ills of modern urban life such as overcrowding and impersonality, prompting one critic to call it a "gaslight romance" because it focuses on the dark side of the past. When McIlvaine ponders Martin's startling claim that he has seen his late father, McIlvaine interprets the words metaphorically to characterize the city that neither man could love nor bear to leave. Part of the city's attraction has often been attributed to its unparalleled energy, especially obvious in a boom time such as the 1870s. But much of this energy flows from the corrupt and/or opportunistic people who make money at the expense of others. In the decade following the Civil War there was in fact tremendous economic growth; many had acquired wealth in this war, and McIlvaine reports, in the postwar decade there was "nothing to stop progress," or the advent of modernity. Throughout I have argued that Doctorow has been critical of notions of progress, and in this novel the trappings of progress in reservoirs, aqueducts, tunnels etc. are inextricably bound with Sartorius's instruments of destruction, prompting one critic to speculate Doctorow is implying ". . . that progress is a slippery matter, that change does not move in a straight line." Ultimately, the question is what constitutes progress and at whose expense it is achieved.

In a short interview Doctorow remarked that in *The Waterworks* he was writing about the New Yorkers whom Edith Wharton left out, the ordinary people. These include those whom we would call the disenfranchised. As McIlvaine describes the city "falling into ruins, a society in name only," he mourns a lack of community. The narrator's sense of loss was likely shared with many of his contemporaries; as was stated in a previous chapter, a common and often explicit theme underlying the responses of writers and social critics in the nineteenth century is the estrangement of urban inhabitants from cities too rapidly growing and changing. One consequence of such rapid growth in a community is that it becomes unable to account for its members. To McIlvaine, the newspaper is itself an urban artifact; in villages a newspaper is unnecessary because people can see what happens and quickly relay events to one another. The anonymity of the city is further suggested in McIlvaine's failure to notice that Martin did not come into the office for several days, "In modern city life you can conceivably experience revelation and in the next moment go on to something else. Christ might come to New York and I would still have a paper to get out."

Swelling populations and densely-packed urban spaces, according to some critics, breed certain kinds of pathology. The notion of the spatial pathology of the city was first articulated in European romantic writing and later in the emerging social sciences and psychoanalysis. Georg Simmel, for one, in his "Metropolis and Mental Health" speculated that urban social relationships would be impersonal and that objective distance would replace subjective empathy. According to some psychologists, the impersonality and crowded conditions of the city caused modern maladies such as claustrophobia and agoraphobia. Feelings of claustrophobia can be detected in McIlvaine's reactions to Sartorius's environs; viewing the reservoir as "unnatural," McIlvaine is ready to "believe in every dark vision if it appeared [there]." The reservoir is further described as a windowless and gasless, resembling a hermetic undersea vault. In this world of water, McIlvaine feels oppressed, trapped, much as did the characters in the recent popular movie *Waterworld*, and in sharp contrast to the characters in *Lives of the Poets*: A Novella and Six Stories and *World's Fair*. *The Waterworks* transforms a life-giving, liberating image into a suffocating one.

Agoraphobia and claustrophobia were diseases primarily of the middle class in the nineteenth century, but *The Waterworks* represents maladies more commonly found among the unemployed and working classes in this period: "ambulatory automatism" (whose sufferers resembled the living dead) and hysterical amnesia. Sartorius disappears, seemingly forgetting who he is, and eventually becomes one of the necropholictics so well described by Simon Schama in his review. Similarly Martin appears to forget his own life in pursuit of his late father, and later is enthralled by Sartorius's operation. The text is filled with characters who are exaggerated, urbanized versions of Selig Mindish: those who attempt to deny their pasts and their mortality, in the process losing their class privilege, and end up among the living dead.

In the popular American imagination especially, the city has often been viewed as nature's antithesis, but *The Waterworks* calls this conception into question, depicting the city as, like nature, naturalistic and Darwinian. McIlvaine tells us, "I had always made a distinction what was nature and what was . . . City. But that was no longer tenable, was it? I longed to be back in my newsroom . . . not in this wild—I was not one for the wild." The wildness associated with the city and nature is a state without controls, such as strict deadlines, formulas for composing news stories and the like. Sartorius and the city in which he thrives may, in Doctorow's terms, be viewed as grotesques only if nature itself never indulged in excess or propagated itself at the expense of others. McIlvaine himself describes nature as resembling the city by being spendthrift enough to produce great wealth for itself.

The narrator identifies himself as the penultimate urban dweller, "a street rat in [his] soul." For himself and his city, he dreams of revival, suggested in the image of new skin sprouting that from the pipes, tunnels and other underground apparatus. Throughout the novel the hope/promise of redemption is repeated, most notably in the image of the Croton Holding Reservoir itself which, O'Connell argues, represents an ignored font of absolution as opposed to the Roman bath that comes to McIlvaine's mind upon entering Sartorius's premises.

Contrasting with the images of redemption are the daily acts of sin and corruption in the city. Indirectly, McIlvaine suggests evil in comparing the sense of foreboding he has at Martin's disappearance with that he had at President Lincoln's death, commenting the audience must trust that this death "like everything I tell you, has a bearing on the story." With Lincoln's murder, we may infer, the nation became vulnerable to carpet-baggers and profiteers similar to the Tweed ring in New York. Though Tweed is destroyed, the evil he represents still persists and intensifies during later "gilded ages." The narrator McIlvaine states that the inhabitants of New

York practiced excess in everything from pleasure to death, that vagrant children slept in alleys while self-satisfied novueau riche flaunted their wealth.

It is no accident that Sartorius's downfall coincides with Boss Tweed's, patron of the rich and corrupt. *The Waterworks* might be read as a parable of this boss's demise. One reviewer argues that Sartorius, though he has the trappings of villainy, is not truly evil. Instead, his scientific experiments function in the novel to put into relief two extremes of the New York population: the urchins and the wealthy, powerful men. The novel's narrator spares no words in describing Tweed's "manifestly murderous," acts claiming one could literally feel Tweed's force and comparing the man's hold on the city to a "vampire suck." Having held so much power, Tweed could not conceive of the ultimate loss of power, his own death. Rather, "The Ring, with their vaulting ambition, would carry ambition to its ultimate form," thus supporting Sartorius's research to ensure their own immortality. Hence, the relationship between Tweed and the novel's other villains is symbiotic. The narrator knows Augustus Pemberton was sustained by a culture; Tweed and his dignitaries in fact attended Augustus Pemberton's mock funeral. Sartorius freely admits that he chose his subjects not for virtue or intellect, but for their wealth, as they would endow his experiments. Though Tweed is a defining part of New York City at this time, his corruption is representative of corruption in general; when McIlvaine journeys from the city to Ravenwood he thinks of Tweed, juxtaposing him with the nation as a whole. The image of Tweed landing on Cuba, dreaming of the New York City where he believes immortality is now possible, represents the hubris of all the powerful men whom Sartorius courted.

The Darwinian essence of nature is personified in both Sartorius and his seeming victim, Augustus Pemberton. On the surface Augustus, a penniless immigrant who earned a small fortune and prominence among New York dignitaries, appears to be an American success story. Yet like so many Doctorow characters—Bennett from *Loon Lake*, Zar from *Welcome to Hard Times*, and Dutch Schultz from *Billy Bathgate*—Augustus has made his fortune at the expense of others' flesh, his "economic opportunity" is his capacity for ruthlessness. He not only sold shoddy equipment to Union soldiers (yet testified at the Senate Subcommittee on War Profiteering), but also likely participated in slave trading, even though slavery was abolished in New York in 1799. His indifference to and contempt for others extends to his own family, whom he views as equivalents to Ravenwood: monuments to himself rather than human beings. So despicable is Augustus that when Martin first claims that his father is still alive, McIlvaine thinks the dramatic man is speaking of "the persistence of evil in general."

Ultimately, Augustus Pemberton becomes a fool in Sartorius's hands. Sartorius himself is the novel's most formidable personage, embodying evil's complexity as well as villainy's tendency to "absent itself, even as it stands before you," that is to be evasive, hard to pinpoint or confront. In his interview with me Doctorow agreed that Sartorius's scientific hubris has much in common with characters of nineteenth-century American novelists such as Hawthorne and Poe. Yet there are more modern roots for the skepticism toward scientific experimentation exemplified in this novel. In their history of science, Appleby et al. note that the generation of the 1960s, born in the shadow of the Bomb, had a more cautious attitude toward science than did its predecessors. Primarily the younger generation asked new questions in an effort to understand how specific ideologies and interests affected science. Though not of the 1960s generation, Doctorow has in numerous essays commented on the pervasive if subtle effects nuclear weapons have had on the population as a whole and on writers specifically. In addition to the Bomb, Doctorow in conversation has mentioned modern controversies, around the use of science to alter life, particularly the Nazi experiments. While we might be tempted to see Sartorius as an unscrupulous villain, he could also conceivably be viewed as "inanely excessive," a grotesque scientist—and again here I refer to Doctorow's notion expressed in "A Gangsterdom of the Spirit" that a truth embraced fanatically often becomes a lie and/or a grotesque. Sartorius in carrying the ideals of his profession too far embodies this notion of the grotesque. His "noble lineaments of the grotesque" include innovative and successful operations during the Civil War, as well as his belief in the germ theory and even heart transplants on animals. The picture of Sartorius is one of mental brilliance and emotional impoverishment. He is like the criminals who are often the subjects of modern detective novels: completely unable to empathize and extremely arrogant. That Sartorius was indifferent to the laws of society is suggested not only in his blatant disregard of them, but also in more subtle antisocial gestures, such as his lack of affiliation with any professional organizations. In trying to explain how someone so socially removed could marshal support for his work, Martin speculates that rather than actively seek support, Sartorius simply accepts what the disciples who gather offer him, "It's as if . . . there's an alignment of historical energies magnetized around him which . . . for all I know, is probably all . . . that makes him visible." Here the word "visible" suggests making the work Sartorius imagines possible, and ironically, making it appear so that it can be discovered and stopped by McIlvaine and Donne.

In a pre-modern ideal model of science, there was presumably a relatively tight fit between nature and human knowledge of it. That is, the clear scientific mind would be transparent as it faced nature rather than driven by personal interest, ideology, or some irrational force. Such an ideal is another dimension of positivism, and though *The Waterworks* is more determinate than some earlier Doctorow fiction, the positivist ideal is nonetheless questioned through the novel's depletion of scientific experimentation. As McIlvaine tells us, in Sartorius the scientific temperament produced a man who was unshockable, one for whom there was no sacrilege.

Sartorius is, like many Doctorow characters, a Gatsbyesque creation. His name itself is the composition of a self-made man. *The Waterworks* tells us that in the Middle Ages members of the German bourgeoisie who wanted to elevate their status took Latin forms of their names, hence, tailor became Sartorius; one who merely altered existing garments became a creator. Throughout the novel the image of a guided boat in the reservoir recurs, and finally McIlvaine imagines this boat being guided by Sartorius, suggesting his evil hand controlling all. (The image of the controlled boat is particularly chilling given Sartorius's associations with slavery.)

At one point McIlvaine says that he is haunted "not by ghosts, but by Science," suggesting—especially with the capital "S'—that while Sartorius may be a grotesque he and his operations are terrifyingly characteristic of the discipline. Indeed, Sartorius, exploiter of orphans, tells the doctors examining him that he's no different from his colleagues in observing laws of selective adaptation. Martin Pemberton likewise describes Sartorius's home as filled with the "menacing furniture of science," an obverse Eden reminiscent of Rappaccini's garden where the scientist, not God, is a dangerous creator. This image is, as I have already suggested, perhaps more terrifying in the twentieth century than it was in the nineteenth because science and technology have more power to destroy.

As was Rappaccini, Sartorius is a respected scientist who had generally worked within the bounds of his discipline. His orphanage, The Home for Little Wanderers, is scientifically managed according to the latest principles of child-rearing. What is lacking in this technically superior environment is any concern for the children's well-being. It is thus somewhat ironic when McIlvaine describes the orphanage as an "outpost of advancing civilization . . . like all our institutions at the edge," indicating that the institution was part of what Doctorow might call the illusion of modernity, the sense that modern civilization fails to moderate nature's laws of survival of the fittest and meet human needs for community. Equally important, the men who approached Sartorius in the hopes of immortality are representatives of modern society, as McIlvaine says, hard-nosed realists turned "acolytes." Sartorius's brand of charisma is best represented in the astonishing conversion of Martin Pemberton, who rather than being outraged by the nature of Sartorius's experiments, actually works for him, describing Sartorius's mind as "a field of gravity, drawing him to me." In part, Martin is drawn in by the "aristocratic dominance" the scientist has over men who seemed impossible to dominate. Described as "recomposing" patients' lives, Sartorius behaves as an author who might recompose a literary character. The description of Sartorius swaddling his patients suggests he is infantilizing them, which he would have been unable to do had they not turned their lives over to him. Like a con man who chooses a mark by the person's vulnerability to extravagant promises, Sartorius plays upon the hubris of his victims, a desire to be immortalized perhaps especially prominent in the rich and famous. Their vulnerability is suggested by the frequent practice of having portraits created by artists such as Harry Wheelwright; Martin himself questioned who among the wealthy would refuse a portrait and "immortality." As Sartorius's subjects are recomposed, so too is Martin, for the intelligent investigative reporter denies the obvious evidence that children are being destroyed. Yet Martin's blindness to Sartorius is in a sense mirrored by the medical profession's unwillingness to fault the scientist because he was not *directly* responsible for the death of any child, suggesting the discipline's legalism which fails to acknowledge personal responsibility and to recognize the interrelationship of human lives.

Sartorius justifies his actions as consistent with contemporary science and even nature, claiming that nature is continuously profligate on its own behalf, immune to the agony of the species. In claiming that bodies have cycles and are subject to tides, he evokes the recurring image of the model boat in the water, here again suggesting he is a controlling creator. Equations between his work and natural processes are intensified in his statement that he is motivated by a search for truth about nature, which is reminiscent of nineteenth-century rationalizations such as Frederick Jackson Turner's that the displacement of Native American tribes was a result of natural forces. Sartorius's grotesque pursuit of scientific truth is then not a personal deformity but a symptom of social malaise. For this reason, McIlvaine and Grimshaw yearn to expose and purge it through a public trial, through a report in which the newspapers could provide the beginning of a "spiritual chastening," "That we would . . . drop to our knees and gather our children to us."

Evoking children is particularly significant since Sartorius's exploitation of them to perpetuate the lives of ailing old men evokes the theme of a society exploiting its children so aptly expressed in Doctorow's "An Open Letter to the President." Christopher Morris in *Models of Misrepresentation* notes that Doctorow frequently represents the writer as an orphan, but in *The Waterworks*, as in *Welcome to Hard Times*, the orphan characters are not creators at all, only vulnerable children. As Doctorow notes in his interview, in nineteenth-century New York there were "thirty to forty thousand vagrant children running around." The novel represents these children as the failures of modern life: vagrant children who had, like *Billy Bathgate*, lost their family names, something that would never happen in a village society. McIlvaine is familiar with one group of often-vagrant children, the "undersized" newsboys whose faces he describes as etched with "shadows of serfdom," and who frequently die young. The narrator's sympathy for children is established in his fondness for the young Noah; hence, we can easily understand this bachelor's distress at their treatment. Again, the governing metaphor of the boat sailing at sea is compared to the child who drowned in the reservoir. More important, in McIlvaine's dream vision the child is a miniature like the boat, indicating children are seen as miniature adults rather than as developing beings with special needs.

Another representation of failed nurturance, again typical of Doctorow's fiction, is in Augustus and Martin's severed father-son relationship, and in the extent to which the narrator and Sartorius both become father figures to the symbolically orphaned Martin Pemberton. Donne quickly perceives the gravity of the Pembertons' differences, referring to a profound derangement of fathers and sons. Such an analysis helps to explain Martin's failure to resist Sartorius. As Schama notes, Martin is motivated to unearth the truth about his father not by filial love, as is Daniel Isaacson, but by hatred. Martin Pemberton is, in fact, a foil to numerous myths about men and ancestry. According to Friedman, for example, "The missing father is the link to the past that, for the protagonist, determines identity." In contrast, McIlvaine says Martin had seen renouncing his father as gaining his own redemption. In forging his own identity, Martin rejects his father in every way, living by his wits rather than financial dealings, choosing a financially precarious life of a freelance, and even investigating his father as a Civil War profiteer. Yet Martin's renunciation of his father is no less problematic than Gatsby's reinvention of himself or Joe's rejection of his parents. It matters little whether Martin is motivated by love or hate; he is nonetheless driven to search for his father and is as altered by his discovery as Marlow in *Heart of Darkness* was.

Finding his father involved in such bizarre experiments is profoundly disturbing to the son who had viewed him as "merely a scoundrel and a thief and a murderer." And as in *The Book of Daniel*, a man who seemingly embodies evil has become a vacant shell, not even recognizing his son, his face devoid of any human character, his body mindlessly dancing at Sartorius's balls. Where we might expect the final break between father and son, a bond is forged: Martin comes to mimic his father's death-in-life state. Even after his rescue, Martin seems engrossed in a profound philosophic meditation that intrudes upon daily life, similar to Marlow in *Heart of Darkness* who after relating the story of Kurtz assumes a Buddha-like stance and otherworldly countenance. Martin, like Marlow, is altered, no longer the arrogant and often angry man he was before this episode, but rather someone who could speak of Sartorius "from some sort of peaceful resolution. . . ."

While Martin has rejected his biological father, he like Joe in *Loon Lake*, is given two surrogate fathers between whom to choose. Throughout the novel McIlvaine indicates that Martin belongs to a younger generation the narrator finds hard to understand. Part of Martin's recuperation involves his embracing McIlvaine after Sartorius has been defeated. However, his initial attraction to the scientist may be viewed as an Oedipal admiration for the man who is powerful enough to conquer his own father. In a sense Sartorius helped Martin to more completely reject his father by enabling the young man to see his father as only an impersonal subject for scientific experiments. When Martin himself is betrayed by Sartorius, he unlike Joe in *Loon Lake*, can renounce his evil surrogate parent and thus save his soul.

Despite the optimism inherent in Martin's choice and in the novel in general, Martin can never be completely released from the hold his father or Sartorius have had on him. Doctorow has said that one of the themes of *The Waterworks*, as in much of his other fiction, is the despair of being locked in history. Certainly throughout his fiction, especially in *The Book of Daniel* and *Welcome to Hard Times*, Doctorow has suggested that the burden of history cannot be negated. The narrator McIlvaine acknowledges this history in positing that perhaps the reason he never wrote the story was that it was part of Martin's patrimony, part of the young Pemberton's ongoing struggle toward resolution.

Martin's struggle, like the struggle against evil itself, is of course conveyed to us through McIlvaine's oral recounting of his memories. Like Doctorow's other narrators, McIlvaine is a somewhat detached figure highly engaged in the act of narration itself: "I'm reporting what are now the visions of an old man. All together they compose a city, a great port and industrial city of the nineteenth century. I descend to this city and find the people I have come to know and for whose lives I fear. I tell you what I see and hear." These words indicate the lifelong bachelor fits Sloterdijk's definition of the cynic as an urban figure who maintains a cutting edge in the goings-on of the metropolis. In reflecting on the writer's relation to his/her society, Budick states that writers do not/cannot break out of ideology, but may interpret or reformulate it by recasting it to make it explicit. That McIlvaine struggles for such an interpretation is suggested in the extent to which the story occupies him, "[has] grown into the physical dimensions of [his] brain." In explaining his attempt to find Martin Pemberton, he underplays any fatherly or collegial concern, admitting that he "smelled a story" and was propelled. His desire to uncover the story is similar to Blue's efforts to keep the ledgers; McIlvaine's motives are apparently positivist, glorifying primary documents and newspapers as evidence of a stable universe. Yet he is simultaneously aware of the limits of his epistemology; for example, he says, "I want to keep the chronology of things but at the same time to make their pattern sensible, which means disrupting the chronology." He understands the gaps between his understanding of Grimshaw's and Martin's accounts and his rendering of them, and fears that readers may dismiss his stories as an old man's delusions.

In these concerns, he is also very similar to Blue moving away from positivism. Though a lifetime reporter, he is skeptical about recent claims for reporters' objectivity, calling it "a way of constructing an opinion for the reader without letting him know you are." Significantly, he dreams of a story "the writing of which might transcend reporting," indicating his desire to become a novelist or memoirist who would bear witness or as he says to give voice to the events of his life and times. In the end, this is perhaps the story McIlvaine tells, one that conveys the importance of a historical event, but with the idiosyncrasies and gaps of an old man remembering and reflecting. Thus McIlvaine touches upon the idea that the novelist's world, unlike the historian's, is continually being created. The past has a "perpetual presentness" that is created in part by interpretation. It is this fictionalized story—one that is filled with interpretations of Sartorius and Tweed, but unlike *The Book of Daniel* , one in which the interpretations are quite clear—that McIlvaine wants to tell. But unlike the Romantic writer, he does not have complete control over the story. Rather, he believes the story must almost tell itself in its own time: "Possibly it can't be rationalized . . . but there is some instinct that prefers the unintruded-upon meaning. That whoever tells our moral history . . . must run behind, not ahead of it. That if, in fact, there is meaning, it is not tolled out of the church bells but suffered into luminous existence." Such words are echoed in Sartorius's prediction that McIlvaine will not be able to write the story until the distant future, when the city is ready to hear it. (This possibility, which is reinforced by McIlvaine's own comment that there are limits to the use of words in a paper, provides another possible explanation as to why McIlvaine never publishes his exclusive.)

Unlike *The Book of Daniel* and *Loon Lake*, which tease readers' desire for closure, *The Waterworks* concludes with a romance ending of two weddings on a day when it seems the city might be forever captured, postcard-like "encased and frozen, aglitter and God-stunned." The almost artificial peace of this moment underscores its illusory and temporary qualities, much as the number of ellipses moderates a sense of certainty that marks the end of this novel. Sartorius and Tweed have been vanquished, but evil has not been finally defeated, and Martin has not and probably never will again be the person he once was.

While the narrator McIlvaine is, as previously mentioned, someone whom we might expect to have cynical traits, he, unlike the modern cynic, does not refuse optimism when he learns from experience and does not withdraw into mournful detachment after gaining disturbing knowledge. Rather, he seems to see Sartorius's downfall as he does the dual weddings: a precious triumphant moment to be cherished. Because of its optimism, *The Waterworks* fulfills some of the goals of the new historicism as expressed by Frank Lentricchia in "Foucault's Legacy": it offers a vision of effective action to free us from a world in which we are forced to become what we do not wish to become. That is, the novel suggests an alternative to cynicism and alienation. Readers of this novel not only become aware of their complicity in their society's evil, but they become aware it is possible to act against evil. Although such action may not free people from being complicit, it may mitigate the wrongdoings of which we are often unwittingly a part. If we draw upon Alan Wilde's theory of postmodern midfiction, we can see that *The Waterworks* in particular and Doctorow's work in general often exemplifies a postmodern vision, "If, as I have several times suggested, the defining features of modernism is [sic] its ironic vision of disconnection and disjunction, postmodernism, more radical in its perceptions, derives instead from a vision of randomness, multiplicity, and contingency; in short, a world in need of mending is superseded by one beyond repair." But if the world is beyond repair, the community is not, and individual local actions are effective, if limited, against the powerful collusion of wealth, science, and government. In Foucauldian terms, *The Waterworks* is about truth and power; in their use of reportorial and police skills, Donne and McIlvaine produce truth that has the effect of producing power for agency. *The Waterworks*, like *The Book of Daniel*, has similarities to the detective novel, but while in *The Book of Daniel* the truth is "beyond reclamation," in *The Waterworks* a truth that has ramifications for many lives is discovered. Moreover, all truths are not equal. Sartorius's relentless search for "scientific truth" is condemned. Like *The Book of Daniel* and Marxist critics such as Terry Eagleton, *The Waterworks* indicates there are objectively verifiable categories.

The possibility of praxis was first suggested in the novella *Lives of the Poets* with Jonathan's decision to hide refugees and teach a young boy to type/write, a scenario some critics faulted as unbelievable. The ending of *The Waterworks*, in contrast, falls within the romance tradition and is thus not subject to the same tests of veracity. As in all romances, there are realistic elements, such as Sartorius's commitment to an asylum and Boss Tweed's fall. These elements represent a serious strike against injustice. The novel's optimism is all the more noteworthy given its gritty, historically-based representations of the nineteenth century city as ruthless and alienating. Indeed, *The Waterworks* implies the possibility and necessity of intervention against both harsh urban conditions and "nature's course," that is, survival of the fittest. The novel implies that it is possible to go beyond merely recognizing one's complicity in evil to taking action that will mitigate, although never negate, evil. Like the newspaper's seven columns, the novel finally suggests that human lives are interconnected and can positively affect one another. For these reasons, the possibility of praxis in *The Waterworks* is more convincing and aesthetically satisfying than in *Lives of the Poets* with its image of the cautious writer sheltering illegal aliens or in *Ragtime* with its sentimental descriptions of the conception of *The Little Rascals*. *The Waterworks* stands as a fine development in Doctorow's work and a strong addition to the evolving American political novel.

Chronology

1931 Edgar Lawrence Doctorow is born in New York City on January 6 to David R. and Rose Lenin Doctorow.

1952 Graduates with honors and receives a degree in philosophy from Kenyon College, Gambier, Ohio.

1952-53 Does graduate work in drama at Columbia University.

1953-55 Serves in U.S. Army.

1954 Marries Helen Seltser on August 20, and eventually they have three children together.

1955-59 Works as a reservations clerk at LaGuardia Airport. Then, as a senior editor, reads scripts for CBS Television and Columbia Picture Industries, New York City.

1959-64 Editor and then senior editor at New American Library in New York City.

1960 Publishes *Welcome to Hard Times.*

1964-69 Editor in chief at Dial Press; vice president from 1968-69. In 1969, quits to write full time.

1966 Publishes *Big as Life.*

1969-70 Writer-in-residence at the University of California, Irvine.

1971 Publishes *The Book of Daniel*, which is nominated for the National Book Award.

1971-78 Teaches at Sarah Lawrence College, Bronxville, New York.

1975 Publishes *Ragtime*.

1978 *Drinks before Dinner* is produced off-Broadway at the Public Theatre.

1979 *Drinks before Dinner* is published.

1980 Publishes *Loon Lake*.

1984 Publishes *Lives of the Poets: Six Stories and a Novella*.

1985 Publishes *World's Fair*.

1986 Awarded the American Book Award for *World's Fair*.

1989 Publishes *Billy Bathgate*. With Eric Fischl, publishes *Scenes and Sequences*.

1993 Publishes *Poets and Presidents*, a collection of essays. Announces his collaboration with two partners to create Booknet, a 24-hour, books-only cable TV service.

1994 Publishes *The Waterworks*.

2000 Publishes *City of God*.

Contributors

HAROLD BLOOM is Sterling Professor of the Humanities at Yale University and Henry W. and Albert A. Berg Professor of English at the New York University Graduate School. He is the author of over 20 books, including *Shelly's Mythmaking* (1959), *The Visionary Company* (1961), *Blake's Apocalypse* (1963), *Yeats* (1970), *A Map of Misreading* (1975), *Kabbalah and Criticism* (1975), *Agon: Toward a Theory of Revisionism* (1982), *The American Religion* (1992), *The Western Canon* (1994), and *Omens of Millennium: The Gnosis of Angels, Dreams, and Resurrection* (1996). *The Anxiety of Influence* (1973) sets forth Professor Bloom's provocative theory of the literary relationships between the great writers and their predecessors. His most recent books include *Shakespeare: The Invention of the Human*, a 1998 National Book Award finalist, and *How to Read and Why*, which was published in 2000. In 1999, Professor Bloom received the prestigious American Academy of Arts and Letters Gold Medal for Criticism.

DOUGLAS FOWLER is Professor of English at Florida State University. His books cover Nabokov, S. J. Perelman and Ira Levin.

MARSHALL BRUCE GENTRY teaches English at the University of Indianapolis. He is the author of *Flannery O'Connor's Religion of the Grotesque and Conversations with Raymond Carver.*

SAM B. GIRGUS is Professor of English at Vanderbilt University. He has written books on literature as well as film.

GEOFFREY GALT HARPHAM teaches English as Tulane University. He has published a book on Joseph Conrad, as well as titles on criticism, culture and ethics.

MATTHEW A. HENRY has taught at Syracuse University.

PAUL LEVINE has taught at the University of Copenhagen in Denmark.

STEPHEN MATTERSON has taught at Trinity College, the University of Dublin. He has written *Studying Poetry* and edited a book on Herman Melville.

CHRISTOPHER D. MORRIS has interviewed E. L. Doctorow. Aside from his book on this author, he has published books on social theorists, tudor anthems and southern living.

JOHN G. PARKS teaches English at Miami University

CUSHING STROUT has written about the work of Henry James, Edith Wharton, Nathaniel Hawthorne and others.

MICHELLE M. TOKARCZYK is Associate Professor of English at Goucher College. In addition to work published on contemporary and literary cultural studies, she has written *E. L. Doctorow: An Annotated Bibliography* and co-edited a book on women working in higher education.

JOHN WILLIAMS has written a book on Mary Shelley as well as many others on a wide range of topics.

Bibliography

Arnold, Marilyn. "Doctorow's *Hard Times:* A Sermon on the Failure of Faith." *Literature and Belief* 3 (1983): 87-93.

Baba Minako, "The Young Gangster as Mythic American Hero: E. L. Doctorow's *Billy Bathgate*." *MELUS* 8 (Summer 1993): 33-46.

Berryman, Charles. "*Ragtime* in Retrospect." *South Atlantic Quarterly* 81 (Winter 1982): 30-42.

Bevilacqua, Winifred Farrant. "Narration and History in E. L. Doctorow." *Studies in Scandinavia* 22 (1990): 94-106.

Bloom, Harold, ed. *Ragtime*. Philadelphia: Chelsea House, 2001.

Campbell, Josie. "Coalhouse Walker and the Model T Ford: Legerdemain in *Ragtime*." *Journal of Popular Culture* 13 (Fall 1979): 302-9.

Claridge, Henry. "Writing on the Margins: E. L. Doctorow and American History." *The New American Writing: Essays in American Literature* Since 1970. Graham Clarke, ed. New York: St. Martin's Press, 1990, 9-28.

Clerc, Charles. "Dutch Schultz's Last Words Revisited." *Journal of Modern Literature* 18 (Fall 1993): 463-65.

Cooper, Barbara. "The Artist as Historian in the Novels of E. L. Doctorow." *The Emporia State Research Studies* 29 (Fall 1980).

Cooper, Stephen. "Cutting Both Ways: E. L. Doctorow's Critique of the Left." *South Atlantic Review* 58 (1993): 111-25.

Culp, Mildred. "Women and Tragic Destiny in Doctorow's *The Book of Daniel*." *Studies in American Jewish Literature* 2 (1982): 155-66.

Doctorow, E. L. "The Art of Fiction." Interview with George Plimpton. *Paris Review* 28 (1986): 23-47.

Emblidge, David. "Marching Backwards into the Future: Progress as Illusion in Doctorow's Novels." *Southwest Review* 62 (Autumn 1977): 397-409.

Estrin, Barbara L. "Recomposing Time: *Humboldt's Gift* and *Ragtime*." *Denver Quarterly* 17 (1982): 16-31

Evans, Thomas G. "Impersonal Dilemmas: The Collision of the Modernist and Popular Tradition in Two Political Novels, *The Grapes of Wrath* and *Ragtime*." *South Atlantic Reivew* 52 (January 1987): 71-85.

Friedl, Herwig, and Dieter Schulz, eds. E.L. Doctorow: *A Democracy of Perception: A Symposium with and on E. L. Doctorow*. Essen: Blaue Eule, 1988.

Garrison, David. "Ovid's Metamorphoses in E. L. Doctorow's *Ragtime*." *Classical and Modern Literature* 17, no. 2 (Winter 1997): 103-15.

Gentry, Marshall Bruce. "*Ragtime* as Auto Biography." *Kansas Quarterly* 21 (Fall 1989): 105-12.

Harter, Carol and James R. Thompson. *E. L. Doctorow*. Boston: Twayne, 1990.

Heber, Janice Stewart. "The X-Factor in E. L. Doctorow's *Billy Bathgate*: Powerless Women and History as Myth." *Modern Language Studies* 22 (1992): 33-41.

Henry, Matthew A. "Problematized Narratives: History as Fiction in E. L. Doctorow's *Billy Bathgate*." *Critique* 39 (Fall 1997): 32-40.

Iannone, Carol. "E L. Doctorow's 'Jewish' Radicalism." *Commentary* 81 (March 1986): 53-56.

Keener, John F. "The Last Words of Dutch Schultz: Deathbed Autobiography and Postmodern Gangster Fiction." *Arizona Quarterly* 54, no. 2 (Summer 1998): 135-63.

Knorr, Walter K. "Doctorow and Kleist: 'Kohlhaas in *Ragtime* [editor: no ital here].'" *Modern Fiction Studies* 22 (Summer 1976): 224-27.

Lorsch, Susan. "Doctorow's *The Book of Daniel* as *Kunstlerroman*: The Politics of Art." *Papers on Language and Literature* 18 (1982): 384-97

Miller, Ann V. "Through a Glass Clearly: Vision as Structure in E. L. Doctorow's 'Willi.'" *Studies in Short Fiction* 30 (1993): 337-42.

Moraru, Christian. "The Reincarnated Plot: E. L. Doctorow's *Ragtime*, Heinrich von Kleist's *Michael Kohlhaas*, and the Spectacle of Modernity." *Comparatist* 21 (May 1997): 92-116.

Morris, Christopher, ed. *Conversations with E. L. Doctorow*. Jackson: University Press of Mississippi, 1999.

Nadel, Alan. "Hero and Other in Doctorow's *Loon Lake*." *College Literature* 14 (1987): 136-45.

Neumeyer, Peter F. "E. L. Doctorow, Kleist, and the Ascendancy of Things." *CEA Critic* 39 (May 1977): 17-21

Osland, Dianne. "Trusting the Teller: Metaphor in Fiction, and the Case of *Ragtime*." *Narrative* 5, no. 3 (October 1997): 252-73.

Ostendorf, Berndt. "The Musical World of Doctorow's *Ragtime*." *American Quarterly* 43 (1991): 579-599.

Parks, John G. "The Politics of Polyphony: The Fiction of E. L. Doctorow." *Twentieth-Century Literature* 37 (1991): 454-63.

Piehl, Kathy. "E. L. Doctorow and Random House: The *Ragtime* Rhythm of Cash." *Journal of Popular Culture* 13 (Winter 1979): 404-11.

Quart, Leonard and Barbara. "*Ragtime* Without a Melody." *Literature/Film Quarterly* 10 (1982): 71-74.

Rapf, Joanna E. "Volatile Forms: The Transgressive Energy of *Ragtime* as Novel and Film." *Literature/Film Quarterly* 26, no. 1 (1998): 16-22.

Ree, T. V. "Genealogy/Narrative/Power: Questions of Postmodernity in Doctorow's *The Book of Daniel*," *American Literary History* 4 (1992): 288-304.

Robertson, Michael. "Cultural Hegemony Goes to the Fair: The Case of E. L. Doctorow's *World's Fair*." *American Studies* 33 (1992): 31-44.

Shelton, Frank W. "E. L. Doctorow's *Welcome to Hard Times*: The Western and the American Dream." *Midwest Quarterly* 25 (Autumn 1983): 7-17.

Solataroff, Ted. "Of Melville, Poe, and Doctorow." *Nation* 6 (June 1994): 784-90.

Sutherland, John. "The Selling of *Ragtime*: A Novel for Our Times?" *The New Review* 4 (1977): 3-11.

Tanner, Stephen. "Rage and Order in Doctorow's Hard Times." *South Dakota Review* 22 (1984): 79-85.

Thomas, David Wayne. "Godel's Theorem and Postmodern Theory." *PMLA* 116 (1995): 248-61.

Thompson, James R. "The Artist as 'Criminal of Perception': E. L. Doctorow and the Politics of Imagination." *Hungarian Journal of English and American Studies* 1 (1996): 147-55.

———. "Categories of Human Form: Some Notes on E. L. Doctorow and Historical Consciousness in American Fiction Since 1960." *Caliban: Le Roman Historique* 28 (1991): 17-24.

Tokarczyk, Michelle M. "The City, *The Waterworks*, and Writing." *The Kenyon Review* 17 (Winter 1995): 32-37.

———. E. L. Doctorow: *An Annotated Bibliography*. New York: Garland Publishing Co., 1988.

———. "From the Lions' Den: Survivors in E. L. Doctorow's *The Book of Daniel*." *Critique* 29 (Fall 1987): 3-15.

Trenner, Richard, ed. *E. L. Doctorow: Essays and Conversations.* Princeton: Ontario Review Press, 1983.

———. "Politics and the Mode of Fiction." *The Ontario Review* 16 (Spring-Summer 1982): 5-16.

Vieira, Nelson H. "'Evil Be Thou My Good': Postmodern Heroics and Ethics in *Billy Bathgate* and *Bufo & Spallanzani*." *Comparative Literature Studies* 28 (1991): 356-78.

Wagner-Martin, Linda. "*Billy Bathgate* and *Billy Budd*: Some Recognitions." *Notes on Contemporary Literature* 20 (1990): 4-7.

Wright, Derek. "*Ragtime* Revisited: History and Fiction in Doctorow's Novel." *IFR* 20, no. 1 (1993): 14-16.

Acknowledgments

"A True Radical History: E. L. Doctorow," by Sam B.Girgus. From *The New Covenant: Jewish Writers and the American Idea*. ©1984 by The University of North Carolina Press. Reprinted by permission.

"E. L. Doctorow and the Technology of Narrative," by Geoffrey Galt Harpham. From *PMLA* 100, no. 1 (January 1985): 81-95. ©1985 by The Modern Language Association of America. Reprinted by permission.

"Politics and Imagination," by Paul Levine. From *E. L. Doctorow*. ©1985 by Paul Levine. Published by Metheun & Co., New York. Reprinted by permission.

"Twain, Doctorow, and the Anachronistic Adventures of the Arms Mechanic and the Jazz Pianist," by Cushing Strout. From *Making American Tradition: Visions and Revisions from Ben Franklin to Alice Walker.* ©1990 by Cushing Strout. Reprinted by permission of The Continuum Publishing Company, Inc.

"Art and Memory: *Lives of the Poets* and *World's Fair*," by John G. Parks. From *E.L. Doctorow*. ©1991 by John G. Parks. Reprinted by permission.

"Illusions of Demystification in *Ragtime*," by Christopher D. Morris. From *Models of Misrepresentation: On the Fiction of E. L. Doctorow*. © 1991 by the University Press of Mississippi. Reprinted by permission.

"Billy Bathgate," by Douglas Fowler. From *Understanding E. L. Doctorow*. © 1992 by the University of South Carolina. Reprinted by permission.

"Ventriloquists' Conversations: The Struggle for Gender Dialogue in E. L. Doctorow and Philip Roth," by Marshall Bruce Gentry. From *Contemporary Literature* 34, no. 3 (Fall 1993): 512-535. ©1993 by the Board of Regents of the University of Wisconsin System. Reprinted by permission.

"Why Not Say What Happened? E. L. Doctorow's *Lives of the Poets*," by Stephen Matterson. From *Critique* XXXIV, no. 2 (Winter 1993): 113-125. ©1993 by the Helen Dwight Reid Educational Foundation. Reprinted by permission. Published by Heldref Publications, 1319 Eighteenth St., NW, Washington, D.C., 20036-1802 ©1993.

"Canonizing *Welcome to Hard Times* and *The Book of Daniel* 1980-85," by John Williams. From Fiction as False Document: *The Reception of E. L. Doctorow in the Postmodern Age*. ©1996 by Camden House. Reprinted by permission.

"Problematized Narratives: History as Fiction in E. L. Doctorow's *Billy Bathgate*," by Matthew A. Henry. From *Critique* 39, no. 1 (Fall 1997): 32-40. ©1997 by the Helen Dwight Reid Educational Foundation. Reprinted by permission.Published by Heldref Publications, 1319 Eighteenth St., NW, Washington, D.C., 20036-1802 ©1997.

"Postmodernism Reconsidered on an Urban Landscape: *The Waterworks*," by Michelle M. Tokarczyk. From *E. L. Doctorow's Skeptical Commitment*. ©2000 by Peter Lang Publishing. Reprinted by permission.

Index